Andr
Shepherd
AF804021

The World Bank

The World Bank is the key institution through which rich nations channel resources to poorer ones. Established over fifty years ago in a radically different international environment, the World Bank has constantly re-invented itself in the intervening decades. What drives this evolution?

This book considers the nature of change at the World Bank, exploring both the external impetus for change, and the impact of the Bank's internal organization and culture. The author's findings are supported by detailed case studies of three of the Bank's most important new agendas: private sector development, participation, and governance.

Michelle Miller-Adams finds that traditional international-relations based approaches, which focus on states and power, are inadequate for explaining institutional change at the World Bank. Attention must also be paid to the Bank's internal processes, especially the technical and apolitical norms that form an intrinsic part of its identity. This identity, which dates from the Bank's earliest days, continues to shape its response to new demands and affect its ability to meet the needs of a changing world.

Michelle Miller-Adams is a writer and editor of publications in the field of international affairs, and teaches political science at Western Michigan University. She holds a PhD and Master of International Affairs from Columbia University. She has worked in New York as vice-president for programs at the Twentieth Century Fund and as vice-president of research at Salomon Brothers, where she wrote numerous reports about the World Bank.

Routledge Studies in Development Economics

1 **Economic Development in the Middle East**
Rodney Wilson

2 **Monetary and Financial Policies in Developing Countries:** Growth and stabilization
Akhtar Hossain and Anis Chowdhury

3 **New Directions in Development Economics:** Growth, environmental concerns and government in the 1990s
Edited by Mats Lundahl and Benno J. Ndulu

4 **Financial Liberalization and Investment**
Kanhaya L. Gupta and Robert Lensink

5 **Liberalization in the Developing World:** Institutional and economic changes in Latin America, Africa and Asia
Edited by Alex E. Fernández Jilberto and André Mommen

6 **Financial Development and Economic Growth:** Theory and experiences from developing countries
Edited by Niels Hermes and Robert Lensink

7 **The South African Economy:** Macroeconomic prospects for the medium term
Finn Tarp and Peter Brixen

8 **Public Sector Pay and Adjustment:** Lessons from five countries
Edited by Christopher Colclough

9 **Europe and Economic Reform in Africa:** Structural adjustment and economic diplomacy
Obed O. Mailafia

10 **Post-apartheid Southern Africa:** Economic challenges and policies for the future
Edited by Lennart Petersson

11 **Financial Integration and Development:** Liberalization and reform in Sub-Saharan Africa
Ernest Aryeetey and Machiko Nissanke

12 **Regionalization and Globalization in the Modern World Economy:** Perspectives on the Third World and transitional economies
Edited by Alex F. Fernández Jilberto and André Mommen

13 **The African Economy:** Policy, institutions and the future
Steve Kayizzi-Mugerwa

14 **Recovery from Armed Conflict in Developing Countries**
Edited by Geoff Harris

15 **Small Enterprises and Economic Development:** The dynamics of micro and small enterprises
Carl Liedholm and Donald C. Mead

16 **The World Bank:** New agendas in a changing world
Michelle Miller-Adams

The World Bank

New agendas in a changing world

Michelle Miller-Adams

ROUTLEDGE

London and New York

First published 1999 by Routledge
11 New Fetter Lane, London EC4B 4EE

Simultaneously published in the USA and Canada by Routledge
29 West 35th Street, New York, NY 10001

© 1999 Michelle Miller-Adams

Typeset in Garamond by Curran Publishing Services
Printed and bound in Great Britain by Biddles Ltd., Guildford and King's Lynn

All rights reserved. No part of this book may be reprinted or reproduced or utilised in any form or by any electronic, mechanical, or other means, now known or hereafter invented, including photocopying and recording, or in any information storage or retrieval system, without permission in writing from the publishers.

British Library Cataloguing in Publication Data
A catalogue record for this book is available
from the British Library

Library of Congress Cataloging in Publication Data
Miller-Adams, Michelle, 1959–
The World Bank: new agendas in a changing world /
Michelle Miller-Adams
192 pp. 156 x 234 cm.
Includes bibliographical references and index
1. World Bank. I. Title.
HG3881.5.W57M55 1999
332.1'532–dc21 96-42331
CIP

ISBN 0-415-19353-2

To Richard Adams, with love

Contents

Figures

Tables

Preface

Early in the research project for this book, I was offered two comments that have stayed with me throughout the writing process. The first was made by one of the authors of a major study of the World Bank's first half-century. After several years immersed in analyzing the Bank's history, he had concluded that the complexity of the institution makes it possible for social scientists to find evidence for every hypothesis and its opposite in their investigations of the World Bank. This note of caution rang true as I plunged into the details of Bank policy and practice. From some vantage points, the extent of change undergone by the World Bank over the past decade appears truly staggering. From others, it seems that the Bank is indeed immutable. In such a complex environment it is difficult to generalize about the nature or extent of change, let alone the processes that underpin it. Yet I believe that generalizations are possible, although they must be informed by the specifics of each case: hence my attention to uncovering the stories of how the new agendas studied here came about.

The second remark was made by one of the Bank's top managers. Referring to the rapid pace of change under way at the Bank, he said, "I hope we make your study obsolete before it's done." His point was that the World Bank is making a sincere effort to respond to the new demands of its environment and to allay the concerns of its critics. This, too, complicates the task of analysis and makes it difficult to reach conclusions that will remain valid several years down the road. It is not enough to offer a snapshot of the institution today. Neither is it sufficient to provide a history of some of the most important recent changes undergone by the Bank. Instead, while focusing on three new agendas introduced at the World Bank in the 1990s, I have also tried to reach a level of generality about the nature of change at the Bank. I hope this will be useful going forward and will provide Bank-watchers with some guidelines on what precisely they should be looking for as they assess the institution's evolution.

This book thus represents my effort to tread the fine line between details and broad trends, time-bound analysis and more lasting generalizations. Having observed the Bank in a variety of capacities for more than a decade, I am impressed by the extent of change that has occurred, and convinced that the attempts on the part of Bank staff and management to "do better" are genuine. But I also believe that strong forces are at work that make the process of change exceedingly difficult. My curiosity about how the competing dynamics of change and stasis will play out drew me to this topic, sustained me through my research, and will keep me watching the World Bank in the years ahead.

A number of individuals deserve my gratitude. My thanks go to David Baldwin, Deborah Brautigam, Jonathan Fox, Jonas Haralz, Arvid Lukauskas, Chuck Myers, Paul Nelson, Salvatore Schiavo-Campo, Ibrahim Shihata, Michael Stevens, Warren Van Wicklin, and Andrew Vorkink for their careful reading and comments on the manuscript. Moisés Naim and Kenneth Lay acted as knowledgeable guides early in my research. Martha Finnemore helped me clarify my thinking at the outset of the project. Amy Corning generously assisted with the charts.Craig Fowlie and Liz Brown of Routledge and Susan Curran of Curran Publishing Services handled the publication process in a highly professional and expeditious manner. I would also like to thank the many individuals I interviewed at the World Bank and elsewhere who shared their time and ideas graciously. Without them this study would not have been written.

I am further indebted to the institutions that helped make this research possible: the Joint Bank-Fund Library; the University of Michigan Libraries; and the Twentieth Century Fund, which offered tangible support early on and allowed me to combine my work as a professional with my role as a scholar. Looking further back, it was in my capacity as a vice president in the research department of Salomon Brothers that I first encountered the World Bank, was confronted by its complexity, and challenged by its nuances. My thanks go, belatedly, to those staff members of the World Bank who in the mid-1980s spent considerable time explaining their institution to a 25-year old investment banker who had no inkling that the time she spent wandering the corridors would lead back to graduate school and then to authorship of this volume.

Above all, I am deeply grateful to my family for instilling in me a conviction of the value of higher education, making me feel that I was engaged along the way in a worthy endeavor, and always believing that I would accomplish it with aplomb. A final word of love and thanks is due to my husband, Richard Adams, who offered continual support and encouragement and whose presence in my life kept this undertaking in its proper perspective.

Michelle Miller-Adams

Abbreviations

ADB	Asian Development Bank
AFIC	Asian Finance and Investment Corporation Ltd
AfDB	African Development Bank
AID	(US) Agency for International Development
CAS	(World Bank) Country Assistance Strategy
CGAP	Consultative Group to Assist the Poorest
DAC	(OECD) Development Assistance Commission
DFC	Development Finance Corporation
EBRD	European Bank for Reconstruction and Development
EDI	Economic Development Institute
FIAS	Foreign Investment and Advisory Service
FPD	Finance and Private Sector Development (World Bank Vice Presidency)
IBRD	International Bank for Reconstruction and Development
IDA	International Development Association
IDB	Inter-American Development Bank
IFC	International Finance Corporation
IIIC	Inter-American Investment Corporation
IMF	International Monetary Fund
ICSID	International Center for the Settlement of Investment Disputes
LGPD	(World Bank) Learning Group on Participatory Development
MIGA	Multilateral Investment Guarantee Agency
NGOs	non-governmental organizations
OECD	Organization for Economic Cooperation and Development
PIC	(World Bank) Public Information Center
PSA	(World Bank) Private Sector Assessment

1 Introduction

> There is almost nothing . . . about the World Bank that cannot be changed, dropped, or expanded if the will is there. It is much more flexible than it looks, and its methods and practices have never been reduced to any formal code.
>
> James Morris, *The Road to Huddersfield*, 1963, p. 226

> That the Bank . . . has survived more than half a century of dramatic global economic and political changes is due largely to its ability to redefine itself. Among the personas it has adopted are those of a capitalist tool, a friend of big government, an international mediator, a force for industrialization, a voice for social justice, a hard-nosed financial institution, a coordinator of the global economy, a social services agency, and an advocate of private entrepreneurship.
>
> Catherine Caufield, *Masters of Illusion,* 1996, p. 2

The World Bank is the key institution through which rich nations channel resources to poor nations in support of their economic development. Established over fifty years ago in a radically different international environment, the Bank has reinvented itself continually in response to demands from its member states, the predilections of its staff, changes in the developing world, and shifts in the broader understanding of economic development.

The Bank's evolution in the last decades of the twentieth century has been driven in part by sudden and sweeping changes in the developing countries that are the recipients of World Bank loans. In the 1980s and 1990s, the political and economic systems of the developing world were transformed. Democratic regimes emerged in Latin America; one-party rule ended in Eastern Europe, the former Soviet Union, and much of Africa; and pressure for greater openness created a new political climate in Southeast Asia. On the economic front, state-centered development models were rejected in Latin America, communist economic systems dismantled in Eastern Europe and the former Soviet Union, and market-oriented economic reform embraced throughout the developing world.

The evolution of the World Bank has also been stimulated by more gradual shifts in beliefs about economic development. In the 1950s and 1960s, the development community – in which the World Bank plays a central role – stressed the importance of providing poor countries with the infrastructure necessary for industrialization. By the early 1980s, development experts had begun to focus on the economic policy reforms needed to secure growth and the benefits of a vibrant private sector. Over the past decade, there has been a greater recognition of the negative environmental consequences of past development approaches, renewed attention to the plight of the poor, and growing awareness of the political impediments to growth.

As a result of these trends, a series of new agendas emerged at the Bank in the late 1980s and 1990s regarding the environment, poverty reduction, the private sector, the participation of local communities in Bank programs, the role of women in development, and the nature of governance in developing countries. These new agendas represent both the Bank's response to the dramatic international transformations of the late twentieth century and a pragmatic effort to adjust its policies in light of new evidence about how it might best help its borrowers.

Three of these agendas – private sector development, participation, and governance – are the focus of this book. In all three cases the Bank's new approach signified an important departure from business as usual. For most of the Bank's history, its policies were marked by reliance on the state as the chief engine of growth. In contrast, the private sector development agenda recognizes explicitly the role of private actors in economic development. In the past, the Bank's staff made little effort to include groups or individuals within developing countries in decisions that would affect them. Today, the participation agenda solicits the participation of beneficiaries in at least some of the Bank's policies and programs. Finally, the recent emphasis on governance constitutes an admission that the World Bank had paid insufficient attention to whether borrowing-country governments truly supported the policies called for in its programs. Those responsible for setting policy at the Bank have come to recognize that a strong private sector, the participation of civil society, and capable and committed governments are essential if the World Bank is to help bring about renewed economic growth and the reduction of poverty in the developing world. Whether and how the Bank can play an active role in fostering private sector development, participation, or governance is, however, less clear.

The three agendas discussed in this book have met with very different fates since their introduction at the Bank. Private sector development has been defined broadly, embraced enthusiastically by management, and given substantial new resources and a prominent bureaucratic location. The Bank's private sector initiative has been supported by the hiring of new personnel, a trend all the more notable at a time of staff downsizing. Reports designed to evaluate the condition of the private sector in major borrowing countries are being prepared, and the private sector is among the issues that must be considered when the Bank sets its strategy toward a given country. The Bank has stepped up the use of its guarantee authority to promote private investment in the developing world. And a high-level effort is under way to coordinate the private-sector-related activities of the three institutions that make up the World Bank Group.[1]

The Bank's participation agenda is more circumscribed. Participatory development, which involves greater collaboration by the Bank with the non-governmental organizations (NGOs) and individuals that make up civil society, is based on the premise that groups affected by Bank projects should have some say in their development and implementation. The importance of participation has been highlighted by the Bank's management as a central part of the organization's mission. It has received some new resources in the form of personnel, training activities, and publications, but it has not been given a high profile bureaucratically. Projects involving the participation of beneficiaries are developed mainly by staff members who are personally committed to such approaches. Significant participatory components are found only in a small subset of targeted anti-poverty programs, rather than being integrated into the mainstream of Bank operations.

The Bank's governance agenda is the most tentative of the three cases examined here. After an initial surge of attention to political issues writ large, the scope of the Bank's concerns in this area narrowed. Although the Bank has begun to pay greater attention to questions of institutional capacity and political management in its borrowing countries, most recently through the anti-corruption initiative of the late 1990s, these efforts have been tailored to fit comfortably with the Bank's technical and apolitical orientation. Governance has met with an ambivalent reception by management and staff and has not been given a central bureaucratic home within the Bank nor allocated additional staff resources. Confusion remains as to how the Bank defines governance and how it should be pursued operationally. In the meantime, governance concerns remain marginal to the Bank's work on the ground, in spite of their prominence in its rhetoric.

Why have these three agendas unfolded in such different ways? Each has been deemed critical to the Bank's ability to accomplish its stated goals and each marks a major departure from past practice. What is it about these issues – or about the Bank – that has led to their variable treatment? In answering this question, I draw on two bodies of theory that take very different approaches to explaining how and why institutions evolve.

Traditional international relations theory, based in the discipline of political science, locates the sources of institutional change in the power and preferences of the states that make up the international system. In this view, the agendas of multilateral organizations like the World Bank evolve in response to pressure from actors outside the Bank, particularly the member states that own the institution, but also other well-organized groups, such as NGO coalitions or members of the financial community from which the Bank raises the funds it lends. To most international relations scholars, institutional change is a fairly efficient process: as the configuration of the international system changes, or as the preferences of its key actors evolve, international organizations like the World Bank will change as well.

International relations theorists would find no mystery in why private sector development has been more deeply incorporated into the World Bank's activities than governance or participation. The World Bank is formally owned and run by its member countries. Of these, the United States is the largest and most powerful member, and has been since the Bank's inception. US pressure on the Bank to pay greater attention to the private sector intensified in the 1980s. The United States had the leverage to carry out its preferences, and eventually exercised that leverage to bring about an explicit change of policy on the part of the Bank. The other two agendas under consideration were pushed by less powerful actors, such as smaller member states or NGOs; as result, they met with a more muted institutional response.

This argument, while plausible on the surface, has serious shortcomings which are revealed by attention to the timing and details of Bank action. Although the Bank adopted a stronger private sector focus in the 1990s, it did not do so in direct response to the US campaign. Moreover, the changes that were enacted unfolded along the lines of the Bank's own preferences, not those of the United States. Innovations in the area of participation, while less widespread than those related to the private sector, were none the less significant. NGOs and some member countries played a part in bringing them about, but the efforts of individuals within the Bank were crucial to their success. Even more important in furthering the participation agenda was the interaction between external and internal advocates, a dynamic not easily captured by international-relations-based theories that look to entities outside an organization as the main sources of institutional change. For its part, the governance agenda seems to have been stimulated more by the Bank's own learning processes and broad international changes than by the pressure of any particular actor. In short, while external actors have clearly played a role in bringing new issues to the attention of the World Bank, theories that focus on their influence alone tell an incomplete story about how new agendas emerge and what happens once they surface. How are new issues defined and made operational within the Bank? What level of resources do they receive? How deeply are they incorporated into the fabric of the organization? Ultimately, it is these factors that determine the impact an organization will have in a given area.

To answer these questions, I have turned to organization theory, a body of work that is attuned to the internal dynamics of institutions. Based in the discipline of sociology, the many variants of organization theory direct attention to the rules, both formal and informal, that guide the operation of an organization, and to the norms, values, and beliefs of its management and staff. An organization's culture, the pattern of norms and attitudes that cuts across the entire social unit, is an embodiment of these rules, norms, and beliefs. Despite the continual evolution of its mission over half a century, the World Bank's organizational culture remains clearly defined.

The World Bank is a government-oriented institution. In part, this is because its founding charter, called the Articles of Agreement, requires it to lend only to governments. But the focus on the public sector goes beyond this formal rule to everyday practice in which Bank staff members interact primarily with government officials and have minimal contact with civil society.

At the same time, the World Bank adheres strongly to the notion that its work is apolitical, a provision that is also expressed in its founding charter. The Bank's identity as an institution "above politics" helps preserve its legitimacy with its 180 member countries and forges a degree of unity among its multinational staff. Most important, the apolitical provision has allowed the Bank throughout its history to work with and lend to a wide range of political regimes. The idea that development, at least as practiced by the Bank, is an apolitical process forms a linchpin of the Bank's organizational culture.

The World Bank is a mover of money. Since the 1970s, the Bank's member countries and managers have judged its success in terms of the number and size of the loans it makes. Only by steadily increasing its lending volume could the Bank make claims on its member countries for capital increases. And, in the development field where the criteria for success are so long-term and uncertain, lending volume was one of the few ways in which the Bank could be judged as having had an impact. As a result, the Bank's organizational culture puts a premium on concluding loans, especially large loans, and staff members have been evaluated and promoted on their success in doing so. The Bank's current management has downplayed the importance of lending volume and tried to establish criteria to evaluate staff members by the quality of the loans they make, not their size, but this is a difficult and long-term process. Most staff members believe the "approval culture" is still in place, that their success at the Bank is tied to their ability to move projects quickly from the development phase to approval by the Bank's board.

The World Bank is centralized and hierarchical. More than 85 per cent of the Bank Group's 10,000-plus staff members are based in Washington. Of the 15 per cent of staff located in developing countries, only about half are regular staff members, as opposed to short-term consultants. Until recently, virtually all Bank decision-makers were located in Washington as well. Efforts to decentralize operations, along with managerial authority, began in the late 1990s but are still in their infancy and it is not clear how far they will progress. In addition to its centralized nature, the Bank is an extremely complex organization. Sweeping plans to revise and streamline its bureaucratic structure have become regular features of Bank life. Usually occurring when a new president assumes control, Bank reorganizations have resulted in a high degree of organizational turmoil and often a loss of staff morale, but do not seem to have achieved either greater simplification or enhanced efficiency.

Above all, the World Bank is a technocracy. Throughout its history, the Bank has relied on well-honed lending techniques that can be measured quantitatively and applied in a wide range of countries. This technical orientation has its roots in the Bank's need early on to establish its creditworthiness in international capital markets and claim for itself a measure of competence in a field where the standards for success are highly uncertain. It has been maintained throughout the institution's history by the selective recruitment, training, and socialization of staff members with a clearly defined set of professional norms. Economists, financial experts, and those with other specialized skills are most highly prized within the Bank's organizational culture and help to preserve its technical bent.

The Bank's approach to lending derives from this orientation. Michael Cernea, who for twenty years served as the chief advocate within the Bank for social development concerns, has written that "the characteristics and biases of an institution's culture tend to put their imprint on the institution's products" (Cernea 1996: 15). From its earliest days, the Bank has taken a blueprint approach to development that compartmentalizes its different stages and is imposed or "induced" from above. Cernea identifies three conceptual biases in the Bank's approach to development: the econocentric model that regards economic and financial variables as the only ones that matter; the technocentric model that addresses the technological variables of development apart from their contextual social fabric; and the commodocentric model that emphasizes the "thing" more than the social actors that produce it, highlighting, for example, the Bank's tendency to focus on coffee production but not coffee growers, or water provision but not water users (Cernea 1996: 15–16).

An organizational culture that is technocratic, apolitical, centralized, and biased toward large lending programs and a blueprint approach to development will provide a more receptive environment for certain kinds of activities than for others. To return to the question posed earlier, private sector development fits readily with key elements of the World Bank's organizational culture, whereas both participation and governance pose greater challenges to it. In seeking to explain the fate of each of these agendas, an organization-theory-based approach would look at the closeness of their fit with the World Bank's organizational culture as well as the malleability of that culture.

In weighing the two explanations presented above, political scientists might argue that international relations theory is successful at explaining most of what we need to know about the behavior of organizations, and that it is less important to understand the details of implementation than the general orientation of the World Bank's policies. There are three problems with this argument. First, in some cases, international-relations-based explanations are insufficient to explain even broad policies. For example, the Bank's adoption of policy-based adjustment lending around 1980 – a move that had significant implications for both the Bank and the developing world – had almost nothing to do with external pressure. Second, the Bank may commit to certain policies but not carry them out in practice. For example, the Bank's policy regarding forcible resettlement has been in place since 1980, but was not taken into account in most of the Bank's lending until the 1990s. Third, it is essential to look at how a new agenda, once adopted, is pursued in practice. For example, it is not enough to know that the Bank now supports the participation of affected groups in the design and execution of its projects. Without examining the resources, leadership, and organizational activities through which the Bank is pursuing this agenda, it is impossible to determine whether participation has actually become a feature of Bank lending, let alone whether the new approach has had any impact. It is this insight into the implementation of Bank policies and their attendant impact that can be gained through an organizational analysis and that international relations theory cannot provide.

Conversely, organization theorists might argue that they, too, can explain recent changes at the World Bank without recourse to international-relations-based approaches. According to such an argument, the Bank's most energetic initiatives in the 1980s and 1990s would have focused on areas where there were clear payoffs and where success was relatively easy to measure, a natural strategy under a decision-making model where actors seek to maximize their bureaucratic interests in ways that are congruent with an organization's culture. This approach, however, underestimates the role of the Bank's member countries in shaping its actions and neglects issues of power that determine why some parties are in a position to make their interests felt and others are not. It also fails to explain why the Bank has gone to great lengths to cast itself as an intellectual leader and activist on issues where, in reality, it can have very little impact and where the payoffs are minimal, if they exist at all.

When the timing and sequence of decisions regarding new agendas at the Bank are examined, it becomes clear that neither international relations theory nor organization theory alone can explain the Bank's evolution. The answer to the question of why private sector development, participation, and governance have met with varying fates lies both with the member states and other actors that constitute the environment within which the Bank operates and with the norms, values, and beliefs that make up its organizational culture.

Students of the World Bank have long faced the problem that most of the material written about the Bank is written or published by the Bank. In investigating the three cases presented in this book, I have made an effort to go beyond the Bank's formal pronouncements and sponsored research by relying on secondary sources and interviews with Bank personnel and others.[2] I am fortunate to have undertaken this project during a period in which "Bank-watching" became both easier and more prevalent. The fiftieth anniversary in 1994 of the Bretton Woods institutions marked the publication of many studies of the Bank and its sister institution, the

International Monetary Fund (IMF), by outside observers. At the same time, heightened attention to the Bank by NGOs in the United States and abroad resulted in a greater availability of independent information. The Bank itself made the job easier by becoming a markedly more open institution.[3]

This study does not attempt to assess comprehensively the changes undergone by the Bank in the 1990s.[4] It is a more limited endeavor that examines three areas in detail and develops from them some broader ideas about the dynamics of institutional change at the World Bank and at other multilateral organizations. I selected the cases of private sector development, participation, and governance for several reasons. First, although they are important areas of Bank activity, they have not received sustained attention from either the academic or policy world.[5] Even the monumental history of the World Bank's first fifty years (Kapur et al. 1997) does not focus to any significant degree on these issues. Yet the agendas covered here are extremely important, in part because they mark the Bank's responses to the most notable trends in the developing world in the 1990s, market-oriented economic reform, democratization, and the growing strength of civil society. In this sense, they serve as excellent bellwethers for judging how and to what degree the Bank has been able to respond to a changing world. Finally, each area represents a significant departure from past Bank practice and, as such, provides insight into the malleability of the institution.

Understanding the factors that underpin changes in the goals and activities of one of the world's most important international organizations has both theoretical and practical significance. By providing a partial answer to the question of when and why multilateral institutions evolve, the stories presented here weigh in on the ongoing debate over the degree of autonomy enjoyed by international organizations. This research also speaks to debates on whether institutions adapt quickly and smoothly to exogenous changes or whether their evolution is more gradual and sometimes takes unexpected turns. At a policy level, this book is intended to inform policymakers' understanding about the degree to which the goals of the World Bank reflect the national interest of its members, and how member state preferences are translated into practice. For development practitioners and NGOs, as well as Bank managers and staff, this book provides some answers to the following questions. How effective will the World Bank be in achieving its stated mission of poverty reduction and renewed growth in the developing world? What constraints does it face in pursuing the new agendas necessary to achieve this mission? And which strategies are most appropriate for those seeking further change in the Bank's activities and goals?

2 Understanding the World Bank

A theoretical overview

As with any organization, it is a challenge to understand the dimensions and dynamics of change at the World Bank. Can patterns be discerned in how the Bank has evolved over time? Do similar causes lie behind shifts in the Bank's mission and activities? Are there bodies of theory that can be drawn upon to shed light on the Bank's institutional development? A central finding of this study is that neither international relations theory nor organization theory alone provides an adequate explanation of change at the Bank. The World Bank is a prominent actor in the international system, created by states to help govern that system and subject to the kind of state-centered analysis that has dominated the study of international relations. Yet it is also a large and complex institution that enjoys significant autonomy in its operations and goal-setting; hence, it can be analyzed using the tools of organization theory. Each of these approaches provides only a partial picture of the dynamics that drive institutional change at the World Bank.

This chapter begins by viewing the Bank through the prisms of international relations theory and organization theory, then takes a more in-depth look at the key elements of the Bank's organizational culture, how it has been preserved, and how it might be altered. Only by integrating the two approaches considered here can one arrive at an understanding of how the World Bank has evolved in the past and how it may change in the future.

States and power: international-relations-based approaches

While political scientists have studied organizations for many years, the analysis of international organizations – particularly their internal dimensions – has been relegated to second-rate status within the discipline of international relations. The chief explanation for this neglect is that international relations theory focuses on the international system as a whole rather than on the dynamics of the organizations that are part of that system. Neorealists, who for many years dominated the discipline, see international institutions as reflections or embodiments of state power and interests, "only one small step removed from the underlying power configurations that support them"

(Krasner 1985: 28). Kenneth Waltz (1979), the leading proponent of neorealism, provided the classic articulation of this view, but it still has currency, as in a more recent comment that "institutions are basically a reflection of the distribution of power in the world" (Mearsheimer 1994/5: 7). Neoliberals posit more of an independent role for institutions, especially in resolving collective action problems, but their focus is still on system-wide questions of regime formation or cooperation among states (Krasner 1983, Keohane 1984). Part of the debate between these two schools of thought revolves around the significance of international institutions in world politics and the extent to which they mitigate difficulties of cooperation within an anarchical state system (Baldwin 1993). Essentially, though, both neorealists and neoliberals are concerned with how states define their interests and how they behave within the international system, leaving little room for any analysis of the internal processes of institutions.

In seeking to understand institutional change at the World Bank, ncorealists and neoliberals would focus on the interests of powerful external actors, although the two groups would define these somewhat differently. The most influential actors in relation to the Bank are those industrialized nations that provide it with capital backing. The reason for their influence is that the Bank borrows almost all the funds it lends on international capital markets. It is able to borrow this money at highly favorable rates because its developed member countries have pledged "callable" capital, money that has not been appropriated or paid to the institution, but that member countries would be legally bound to contribute if the World Bank were unable to repay its bondholders. The Bank is not allowed to borrow or lend more money than its member countries have pledged, plus its reserves. This means that it depends on the capital support of its members to underpin its lending and must secure from them capital increases if it is to grow.

Voting power is heavily skewed toward those developed countries that provide the greatest capital backing for the Bank. The three most influential members, all of them countries that do not borrow from the institution, together control 28 per cent of its votes. (The United States had 17.0 per cent of voting power at the end of fiscal 1997, Japan 6.0 per cent, and Germany 4.7 per cent.) States that provide capital to the Bank use their voting power to approve loan decisions and determine policy (the United States, for example, retains a *de facto* veto over changes to the Articles of Agreement), but they also influence the Bank by putting pressure informally on other member countries or management. While the voting power of the United States has waned over time, it remains by far the most important IBRD member. The United States has additional leverage because the Bank's president is by tradition an American selected by the United States.[1]

The IBRD's three largest borrowers – China, India, and Russia, each with 2.9 per cent of voting power – account for less than 9 per cent of votes within the organization. But the limited voting power of borrowers understates the influence they can wield. Borrowing countries have a say in Bank policies, although theirs tends to be a "negative" power, the power to say no rather than to place a new issue on the institution's agenda. This source of influence has its roots in the Bank's steady expansion and historical equation of success with higher lending levels. In order for the Bank to grow, and before it can request a capital increase, demand for its loans must rise, and that demand comes from borrowers. Thus, borrowers exert control over the Bank by their willingness or unwillingness to accept the conditions of Bank lending. Those borrowers that have access to other sources of capital (such as middle-income countries that can now borrow on private markets) and large countries in which the Bank needs to do business in order to maintain its loan volume (such as China) are more powerful than the smaller and poorer developing countries.

While neorealists would emphasize the role of the states that subscribe capital to and officially govern the World Bank, neoliberals would point also to those non-state actors that affect Bank policy, especially non-governmental organizations (NGOs) in both industrialized and developing nations. NGOs have had a growing impact on the Bank in recent years mainly through public campaigns to monitor and influence its performance. These campaigns include successful efforts by environmental NGOs to halt several large hydroelectric dam projects funded by the Bank and the "50 Years is Enough" campaign to publicize NGO and grassroots criticism of the work of the Bretton Woods institutions.[2] There are also a number of formal channels through which NGOs provide input into Bank decision making, such as the NGO-World Bank Committee, the World Bank Inspection Panel, and ongoing meetings between Bank staff and NGO representatives.

In addition to NGOs, there are other non-state actors that play a role in shaping Bank policy. The financial community, made up of the investment banks that underwrite World Bank bonds, the rating agencies that rate those bonds, and the investors that hold them, is one such group. These actors exercise power over the institution by their continued willingness to finance the Bank's borrowing program, their role in determining the interest rate at which it is able to borrow, and their insistence that certain financial policies be maintained in order for the Bank to preserve its strong credit standing.

The question addressed in this study is why new agendas introduced at the Bank have become institutionalized in different ways and to varying degrees. Most international relations theorists would interpret the Bank's enthusiastic adoption of private sector development, relative to participation or governance, as a reflection of the power and preferences of external actors. In this view, private-sector-related initiatives were essentially forced on the Bank by its largest member, the United States. Support for participation and governance came primarily from coalitions of NGOs and the Bank's smaller member countries that have less formal power than the United States; thus, these agendas met with a less enthusiastic response from Bank staff and management. At the same time, developing country governments may have been more willing to accept loans tied to the promotion of the private sector (especially given that private sector resources are often concentrated in the hands of elites who also run the government) than they were to accept loans tied to how the government operates or how closely groups within civil society are involved in Bank projects, conditions that could serve to undermine elite power.

But analyses that interpret the behavior of international organizations solely as the outcome of the preferences of external actors, be they states or NGOs, provide a distorted view of institutional change. When one traces how the new agendas examined here actually emerged at the Bank, externally driven explanations reveal themselves to be overly mechanistic and capable of providing only a partial picture of what happened. One shortcoming of this kind of explanation is that it undervalues the substantial resources, financial and otherwise, amassed by the Bank over the years. Instead of relying directly on member contributions (like the United Nations), the IBRD has its own access to worldwide capital markets on extremely favorable terms. With net income of over $1 billion annually since 1985, the Bank has accumulated substantial financial assets, amounting to $18 billion at the end of 1997. A staff of more than 10,000, recruited from every part of the world (and especially its top universities) and an extensive research operation have contributed to making the Bank Group the world's largest single repository of technical expertise about development issues and a major contributor to development thinking. A sprawling (and spreading) physical complex in Washington, DC, and regional offices around the globe provide a physical counterpart to these financial and intellectual resources. Its assets make the World Bank a powerful force in its own right. Even when external pressure is applied, an institution with the size and strength of the Bank may not respond in ways that are expected. The metaphor used most often in regard to efforts to change the World Bank is that of trying to reverse the course of an ocean liner. Both processes are slow, unwieldy, and hard to control.

An additional source of autonomy for the Bank comes from its structural position as an intermediary in the international economy. The Bank stands at the center of a two-part "principal–agent" relationship (Ruttan 1996): donor countries provide the Bank with funds and delegate to it the power over how and to whom they should go. The Bank then lends these funds to developing countries, requiring them to fulfill certain obligations in exchange for the money. In both relationships, substantial asymmetries of information exist, with the Bank in the privileged position. These asymmetries mean greater influence for the Bank *vis-à-vis* its member countries, both donor and borrower.

The three cases examined in this study show how external actors played an important role in bringing new issues to the Bank's attention. But they show that institutional factors were at work as well. Moreover, external actors had very little to do with how these new issues, once introduced, were incorporated into practice. The explanation for that part of the story is often found within the World Bank and is a task for which organization theory is particularly well-suited.

Norms and beliefs: organization-theory-based approaches

Organization theory focuses on the internal aspects of institutions and their relationship to the environments in which they operate. An early body of work relevant to this study is that of Philip Selznick and his colleagues. Believing that an organization should be analyzed as an organic whole, they presented "natural histories" of organizations in the form of case studies. These emphasized the normative aspects of institutions, focusing on social obligation, morals, and values. For institutional theorists like Selznick, organizational behavior is explained not by the formal structure of an organization, but by subterranean processes such as conflicts between informal groups, recruitment policies, dependence upon outside constituencies, and the striving for prestige (Perrow 1972: 180). Newcomers to an organization undergo socialization in which their preferences are shaped by norms and reflected in evaluative judgments. The natural history approach is well suited to explaining how new agendas emerge and are incorporated into World Bank practice. Moreover, in telling stories of institutional change at the Bank, it is essential to pay attention to the role of informal processes first identified by institutional analysts.

A later generation of organization theorists took a somewhat different approach than Selznick and his colleagues. These "open systems" theorists argued that institutions cannot be analyzed as discrete entities because they depend on exchanges and interaction with other systems (Thompson 1967). Analyses of how organizations extract resources from their environment utilized two concepts – task environment and core technology – that help make sense of institutional change at the World Bank today.

The task environment encompasses those aspects of the world outside an organization that affect how it sets and attains its goals. The components of an organization's task environment are its various constituencies: customers, suppliers, regulators, and competitors (Scott 1981). Using this four-part division, the World Bank's task environment can be sketched as follows. (See Figure 2.1 for a graphic representation.)

- *Customers*. The World Bank's primary customers are the developing member countries to which it lends. Membership in the Bank has grown steadily since it was founded, with the increase coming almost exclusively from the addition of new borrowers. The two most rapid increases occurred in the early 1960s as a result of decolonization and in the early 1990s with the break-up of the Soviet Union.[3] The Bank had 180 members at the end of the 1997 fiscal year, compared to thirty-eight at its inception. Not only has the number of borrowers grown, but the Bank in recent years has made its clients an increasingly important focus of its attention. In the past, the Bank often projected an arrogance based on its extensive staff and skills, as well as the fact that its borrowers had few alternative sources of long-term funding. For a variety of reasons (some of

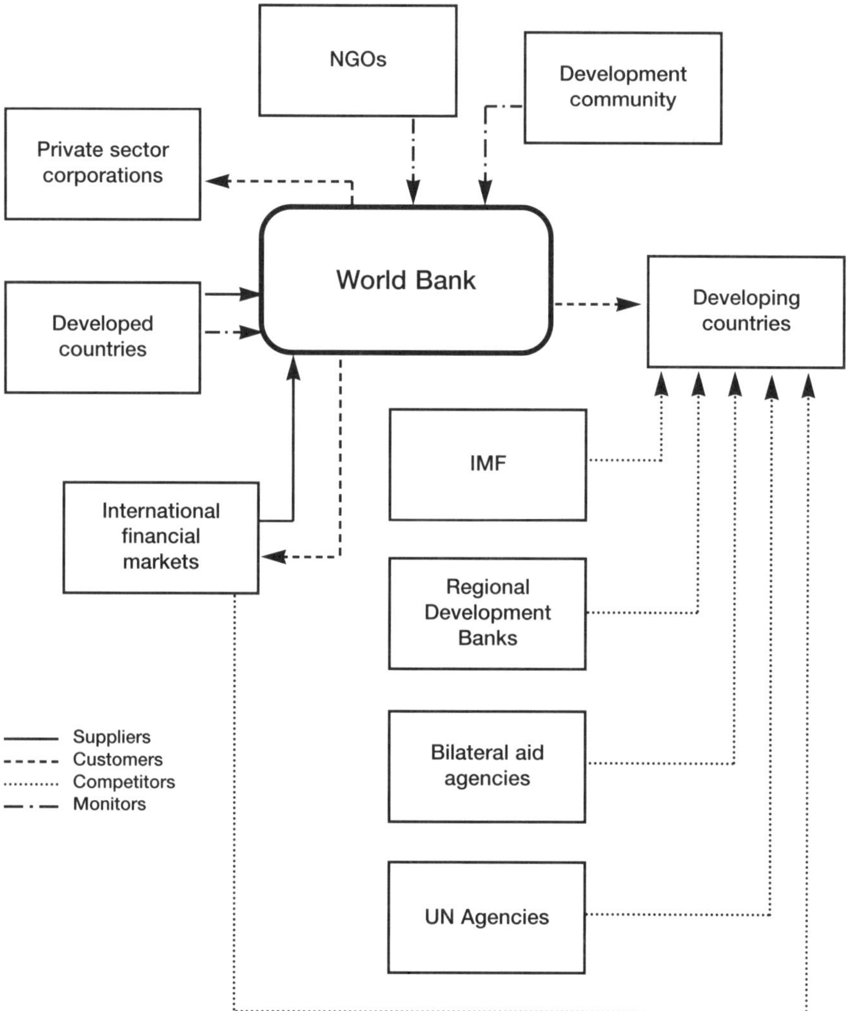

Figure 2.1 The World Bank's task environment

them explored later in this study), the Bank is making changes to ensure that its activities are driven increasingly by its clients' needs and that its attitude is one of partnership.

- *Suppliers.* The World Bank's main resource is its capital. Most of this is supplied by private sector investors who hold World Bank bonds, but the level of Bank borrowing depends, in turn, on the capital backing of its member countries. Thus, the developed member countries that provide capital subscriptions to the Bank can be considered its main suppliers. The key trend here has been the steady decline in US voting share and the gradual diffusion of influence to other industrialized nations. When the IBRD was established in 1947, the United States held 35 per cent of voting power; by the end of fiscal 1997, the US share had declined to 17 per cent, compared to 6 per cent for the second-largest contributor, Japan. When IDA was established in 1960, the United States contributed 32 per cent of its capital and held over 25 per cent of voting power; by 1997, the US voting share was 15.3 per cent, compared to Japan's share of 10.7 per cent.

- *Competitors.* The Bank is part of a larger system of organizations that are charged with financing international development. The bilateral development system comprises the aid agencies of twenty-one industrialized countries represented in the Development Assistance Committee (DAC) of the OECD. The multilateral development system includes not only the World Bank and the International Monetary Fund (IMF), but also the UN specialized agencies that serve sectoral demands in the areas of population, child care, health, agriculture, and so on, as well as an array of regional institutions.[4]

  Bilateral aid agencies, such as the US Agency for International Development (AID) or the United Kingdom's Overseas Development Administration, make many of their decisions about foreign assistance on the basis of political and strategic, rather than economic considerations. Much of their funding is in the form of grants, not loans, and their resources must be provided by national legislatures.

  More similar in structure to the World Bank are the African, Asian, and Inter-American Development Banks, and the European Bank for Reconstruction and Development (EBRD). The first three resemble each other and the World Bank in their activities, although not their regional focus or scale. When the EBRD was founded in 1990, some advocates for the World Bank (including the US Treasury Department) feared that the new institution would prevent the Bank from taking the lead in the economic restructuring just under way in Eastern Europe and the former Soviet Union. In part as a result, the EBRD is set up somewhat differently from the World Bank and distinct roles have been reserved for each in the region.

  Although the IMF is quite different from the World Bank in its size, structure, and operations, the functions of the two agencies have converged in recent years. The division of labor set forth at Bretton Woods, under which the IMF had primary responsibility for short-term exchange rate management and correcting imbalances in external accounts, while the Bank made long-term investments in development projects, persisted through the 1960s. When the Bretton Woods system of fixed exchange rates collapsed in the early 1970s, the Fund became increasingly involved in stabilization and the time frame of its activities lengthened. In 1980, the World Bank began making structural adjustment (that is, non-project) loans that are disbursed over a shorter period and are conditional on economic policy reform in member countries. These changes brought about a state in which the Bank and the IMF were "both providing balance of payments loans, tranched over one to three years, with medium-term amortization periods. Both programs supported macroeconomic and microeconomic adjustments, and focused on improving both external and internal accounts" (Feinberg 1988: 549–50). The blurring of responsibilities between the two agencies became even more evident during the debt crisis of the 1980s when both played a part in channeling capital to heavily indebted countries. This overlap has led to calls for a rethinking of the respective roles of the Bank and the Fund and even consideration of whether they should be merged.

A new competitor for the Bank has arisen recently in the form of private capital markets, which now provide substantial flows of portfolio and equity investment to parts of the developing world. In recent years such flows, which were almost nonexistent following the debt crisis, have surged, especially to those middle-income countries that represent the strongest portion of the World Bank's portfolio. The Bank is forbidden by its charter to compete with private sources of capital. Renewed private investment thus raises questions for the Bank about how to continue its work in these countries without infringing on the activities of private investors.

- *Regulators.* The Bank is not regulated formally by any group other than the governments of its member countries (although its financial operations are governed by the securities laws of the countries in which it borrows funds). However, there are external actors, such as NGOs and development experts, that monitor and evaluate the Bank's activities. The NGO community has become increasingly active in this regard in the 1980s and 1990s, with a variety of implications for the Bank. On the one hand, the Bank has stepped up its dealings with NGOs and is working to involve them in many of its lending activities; on the other hand, the Bank has become a juicy target for NGO attacks over its environmental policies and adjustment lending, leading to institutional changes that have brought with them greater openness and accountability.

The main change in the Bank's task environment is a bewildering growth in the number and variety of its stakeholders.[5] The Bank operates within a more complex environment than at any time in its past, with more member countries, new competitors, and increasingly active NGOs that represent not only concerned populations in donor countries but also groups within borrower countries that are affected by Bank activities. Managing this wider range of stakeholders and extracting from them the resources necessary for the maintenance of the institution has become an increasingly difficult task for World Bank leaders.

Core technology, the second key concept used by open systems theorists, refers to the central tasks around which an organization is built (Scott 1981:

189). The Bank's core technology has changed along with its task environment. Until about 1980, the distinguishing features of the Bank's technology were the detailed specification of project plans before Bank approval of loans, the centralization of decisions regarding the preparation and implementation of projects, and the identification of discrete investment-oriented activities to be financed by the Bank (Crane and Finkle 1981: 531). While project plans are still specified in advance of loan approval, the other two features have changed markedly. The addition of new stakeholders and greater openness to outside views means that project-related decisions are less centralized than in the past, and the emphasis on stand-alone investment-oriented projects has given way to policy adjustment lending and a range of programs designed for purposes other than investment.

A final aspect of the Bank's core technology is its top-down, expert stance, whereby the Bank develops a lending program in line with its own diagnosis of a borrower's problems and brings to bear the technical skills and financing it believes are needed to address those problems. The Bank has begun to acknowledge that it does not have all the answers and is increasingly willing to consult with outside groups, but the top-down, expert-oriented approach to lending remains very much intact.

One of the primary survival strategies of an organization is to "buffer" its technical core from disturbances in the environment. In this regard, organizations strive not just to achieve technical efficiency, but to ensure organizational survival and enhance their bargaining position *vis-à-vis* other systems (Scott 1981: 189). One of the most typical buffering strategies for an organization, and one the World Bank has pursued since its establishment, is growth. Another is cooptation, the incorporation of representatives of external groups into the decision-making structure of an organization. This strategy has been evident in the approach the World Bank has taken toward some of its critics in the NGO community. Scott (1981) points out that as an organization incorporates elements of the environment into its own structure, it may introduce new, alien, and occasionally hostile elements into its own system. This dynamic has contributed to the emergence of networks of individuals within the World Bank who have challenged its dominant culture and in some cases brought about organizational change.

In contrast to earlier organization theorists who stressed the normative aspects of institutions, the "new" institutionalists in sociology emphasize their cognitive aspects, especially the importance of taken-for-granted scripts, rules, and classifications.[6] In this approach, the mechanism of conformity is not socialization, as in traditional organization theory, but "cognitive models in which schemas and scripts lead decision makers to resist new evidence" (DiMaggio and Powell 1991: 15). Formal structures are "manifestations of powerful institutional rules which function as highly rationalized myths that are binding on particular organizations" (Meyer and Rowan 1977: 44). These myths are "rationalized and impersonal prescriptions that identify various social purposes as technical ones and specify in a rulelike way the appropriate means to pursue these technical purposes rationally" (ibid.: 44). Myths "are highly institutionalized and thus in some measure beyond the discretion of any individual participant . . . They must, therefore, be taken for granted as legitimate" (ibid.: 343–4). This concept of institutional rules, or organizational myths (the terms are used interchangeably here) – those values and beliefs that are accepted as "given" by Bank personnel – forms an important element in the analysis of institutional change presented below.

New institutionalists identify three types of processes – regulative, normative, and cognitive – through which institutions "provide stability and meaning to social behavior" (Scott 1995: 33). The World Bank embodies elements of each.

Regulative processes

In their regulative capacity institutions set rules and monitor and sanction behavior. The World Bank's chief role as regulator concerns its relationship with its borrowers. When a country receives a World Bank loan, it becomes bound by a series of requirements embodied in the loan covenants and related documentation. These requirements include not only the terms of the loan (its repayment schedule, interest rate, and so on), but the conditions that are specified by the loan, such as the completion of a given project or the enactment of agreed-upon policy reforms. Only if these conditions are met will the Bank agree to release future installments of the loan. (Virtually all World Bank loans are paid out in tranches over several years.) And only if the country continues to service its World Bank debt will future loans be committed and disbursed.

In reality, there are strong incentives for the Bank to continue to lend, especially to its large borrowers, even if all the terms of a loan are not complied with. One fear is that if lending slows, the Bank will shrink in size and become a less central player in the international economy. Another incentive arises when the Bank is owed a considerable sum by a borrower on the brink of insolvency. In such a case, the Bank's institutional interest lies in ensuring that the borrower is able to service this debt, even if means lending the borrower new money to do so.

A second regulative feature is the formal control vested in the Bank's member countries, particularly those that contribute capital to the organization but do not borrow from it. In this case, regulation flows in the opposite direction, with the Bank itself the regulated party rather than the regulator. The Bank's member countries exercise formal power over the institution by virtue of their capital contributions and voting share. Representatives of member countries sit on the Bank's Board of Executive Directors and are responsible for determining the rules that govern the Bank and for overseeing its operations. In practice, a great deal of decision-making authority resides with the Bank's staff and management; in formal terms, however, the Bank's members are charged with its governance.

Both of these features point to a disjunction between the Bank's formal rules and its actual operation, and suggest that an institution's regulative aspects tell only a small part of its story.

Normative processes

Normative processes involve the prescriptive, evaluative, and obligatory features of an institution. The World Bank is one of the world's largest and most creditworthy borrowers, issuing bonds in global capital markets on highly preferential terms. The Bank's creditworthiness is based not only on formal criteria, such as its one-to-one gearing ratio under which it cannot lend more than its subscribed capital, but on normative standards as well. Participants in the capital markets make ongoing judgments that the Bank is conducting itself appropriately, adhering to strict financial policies, keeping on hand a safe level of reserves, and managing its resources profitably.

Borrowing countries do not repay the Bank only because they are bound to by law. Since its inception, the Bank has been treated by borrowers as a "preferred creditor," the institution a country repays before all others. For example, borrowers continued to service their World Bank debt in the 1980s even as they curtailed repayments and received successive reschedulings of their loans from commercial banks. Countries generally service their World Bank debt promptly not only to continue receiving disbursements of World Bank loans, but also to remain in the good graces of other international lending institutions. The World Bank's preferred creditor status is not a legal requirement, nor is it simply a recognition of the power of the Bank. Over the years a normative consensus has formed among lending institutions and borrowing countries alike that treating the World Bank as a preferred creditor is a central part of playing by the rules of international finance.

There is an evaluative component to the Bank–borrower relationship as well, as Bank staff makes ongoing judgments as to whether a borrower is managing its economy successfully by following policies the Bank has deemed appropriate. In addition to monitoring a country's economic performance, Bank staff and management routinely engage in a dialogue with policymakers in borrowing countries. Informal and off the record, this policy dialogue is none the less influential in shaping the Bank's perception of a given borrower's economic policies. The evaluative function has broader ramifications: Bank approval of a country's economic policy – signalled, for example, by the conclusion of a large adjustment loan – is a key factor in establishing that country's creditworthiness in the eyes of private investors.

An additional normative feature of the World Bank is the leadership role played by management. Although formal authority resides with the Board of Executive Directors, it is the Bank's top managers who set the agenda for the Board and whose proximity to the organization's day-to-day operations gives them substantial *de facto* power.

Finally, the World Bank's staff and management share a common set of values by virtue of their background and academic training, despite the fact that they come from many different countries. An emphasis on technical analysis based in the disciplines of economics and finance, and the official avoidance of politics, are two key norms that contribute to the Bank's organizational culture. (These are discussed in more detail below.)

Cognitive processes

The cognitive aspect of institutions concerns their symbolic systems and shared meanings. One of the shared beliefs of World Bank staff since the late 1970s is that neoliberal policies are the appropriate prescription for its borrowers' ailing economies. Neoliberal policies call for markets, rather than governments, to serve as the key allocative mechanism within an economy; to this end, the Bank favors price, trade, tax, and institutional policies designed to increase the efficiency of resource allocation, especially in the area of domestic investment. These ideas have been espoused by the Bank in its research program and are incorporated into the terms of its structural adjustment loans. The Bank's stance, which coincided with that of the IMF and the Reagan and Bush administrations, contributed to what came to be called "the Washington consensus." As the very term implies, these views are considered conceptually correct by development experts inside and outside the Bank. The Bank's recruitment and hiring processes go a long way toward screening out potential staff members with different conceptual frameworks. More informal socialization mechanisms enforce conformity as well; for instance, interviews with Bank personnel suggest that it is difficult for a staff member to express or act on opinions that are seriously out of step with accepted beliefs about development.

The neoliberal orthodoxy embraced by the Bank has repercussions beyond the institution. The relationship between the Bank and the wider community of development experts (including those in government, academia, and think tanks in both the industrialized and developing world) is mutually constituting. The World Bank is not only an organization that receives and carries out the tenets of development ideology; it is also a contributor to that ideology. The size of the Bank's research effort and the widespread dissemination of pivotal Bank studies suggest the extent of its influence in shaping the views of the worldwide development community. The annual *World Development Report*, for example, has a print run of 120,000 copies, compared to a standard circulation of about 1,000 to 2,000 for an economics journal or monograph (Stern 1997: 591). The input of development experts from outside the Bank into its reports demonstrates the reciprocity of influence between the organization and the broader community of which it is a part.

Organization theorists note that the tendency of similar institutions to imitate each other suggests a cognitive mechanism at work. The World Bank is member (and flagship) of a larger family of regional development banks. Mimetic processes among these institutions are striking. All were configured in a similar way: their creditworthiness is underpinned by members' capital, they borrow money by issuing bonds, and they adhere to the same strict financial policies. These institutions have also tended to behave in similar ways and evolve in similar directions. In the 1980s, most of the development banks implemented some form of adjustment lending and became more concerned with environmental issues, while in the 1990s they became more attuned to the concerns of the private sector and began to consult more closely with NGOs. These trends suggest strong patterns of imitation and replication, with the smaller institutions generally following the lead of the World Bank.

The World Bank is also one of the Bretton Woods institutions, created at the same time as the IMF. The two organizations are dissimilar in structure and operate in different ways, but since the early 1980s they have come to imitate each other in the policy sphere. As noted above, following Mexico's near-default in 1982, both the Bank and the Fund became involved in helping severely indebted countries remain solvent, the Fund by providing stand-by agreements and arranging the rescheduling of commercial bank debt, and the Bank by making fast-disbursing adjustment loans conditioned on policy reform. While there is no official cross-conditionality between the two organizations, their assessments of borrower performance are often carried out in tandem and neither organization will provide funds to a borrower if it is not living up to its obligations to the other. Staff of the Bank and the Fund collaborate closely, work out joint programs for borrowers, track the same issues, and participate in each other's missions to borrowing countries, further strengthening the tendency of the two organizations to move parallel to each other.

The World Bank's organizational culture

The concept of organizational culture refers to a pattern of norms and attitudes that cuts across a whole social unit (Schein 1990: 109–10). An organization's culture reflects the values, beliefs, and practices that give it meaning, identity, and coherence (Nelson 1995: 143). Within an organization as large and complex as the World Bank one can, of course, discern a variety of subcultures. Those staff members who work on the Bank's financial side borrowing and investing its funds exhibit a very different set of attitudes from those who came to the Bank with a background in grassroots development and now work closely with NGOs in borrower countries. The subculture of the former group may resemble that of a private sector bank or firm, while that of the latter may have strong similarities to the Peace Corps. None the less, it is possible to make some generalizations.

First, the Bank's culture is shaped by its founding charter. The IBRD's Articles of Agreement were signed in 1945 and have been amended on only a few occasions. Perhaps because the charter is such a brief document, it has proven quite flexible. The Bank's general counsel points out that, "It has been able to innovate through policy changes and practical measures," rather than resorting to amendment of its charter (Shihata 1991: 1–2). The flexibility of the Articles of Agreement means that they require interpretation, and it is the Bank itself that serves as the chief interpreter of its own legal boundaries (Sullivan 1995: 12). Although referred to frequently in debates over why the Bank can and cannot undertake certain sets of activities, the Articles leave open a wide array of paths through which the Bank can pursue issues that it deems central to the goal of development.

More relevant than the Articles for determining Bank practice are the range of policies, directives, and advice published by the Bank for use by its staff. The most binding of these are Operational Policies that follow from the Articles of Agreement and have been approved by the Board of Executive Directors. They establish the parameters for the conduct of Bank operations. Operational Policies have been issued on topics ranging from instruments for Bank lending, to the preparation of project documents, to the need for environmental assessments. A less binding category of policy is Bank Procedures that spell out the processes and documentation needed to ensure that Bank policies are carried out in a consistent manner. A third category of policy, called Good Practice, consists of advice and guidance on how to implement policy. This is not required to be followed by staff, but represents what are considered to be valuable models.

This set of policies and advice, contained in the Bank's operational manual, are what Bank staff refer to when they seek guidance for their work. They provide an important intermediate level of authority and advice between the formal rules of the Articles of Agreement and the informal norms that shape the Bank's organizational culture.

The Bank's culture is characterized by two key norms. First, development, at least as practiced by the Bank, is an apolitical process. Second, development is best achieved through technical means. What do these ideas mean, where did they come from, and how have they influenced the Bank's structure and function?

The apolitical norm

The Bank's apolitical orientation, embodied both in the Articles of Agreement and in the values and beliefs of its staff, is what sociologists call an "organizational myth." The point about such a myth is not whether it is true or false, but that it plays an essential role in an institution's self-conception and quest for legitimacy.

The accuracy of the Bank's claim to apolitical behavior has long been subject to debate. Officially, the Bank "has deemed political considerations to be generally irrelevant to its operations" (Shihata 1991: 53). At the same time, the Bank acknowledged early on that it "cannot ignore conditions of political instability or uncertainty which may directly affect the economic and financial prospects of the borrower" (IBRD 1954: 61). Various scholars have made the case that the World Bank has never been as apolitical as it maintains, but the apolitical norm is an important part of the Bank's identity and legitimacy in the eyes of the international community for several reasons.[7]

First, the official avoidance of politics has allowed the Bank to work with a diverse group of governments. The 180 countries that are members of the IBRD span a wide variety of ideologies and political cultures. In order to lend to countries with different types of political regimes and maintain enough support to underpin its steady expansion, the Bank has had to adhere to a set of strict technical criteria and portray itself as "above politics." Despite the validity of arguments that question the apolitical myth, there is no disputing the fact that the Bank has worked with regimes as ideologically diverse as Pinochet's Chile, communist China, socialist Zimbabwe, and authoritarian Brazil. This in itself is not evidence that the Bank avoids political considerations in its lending decisions, but it does suggest that the claim of political neutrality enables the Bank to deal with a wide range of governments.

Second, the apolitical norm allows staff members drawn from many different countries to set aside their personal and/or national politics and identify themselves with the institution for which they work. The need for the Bank to maintain its apolitical stance is accepted by staff members when they join the Bank and shapes their career paths from then on. In part to preserve this norm, nationals of a given country are almost never assigned to work directly on that country and a special effort is made to appoint senior managers of regional divisions who come from outside the region. There is also frequent rotation of staff members to keep them from forming too strong an attachment to a given region, nation, or government. The belief within the Bank that it does not – and, moreover, should not – become involved in a country's politics ensures the smooth functioning of an international secretariat staffed with people of many nationalities.[8]

Third, the Bank's apolitical identity increases its legitimacy in the eyes of its borrowers. Pressure to avoid politics has come from some developing countries that oppose what they perceive as Bank interference in their internal politics. The Bank's *World Development Report*, in particular, has suffered from what one observer called "an enforced reticence on political matters. Generally, anything that might offend politicians of particular countries has been avoided . . . In effect, each member country has veto power over material referring to it" (Stern 1997: 571). As most developing countries have become more open politically this has been less of a problem.

The apolitical norm had its origins in the multinational character of the World Bank and the need to obtain support from, and lend to, as broad a range of governments as possible. The onset of the Cold War in the 1950s made this orientation even more pressing. Although Eastern bloc countries (except for Yugoslavia) were not members of the World Bank during the Cold War and thus received no World Bank loans, the Bank's officially apolitical nature enabled it to lend to Third World countries allied with the Soviet Union, as well as to non-aligned countries.

The end of the Cold War brought the entry of formerly communist countries into the World Bank and resolved the decades-long schism between socialist and democratic systems of government in favor of the latter. With the geopolitical reins loosened, the Bank at the end of the 1980s was able for the first time to acknowledge explicitly the importance of political factors in economic development, including the benefits of representative government. Yet, despite some tentative experimentation in the direction of improving borrower countries' governance, the Bank continues to maintain that politics lies outside its mandate and that its apolitical orientation remains central to its effectiveness. It appears that the apolitical philosophy, which emerged at a time when it filled an important need, has become sufficiently institutionalized to persist even though that time has passed.

The technical norm

The World Bank's second key institutional norm is that development can be achieved through technical means. Throughout its history, the Bank has relied on well-honed techniques that, whenever possible, involve quantitative measurement and can be applied in a wide range of countries. In its early days as a lender for infrastructure projects, Bank staff consisted largely of specialists with expertise in a given technical area, such as agronomy, engineering, or hydrology. The influence of economists grew in the 1960s and 1970s, and when project lending was supplemented by policy adjustment lending in the 1980s financial experts joined the ranks. Even now, as the Bank seeks staff with a different "skills mix" to carry out some of its newer activities, these skills are defined exclusively in technical terms. Despite the evolution of the Bank in new directions, the "mastery of technical knowledge based on objective and rational analysis" (Kardam 1990: 117) remains the order of the day.

One reason for the centrality of technical analysis at the World Bank is that economic development is a fairly young field and one where the standards for success are difficult to define:

> [P]rofessional practice in a young field tends to establish itself, almost unconsciously, by holding itself up to the standards that give the classical professions status – often a framework of technical rationality that in law and medicine justified rigorous training and mastery of things technical.
> (Dichter 1992: 91)

As development economics emerged as a discipline in the early 1950s, its professionalization "made it possible to remove all problems from the political and cultural realms and to recast them in terms of the apparently more neutral realm of science" (Escobar 1995: 45). A high degree of technical expertise was essential to the World Bank's claim to leadership in this new field.

The technical norm is also related to the Bank's need shortly after it was founded to establish its creditworthiness in the capital markets. Because of its central role in economic development – both intellectually and in terms of resources – it is easy to forget that the Bank is structured to resemble an extremely conservative financial institution. It is owned by shareholders (its member countries) who commit capital to be used in the event of an emergency. This capital backing, combined with conservative financial policies, allows the IBRD to borrow most of the money it lends on the world's capital markets. (Because it makes funds available on concessional terms, IDA does not issue bonds but is funded directly by member countries and through contributions from the IBRD's annual profits.)

The World Bank has had a triple-A credit rating (the highest possible) since the late 1950s, and its bonds are held by the most cautious of investors.[9] The Bank is judged continually in the capital markets and by the rating agencies on measures of its financial strength, such as capitalization, the level of financial reserves, annual profits, and the condition of its loan portfolio. The Bank's substantial skill in maintaining strict financial policies and performing well in purely financial terms has allowed it to act as an intermediary through which the resources of the world's most conservative investors can be channeled to developing countries for what, under other circumstances, would be considered distinctly risky ventures.

An important aspect of this system is the Bank's adherence to rigorous financial standards in its lending program. IBRD loans are made at market rates and are expected to earn a rate of return of at least 10 per cent or its equivalent in qualitative terms when quantification is not feasible (*Annual Report* 1993: 61). (In practice, rates of return are not quantified for about half of the Bank's portfolio.) Cases of non-payment by member countries are taken seriously and a range of measures are brought to bear against those few governments that are late in servicing their debts to the Bank. The Bank is helped in its financial performance by its preferred creditor status. Of course, the continued willingness of developing countries to repay their Bank debt in the 1980s was due in large part to the fact that the World Bank continued to lend to them when almost all commercial sources of finance had evaporated. For most World Bank borrowers, there continues to be "money in the pipeline" – loans committed to a country but not yet disbursed – that provides a strong incentive for prompt servicing of World Bank debt.[10]

Occasionally, the requirements of the World Bank as a financial institution have been used by management to resist new initiatives pressed on it by member countries or others. Experience suggests, however, that the investor community cares little about what the Bank does with its money, as long as its loans are repaid and its conservative financial policies maintained. In 1959, an observer argued that "It is impossible . . . to raise money for various forms of social investment which the Bank rules out as unproductive; housing, schools, health services, and so on" (Cairncross 1959: 18). The Bank, of course, now raises significant sums precisely for these purposes. In the 1960s, investors grew anxious when the IBRD began to channel surplus funds to IDA to increase Bank lending to the poorest countries in violation of an earlier promise not to mix IBRD and IDA resources, yet this development (which continues to the present) did not affect the Bank's credit standing.[11] Bondholders initially were concerned when the Bank began lending for structural adjustment, but returned rapidly to the usual high level of comfort with the World Bank's creditworthiness. Bank participation in the 1989 Brady Plan for reducing the debt of less-developed countries met with a similar reaction. Despite ongoing evidence of the strength of investor confidence, the fear of a negative reaction by capital markets to new initiatives acts as an additional source of conservatism and reinforces the primacy placed by the Bank on its technical expertise.

An organization that prides itself on its status as a first-class financial institution will staff itself with economic, financial, and other technical experts and will place a strong emphasis on rigorous and quantitative analysis. Like the apolitical norm, the technical norm is rooted in conditions of the Bank's establishment. The context within which an organization is created affects its institutional structure in significant ways. As the noted scholar Arthur Stinchcombe wrote, "Organizations which are founded at a particular time must construct their social systems with the social resources available" (Stinchcombe 1965: 168). In other words, the architects of an organization must design it in such a way that it is able to recruit the resources it needs from society.

When it was founded, the resources the World Bank needed above all were capital and legitimacy, and the two were closely related. In order to ensure that these resources would be forthcoming, the Bank's creators constructed it as a financially conservative organization and repository of technical competence. From the 1950s on, the insistence that the Bank's work was politically neutral was necessary to enable the Bank to maintain the confidence of its member countries while lending to as many different types of governments as possible within the geopolitical framework of the Cold War. (A similar institution created today might look very different, as indeed does the EBRD, with its overtly political mission and commitment of resources directly to the private sector.) These financial and political considerations contributed to an enduring emphasis on quantitative and economic analysis, as well as an insistence that objective judgments of a country's development needs are possible. As its general counsel has written, "the Bank's credibility and strength has traditionally depended on its status as a quintessential technocracy exclusively concerned with economic efficiency" (Shihata 1991: 54).

By the 1990s, the conditions that had given rise to these institutional rules were no longer in place. The Bank's creditworthiness had been established for decades and its credibility as a development institution no longer required the ongoing demonstration of technical expertise. Moreover, the geopolitical environment had changed dramatically with the end of the Cold War. Yet the institutional rules that emerged in the Bank's earliest years continued to shape its activities. A key aspect of institutional theory is its understanding of change as incremental and "channeled in the well-worn grooves of established adaptations" (Perrow 1972: 157). Organization theorists expect institutional rules to remain basically intact, even once the conditions that gave rise to them initially have changed. In contrast, an international relations perspective that treats multilateral institutions as fairly efficient conduits of state interests would expect international organizations to change as the international system changes. The persistence of the Bank's technical and apolitical orientation well into the 1990s, within a radically altered international context, suggests the usefulness of an institutional approach.

Preserving the Bank's culture

The Bank's recruitment and hiring of staff trained almost exclusively in economics, finance, and other specialized fields has contributed to the persistence of the apolitical and technical norms that characterize the Bank's organizational culture. One of the reasons why an organization's culture remains intact over time is because of the role played within it by professionals. Professionalization – "the collective struggle of members of an occupation to define the conditions and methods of their work" (DiMaggio and Powell 1983: 70) – helps explain why institutional norms endure. Organizations staffed and run by members of a given profession will behave according to its norms. Professional norms are preserved through selective recruitment, a fast-track mechanism that promotes people with the "right" set of values, and socialization of newcomers to prevailing beliefs. At elite institutions, such as the World Bank, "professional career tracks are so closely guarded . . . that individuals who make it to the top are virtually indistinguishable" (ibid.: 71). The filtering of personnel is achieved through, among other things, "the recruitment of fast-track staff from a narrow range of training institutions" and "skill-level requirements for particular jobs" (ibid.: 71). For example, the Bank's Young Professionals (YP) program traditionally recruited only from Ivy League institutions in the United States and a few French and British universities; in the 1990s, it expanded its recruitment activities to MBA programs, including those abroad, and the top Japanese universities. Even so, however, it remains focused on the most elite schools in only a few countries.

Reliable details about the professional make-up of the Bank's staff are hard to come by. In fact, the Bank seems to have cut back on the few pieces of information about hiring that historically were presented in the annual report. The staffing data that is available publicly can be misleading; for example, the *Annual Report* 1997 puts the Bank's "regular and fixed-term staff" at 5,443, but provides no indication of the number of temporary staff and consultants, of whom there are several thousand. While many areas of the Bank have become increasingly transparent over the past few years as a result of outside pressure from NGOs and member countries, the new openness does not seem to extend to information about the Bank's hiring practices or personnel profile.

When it comes to determining the number of economists on the Bank's staff, a new difficulty arises. Because of the premium placed by the Bank on economic skills, there is a tendency for staff members to identify themselves as economists even if they do not hold a PhD in economics. One senior staff member has suggested that as a result the standard estimate of around 1,000 economists on the Bank's staff is probably inflated. (A recent estimate by contributors to the World Bank History Project puts the count at 800 (Stern 1997: 524).) Whatever the precise number, it is clear that members of the discipline (along with their colleagues trained in finance) exercise a great deal of influence within the organization. Economists fill many managerial positions and dominate some important units of the Bank. A 1991 survey of the Bank's policy and research department, a key locus of decision-making at the time, found that 46 per cent of undergraduate and 55 per cent of graduate degrees held by staff were in economics or finance (Stern 1997: 586). Another analyst reports that, "In general, most upper-level decision makers are economists. Most non-economists who work at upper levels are 'advisors'." (Annis 1986: 102) In its literature, the Bread for the World Institute claims that "among Bank staff, there are twenty-eight economists for every one non-economic social scientist," and the latter are often consultants or junior staff dependent for their compensation on trust funds rather than on the normal Bank budget (Bread for the World Institute 1996: 9).

Other estimates come from the Bank itself which reported ninety-nine staff members specializing in the social sciences as of 1996, of whom more than 60 per cent had been recruited within the prior three years (*Annual Report 1996*: 55). The standard estimate of the number of professional economists on staff thus puts the economist to non-economic social scientist ratio at ten-to-one. A statistic that sheds further light on Bank hiring patterns comes from the YP program where about one-third of each year's new class hold PhDs in economics, another third have MBAs, and the rest have advanced degrees in some other technical field, such as engineering or environmental science.[12]

Moreover, staff members generally receive their training from a narrow range of institutions. The 1991 study mentioned above found that nearly 80 per cent of staff surveyed had received graduate degrees from institutions in the United States or United Kingdom (Stern 1997: 587).

These similarities in background and training contribute to the preservation of the Bank's organizational culture. One study goes so far as to argue that the Bank resembles a religious institution in its pressure for conformity and belief in a single truth:

> Like any institution, the Bank has its own self-reinforcing culture and its codes which set the limits on what can be reasonably believed and discussed if one hopes to be taken seriously and remain a member of the group . . . Put in the same place several hundred people who have been

> trained in the same schools to think in the same way, recruit them precisely because they have excelled in this training . . . [and the] probable cultural outcome will be – at least among the economists – monolithic and fundamentalist.
>
> (George and Sabelli 1994: 102)

Pockets of staff trained in fields other than economics or finance exist throughout the Bank (there are informal networks of environmentalists, sociologists, those interested in gender and human rights, and even a few political scientists), but the core disciplines of the Bank remain macroeconomics, neoclassical microeconomics, and financial management. One staff member speculates that the reason for this may be that other social science disciplines don't have as many agreed-upon truths or clear-cut methods of assessment as economics. They therefore appear less "scientific," less rigorous, and more interested in case-based analysis. While there may be more pluralism at the Bank than in the past, anything that is inconsistent with the accepted economic wisdom still meets with a strong negative reaction.[13] The concentration of staff trained at US institutions also has important implications. The political philosophy taught in US graduate schools emphasizes individualism over the state and discourages the study of fields like applied welfare economics, poverty, and income distribution that enjoy greater legitimacy elsewhere (Stern 1997: 588). This training reinforces the Bank staff's cognitive bent toward neoliberal policy prescriptions.

The YP program is the Bank's "fast track" recruitment mechanism. Established in the early 1960s, the program served originally as a recruitment stream for economists, many of whom rose to senior management positions within the Bank. It has recently broadened its requirements to include individuals with other technical skills, but the disciplines of economics and finance continue to dominate. The program remains highly selective, in terms of both the number of people it accepts and the range of fields from which they are drawn. Each year, the Bank chooses thirty-five to forty YPs from among 6,000 applicants. According to application material for the YP program, applicants "*must* have a masters degree (or equivalent) in economics, finance, or a technical field" (emphasis in original). Although YPs represent only 15 per cent of the Bank's overall recruitment, they have an importance well beyond their numbers. The competitive selection process assures that YPs are well-trained and highly motivated. The visibility of the program and the favorable perception of YPs by senior managers mean that YPs tend to move quickly into managerial positions. Many of the Bank's most prominent managers, as well as its rising stars, began their careers at the Bank as YPs. The normal recruitment channels for higher-level staff are also extremely selective, with just under 200 professionals selected annually from among 30,000 applicants.[14]

A key to the preservation of organizational culture is the socialization process. That process begins with recruitment and selection. If the organization can find "new members who already have the 'right' set of assumptions, beliefs, and values . . . it needs to do less formal socialization" (Schein 1990: 115–16). The emphasis at the World Bank is on hiring a select group of individuals, with well-developed technical skills in several clearly defined fields, ensuring that new employees arrive with the "right" norms already in place. The lack of any formal training program that all new staff are required to attend, such as those that exist at many other financial institutions, suggests that the Bank relies on recruitment, selection, and on-the-job training to ensure the socialization of new employees.

A recruitment pool made up of people with similar backgrounds and education, reinforced by extremely selective hiring, has contributed to an identifiable belief system for Bank staff, one that accepts the idea that development is an apolitical process and relies overwhelmingly on technical approaches to achieve it. These are not merely values held by the staff; rather, they are taken for granted and embodied in the very nature of the institution and its work.

Existing belief systems are reinforced when those who hold power within the organization seek out successors who have the same values and interests as they do. This occurs because decision makers generally want to preserve what they think is valuable about their organization. At a subconscious level they feel comfortable with, associate with, and understand people like themselves. As one former Executive Director of the Bank put it succinctly, "Managers recruit themselves."[15] This has meant that strenuous efforts have been required to develop a more diverse work force in terms of women, staff from developing countries, and non-economists. Even with these efforts, of the 188 new staff members hired in 1996, only one-third were from developing countries and just under one-third were women (*Annual Report* 1996: 156).

The leaders of an organization control the socialization of their successors both by design and unintentionally. By design, they set up socialization mechanisms like training programs and apprenticeships. Unintentionally, those principles that are used to identify successors become rewards and sanctions governing the whole course of socialization. Those who *want* to work at the World Bank come to believe the set of values and norms held by those who *do* work there; they then seek the training that will enable them to join the institution. In Stinchcombe's words, "If a man of his own volition pursue something which requires holding some value to get, he usually comes to be quite convinced of the sacredness of that value" (Stinchcombe 1968: 110).

Changing the Bank's culture

If the norms of a given profession and mechanisms of institutional self-replication described above lead to institutional stability, the reverse may hold true as well: the introduction of professionals with a different set of norms into an organization and a conscious change in patterns of selection, socialization, and incumbency may bring about institutional change. One case where this process may be under way is in the small but growing number of sociologists and anthropologists on the Bank's staff. From a single position in 1974, the Bank has gradually built up an in-house group of non-economic social scientists which today numbers about one hundred. These professionals are well aware of the difficulty, in the words of one, of "introducing anthropological knowledge within an 'economic fortress'" (Cernea 1996: 4). But they have begun to do so, developing strategies to present their views in such a way that they fit with the Bank's existing techniques and approaches.

While the number of sociologists and anthropologists at the Bank is dwarfed by the much larger number of economists, MBAs, and others with more technical backgrounds, there is evidence that the presence of a group of non-economic social scientists has had an impact on Bank policy in some areas. For instance, sociologists and anthropologists were involved in shaping the Bank's policies on involuntary resettlement and indigenous people and, more important, have helped hold others within the institution accountable to these policies.[16] The very presence of non-economists creates a dynamic in the direction of greater attention to social issues and increasing demand for social specialists. For example, sociologists and anthropologists were instrumental in initiating and carrying out a 1996 exercise called the Task Group on Social Development, the report of which called for recruiting more social specialists and increasing the training of current Bank staff in the social dimensions of development.[17] The path of institutional change through the addition of new staff with a different set of norms is, of course, extremely slow, particularly at an institution as large as the World Bank and in a climate of cutbacks rather than growth, but once a new dynamic has been introduced into an organization it often takes on a life of its own.

Another approach focuses on existing staff. The sociologist James March has argued that in order to change behavior within organizations, managers must change the premises on which individuals base that behavior. A number of strategies flow from this reasoning. One can replace an organization's senior management (although it is likely that viable replacements will share the same perspective as current leaders). One can go outside the organization for new leaders. Or one can change the experiences that will be had by those people destined to become top managers, perhaps by promoting people who have had deviant rather than conventional career paths. The initiative to reshape the World Bank introduced by President James D. Wolfensohn in 1996 includes elements of all these approaches.[18] Among other measures, Wolfensohn:

- established a new top management structure (although it contained many old faces);
- brought in several high-level managers from outside the organization;
- initiated a program for select managers to attend short-term executive training sessions at institutions like the Harvard Business School, INSEAD, and the London Business School;

- announced an exchange program under which managers from private sector firms and senior Bank staff trade places for a year or two;
- expanded the Bank's internal training program, increasing the number and type of courses offered, and changed the incentive structure to encourage attendance;
- proposed that internal training courses include attendees from outside the Bank, allowing Bank staff to build networks that extend beyond the institution; and
- announced a program under which government officials or development experts come to the Bank for short stays or serve longer periods as resident advisers.

These measures suggest a strategy for change that reflects an understanding of the importance of the Bank's organizational culture and an appreciation of its deeply entrenched nature.

Conclusion

We can now return to the puzzle raised in Chapter 1 in light of the two theoretical approaches discussed above. Why have the private sector, participation, and governance agendas evolved in such different ways since their introduction at the Bank? Whereas international relations theory points to a central role for external actors in bringing about change, organization theorists would posit that private-sector-related activities fit better than participation or governance with the World Bank's technical and apolitical rules and the cognitive orientation of its staff and management. Whereas neorealists see institutional change as a fairly efficient process that responds to changes in the international system, organization theorists would expect the Bank's organizational culture to remain intact even if the conditions that initially gave rise to it no longer exist.

The task of mediating between these two explanations – the first emphasizing the role of external actors and their power over the World Bank, the second stressing internal aspects of the institution like norms and beliefs – is complicated by the fact that a cursory view of the status of the three agendas considered here provides evidence for both explanations. Powerful external actors, particularly the United States, intervened more decisively in favor of private sector development than on behalf of either participation or governance, providing support for an international relations-based explanation. And private sector development fits more closely with the Bank's organizational culture than the more political and less technical approaches required for work on participation and governance, making plausible an explanation based in organization theory.

Fortunately, a reconstruction of the process by which these new agendas came about provides greater insight. By looking at the emergence of private sector development, participation, and governance, while paying close attention to the sequence and timing of decisions, it becomes clear that the preferences of external actors were not the decisive factor in the way these agendas became institutionalized at the Bank. This task requires examining not only the process by which new agendas were introduced and their degree of integration into Bank activities, but also the nature of their incorporation. *How* the World Bank has carried out its work in these three areas suggests a central role for institutional norms.

Theoretical approaches based in international relations direct our attention to sources of power in the external environment to which international organizations must respond. They are useful in helping us understand how new agendas come to the attention of a multilateral organization like the World Bank. But they tell us little about how new agendas are defined and pursued operationally, the level of resources they receive, and how deeply institutionalized they become. Sociological approaches that focus on institutional rules and taken-for-granted beliefs help explain how these agendas are transformed into practice.

3 Approaching business
The private sector development agenda

> Inextricably mixed up in [the Bank's] attitudes was a conviction that capitalism was the right way, that private enterprise was best, and, as a rule-of-thumb dogma, that the less State interference, the better.
>
> James Morris, *The Road to Huddersfield*, 1963, p. 43

The World Bank's relationship to the private sector is marked by a central contradiction. The Bank was designed from the beginning to promote a global capitalist economic order, but it can lend only to governments or with a government guarantee. Furthering economic growth became the cornerstone of the Bank's approach early on, but the belief that this is best achieved through infrastructure development – and that infrastructure is the purview of the public domain – led the Bank through the 1950s and 1960s to relate much more closely to governments than to private actors.

In the 1970s, under the leadership of Robert McNamara, the focus on economic growth took a back seat to the goals of transferring resources from rich countries to poor countries and strengthening those sectors that had a direct impact on poverty, such as health and education. In the 1980s, the Bank returned to an emphasis on growth, this time through support for market-oriented economic reform and the creation of a policy environment conducive to a strong private sector. These efforts, however, required Bank staff to work more closely than ever with governments, leading to criticism that the private sector was being neglected. Since 1989, the Bank has explored ways to interact directly with private actors and to coordinate its private-sector-related activities with those of its affiliates, but structural and cultural features of the institution complicate this effort.

In examining the evolution of the Bank's private sector development agenda over the past twenty years it is essential to draw a distinction between policies and practice. The adoption of explicitly pro-private-sector policies occurred around 1980 when the Bank's research apparatus shifted in the direction of neoclassical (as opposed to Keynesian) economics, and its operational apparatus began to make Bank support contingent on market-oriented economic reform through structural adjustment lending. While the terms of adjustment loans helped create a more favorable business environment in many developing countries, the Bank in its day-to-day operation continued to have little to do with private actors. The change in practice came toward the end of the decade, as the Bank began to step up its private sector involvement.

The private sector development agenda was first proposed in 1989. At that time, the Bank identified its priorities in this area as improving the business environment, restructuring or privatizing public enterprises, and developing the financial sector (World Bank 1989a: v). These activities continued to dominate the Bank's private-sector-related work ten years later. Even a face-off with the United States in 1991 over the status of the private sector at the Bank left the core elements of this agenda untouched; US complaints focused not on the choice of these goals but on the intensity with which the Bank pursued them.

Among the three cases examined in this study, the private sector development agenda is the one that has changed least since it was introduced. It is also the initiative that has become most deeply integrated into the Bank's operations. This is no surprise, whether one interprets change at the Bank through the lens of international relations theory or that of organization theory. The Bank's most powerful member has long urged it to become more attuned to the needs of the private sector and to work more effectively with private actors. And the Bank's activities in this area fit well with key elements of its organizational culture.

Work on private sector development relies on the kind of top-down, expert-oriented approaches that characterize the Bank's traditional lending, even though the Bank does not actually lend *to* the private sector. (Rather, it makes loans to governments that contain policy advice and provides technical assistance to government agencies. Direct lending to private entities is reserved for the International Finance Corporation.) Projects are designed by Bank staff in cooperation with government officials; they do not require broad societal support, as do loans in the social sectors or those that aim to increase popular participation. Unlike governance loans, which aim at deep-seated institutional change that unfolds over many years, the results of planned privatizations and financial sector reform may be evident fairly soon and their success is easier to judge. Many of these loans are readily quantified (by, for example, measuring how many companies have been privatized or how many financial institutions made solvent) and techniques for implementing reform are well developed. Large amounts of money can be transferred through adjustment loans with pro-private-sector provisions, an important consideration as the Bank strives to keep its lending levels from declining. Perhaps most important, the goal of strengthening the private sector fits comfortably with the Bank's technical and apolitical orientation. The biggest challenge the private sector development agenda poses to the Bank's organizational culture is that it requires Bank staff to operate on the borderline between government and business – an arena in which the institution has little experience – and interact with a new set of government officials and industry leaders.

The value of a strong private sector is widely accepted inside the Bank, although there is some debate about the relative weight that should be given to the economic as opposed to the social or political dimensions of development. Outside the Bank, the private sector development agenda has met with a more mixed reception. Conservative critics of the Bank (such as the Cato Institute, the Heritage Foundation, and some members of the US Congress), rather than being comforted by the Bank's attention to the private sector, question the continued existence of the organization.[1] Their goal is not a World Bank that is responsive to private sector needs, but the elimination of what they see as an overly large and state-centered bureaucracy. At the other end of the continuum is a group of left-leaning non-governmental organizations (NGOs) which believes that the neoliberal development model supported by the Bank has harmed the poor in borrowing countries to such a degree that the world would be better off with a radically transformed World Bank or none at all.[2] To this group, promotion of the private sector is simply an extension of a set of Bank policies that has always favored the priorities of international and domestic capital over the needs of the poor. Between these extremes are those who acknowledge that a strong private sector is one factor among several that are required for building healthy economies. For some, recent attention to the private sector is a necessary corrective to the public-sector-oriented, infrastructure-based development model supported by the Bank for much of its history. For others, the prominence of private-sector-related activities raises fears that the Bank will minimize or neglect the badly needed institutional and safety net functions that only governments can provide.

Since 1990, the Bank has reemphasized a commitment to poverty reduction as the central element in its mission. The connections between the Bank's private sector development activities and its broader mission of poverty alleviation are threefold. Whether the promotion of the private sector does, in fact, improve the lot of the poor remains subject to debate.

The first argument is that a healthy private sector leads to greater competition within developing country economies, thereby bringing about higher levels of growth. This "rising tide lifts all boats" rationale holds that faster growth benefits all members of a society. But many observers note that growth is usually distributed unequally within developing countries, with the poorest sectors of society receiving fewer benefits than the more privileged.

A second path through which a private sector emphasis is believed to contribute to poverty alleviation concerns privatization and public enterprise restructuring. These policies are intended to reduce the fiscal burden on states, thereby increasing state capacity for greater spending on social sectors like education and health. But state resources freed up by privatization may or may not be used for social services; this depends not simply on the availability of funds but on the priorities and politics of the state in question.

A third connection between the private sector and poverty alleviation is reflected in Bank programs targeted toward microenterprises in borrowing countries. Policies that simplify licensing procedures or increase access to credit for an economy's smallest firms work to the benefit of their largely poor owners. But lending programs devoted to small firms comprise only a tiny fraction of the Bank's private-sector-related activities. The Bank has supported the idea of microenterprise finance but it is not a trend-setter in the area. Observers note that a lack of experience in making small loans and the institutional need to move large amounts of money makes this type of lending difficult for an institution like the World Bank. The alternative has been to provide funds to microenterprises through intermediaries. Programs along these lines have included an allocation of $2 million from fiscal 1994 net income to the Grameen Bank of Bangladesh, a leader in the microenterprise field, and the establishment of a microfinance program administered by the Consultative Group to Assist the Poorest (CGAP), under which up to $30 million of IBRD income is made available to successful microfinance programs (*Annual Report* 1995: 32). Half of this amount was committed by CGAP in its first two years of operation (*Annual Report* 1997: 34).

Despite debate over whether and how the Bank's private sector initiatives help the poor, there is a general consensus among staff and management that the goal of promoting the private sector is in keeping with the Bank's mission. This distinguishes private sector development from the more contested agendas discussed in Chapters 4 and 5. The next section explores how the Bank evolved from an institution that worked mainly with governments on state-sponsored projects to its current identity as a champion of the private sector in developing countries.

The origins of private sector development

The contradiction that lies at the heart of the Bank's approach to the private sector is embodied in its founding charter. The Articles of Agreement require that the Bank promote private investment but prohibit the institution from lending its funds to private sector firms without a government guarantee (Article III, Section 4). This seeming paradox originates in the conditions of the Bank's establishment. Its chief sponsors at Bretton Woods, the United States and the United Kingdom, wanted the Bank to have as its central mission the promotion of the capitalist system internationally, yet they also understood that the Bank's effectiveness hinged on its creditworthiness, hence the requirement that all loans or guarantees extended by the Bank be covered by a sovereign guarantee. This policy was shaped in part by the negative experience of investors who had lost money when companies in developing countries defaulted on their foreign bonds in the early part of the twentieth century. A government guarantee was thought to partially allay the danger of default.[3]

Bank lending has always furthered the interests of private capital and supported the goal of international economic liberalization, but during its first three decades it did so indirectly. The emphasis on economic planning (even in capitalist countries) and prevailing models of industrialization in the 1950s and 1960s led the Bank naturally into support for large, state-sponsored projects. Along with the charter provisions discussed above, this meant that in practice the Bank had very little to do with the private sector.

The Bank's method of operation also differed from what its founders had envisioned. The Articles call for the Bank:

> to promote private foreign investment by means of guarantees or participations in loans and other investments made by private investors; and when private capital is not available on reasonable terms, to supplement private investment by providing . . . finance for productive purposes out of its own capital, funds raised by it and its other resources.
>
> (Article I, Section 2)

What was intended to be a supplemental role – that of the Bank lending its own resources – has thoroughly dominated its history; in fact, the first IBRD participation in a private loan syndicate did not take place until 1983, and the first guarantee of a private loan was not made until 1984. There was little subsequent action in either of these areas for more than a decade.

There are a variety of reasons why Bank practice departed so significantly from what was planned. First, direct lending to governments and state-owned enterprises fit readily with the infrastructure-oriented development approaches of the post-World War II era. Second, developing countries found it cheaper and simpler to borrow directly from the Bank than to seek its guarantee for commercial loans; governments were reluctant to extend their own sovereign guarantee to private borrowers, preferring to have Bank funds go directly to themselves or to public enterprises. In addition, private investors were hesitant to accept loans that carried government guarantees for fear that they might be accompanied by government interference. For its part, the Bank, driven by an imperative to increase the volume of its lending, found it easiest to make large loans to governments and state-owned companies. (The dynamic behind the Bank's drive for continual increases in its lending volume is straightforward. Only by demonstrating to its members that it is using all the capital at its disposal, and that it will be able to make productive use of more, can the Bank expect to persuade them to grant it periodic capital increases, which are necessary for the institution to expand. Declining lending levels, on the other hand, may lead member states and others to question whether the Bank is doing its job or, indeed, whether the institution is needed at all.) Over time, a tradition of working with governments was established and Bank staff had little contact with the private sector in borrowing countries. As one study of the Bank explained:

> The operational staff of the World Bank become quite accustomed, early in their careers, to playing an influential role in important matters of public policy in developing member countries. Visiting or resident staff missions are perceived by their host countries as emissaries of an institution with virtually sovereign weight and prestige, and they find themselves treated as peers of the most senior officials . . . Thus, both the Bank's basic mandate and its staff's everyday experience combine to relegate the private sector, in the organization's collective consciousness, to the status of abstraction.
>
> (Richardson and Haralz 1995: 11)

This is not to say that the private sector was ignored by the Bank. Instead, relations with private actors were handled mainly through the International Finance Corporation (IFC), a World Bank affiliate established in 1956. The IFC's legal framework differs from the Bank's in that it is allowed to provide financing directly to the private sector. While the IBRD and IDA may lend only to governments or with a government guarantee, the IFC is permitted to make equity investments and provide loans without government guarantees. The IFC's autonomy from the Bank – unlike IDA, it has its own leadership, staff, budget, and building – reinforced the perception that the Bank itself was not engaged directly with the private sector.

Two other organizations, the International Center for the Settlement of Investment Disputes (ICSID) and the Multilateral Investment Guarantee Agency (MIGA), also deal mainly with private actors by providing support for foreign investors in World Bank borrowing countries. ICSID, established in 1966, is a separate organization operated out of the World Bank. Its mandate is to encourage flows of international investment through the arbitration of disputes between governments and foreign investors. MIGA, established in 1988, is a World Bank affiliate charged with insuring private investors against political risk, such as expropriation and war. An additional private-sector-related initiative is the Foreign Investment Advisory Service (FIAS), a joint IFC–Bank program that helps governments attract foreign private direct investment. FIAS is funded by the IFC, the Bank, other donors, and paying customers among the developing countries that receive advice. Much of the Bank's increased emphasis on the private sector in the 1990s was manifested in rapid growth in the activities of the IFC and MIGA.

But even in its own operations, the Bank has interacted with the private sector in important ways. For much of its history, the Bank channeled a significant portion of its loans to national development banks that served as intermediaries, on-lending these funds to private sector borrowers. This type of lending has at times amounted to a significant proportion of Bank activities, reaching a high of 17 per cent of total lending in 1968 (Haralz

1997: 834) and averaging 11.5 per cent of total loans during the 1986–1990 period (Shihata 1991: 204). Intermediary lending dwindled in the 1990s as national development banks floundered and borrowers shifted from state-led to market-based development approaches that required a sensibility lacking at most of these institutions.[4] Other examples of interaction with the private sector are the Bank's sizeable lending programs in the areas of agricultural credit for private farmers and export development assistance, both of which were designed to improve the lot of the private sector even though the loans themselves were channeled through state agencies.

These indirect mechanisms of support have been considered inadequate by some and from time to time there has been pressure to amend the Bank's charter to permit direct lending to the private sector. As early as 1963, Bank President George Woods proposed changing the Articles of Agreement to allow direct lending to the private sector without a government guarantee. This proposal was rejected because of concern over its effect on the Bank's credit standing. Instead, the IBRD's articles were altered in 1965 to allow the Bank to lend to the IFC, thereby increasing the IFC's resources and capabilities (Shihata 1991: 205–6). More recently, the US Treasury Department raised the issue of non-guaranteed lending as part of a dispute with the Bank in 1991, and the Institute of International Finance, a think tank owned by banks and other financial institutions, called on the Bank in 1995 to lend to the private sector without a host country guarantee. Efforts are under way to develop an instrument that will allow the Bank to issue guarantees for infrastructure and natural resource projects that do not require sovereign counter-guarantees (World Bank 1997b: 10).

A new attitude toward the private sector emerged around 1980 as the World Bank embraced the view that markets, rather than governments, should serve as the chief allocators of resources and engines of growth in developing countries. This view was reflected in the terms of the Bank's structural and sectoral adjustment loans. Introduced in 1979, policy-based adjustment lending initially emphasized macroeconomic reform, then expanded to include the promotion of free trade, privatization, the deregulation of financial systems, liberalization of investment regimes, and legal and regulatory reform.[5] The impetus for adjustment lending appears to have come from within the Bank as part of a recognition that the success of projects requires not just sound loans but also a supportive policy environment. Adjustment lending expanded in the 1980s in the wake of the debt crisis as the United States acknowledged that the World Bank and the IMF could serve as effective – and cost-effective – proponents of neoliberal economic reform. A key turning point came in 1982 with the Reagan-administration-backed appointment of neoclassical economist Anne Krueger as head of the Bank's research department, an event read by many economists as a distancing of the Bank from the Keynesianism that had shaped both its research and lending activities for many years. The new free market policies supported by the Bank were those favored by much of the private sector worldwide and contributed to a more favorable business climate in many borrowing countries. Yet the Bank was still working with governments – in fact, more closely than ever – and apart from staff at the IFC, hands-on knowledge of the private sector was confined to a few units scattered throughout the institution.

Beginning in the late 1980s, the Bank steadily increased its emphasis on the private sector, promoting a policy environment conducive to business, supporting privatization, and encouraging financial market reform. Several factors were responsible. Pressure from the United States was one of these, but the change was also brought about by the evolution of borrowers' economic policies and global developments. The new approach was stated most clearly in the 1991 *World Development Report* where the Bank announced a strategy of "market-friendly" development, adopting the precept to "let markets work unless it is demonstrably better to step in" (p. 5), while accepting a limited role for government, one confined to creating a legal and regulatory framework within which markets operate and intervening in cases of market failure. This explicit advocacy of market-led development signalled the final break with the state-led approaches that had characterized development ideology and the Bank's activities for several decades, and marked a return to the avowedly capitalist stance of the Bank's pre-McNamara days.

Contextual factors

The Bank's private sector development initiative unfolded amid dramatic changes in the international environment. The economic success of the East Asian newly industrializing countries and Chile, and subsequent embrace of market-oriented reform in much of Latin America, served in the 1980s to delegitimize state-led models of development. The fall of the Berlin Wall, collapse of the Soviet Union, and enthusiastic adoption of free-market policies in Eastern Europe in 1989–91, marked the end of that ultimate form of state-led development, communism. Throughout this period, international aid agencies reoriented their policies to provide support for the private sector and market-based reform.

Among such agencies were the regional development banks. The newest of these, the European Bank for Reconstruction and Development (EBRD), was founded in 1990 in the wake of the collapse of the Soviet Union. Designed explicitly to promote both democracy and the private sector, it may lend only to democratic regimes and, in a proviso added by the United States, is required by its charter to make at least 60 per cent of its loans to private enterprises without a government guarantee.[6]

Other regional institutions added private sector affiliates and took steps to allow some portion of their resources to go to the private sector without a government guarantee.[7] In 1985, for example, the Asian Development Bank (ADB) revised its policies in order to undertake a modest amount of direct lending, without government guarantees, to private enterprises. In 1986, a private sector division was formed within the bank. And in 1989, the Asian Finance and Investment Corporation Ltd. (AFIC) was established as a separate financial organization under ADB sponsorship. The structure of AFIC and its relationship to the ADB differs from that of the IFC and the World Bank. The ADB contributed 30 per cent of paid-in capital to the organization, with the remainder divided among twenty-five private shareholders, including commercial banks, investment banks, insurance companies, and leasing companies.

The Inter-American Development Bank (IDB) also set up a private sector affiliate, the Inter-American Investment Corporation (IIIC), modeled more closely on the IFC. Although established in 1985, it did not begin operations until 1989. The IIIC's gearing ratio was raised in 1995, allowing it to more than double its capacity to provide finance for companies investing in Latin America. In 1994, the IDB's members decided to allow up to 5 per cent of its lending to be committed without a government guarantee, primarily for infrastructure financing, having been assured by the debt rating agencies that this would not affect its credit rating negatively. Unlike the World Bank, the IDB is not prohibited by its charter from this type of lending.[8]

The African Development Bank (AfDB), although not as far along as the other regionals in this area, set up a small private sector development division in 1987. In 1990 the AfDB's directors decided to establish a larger private sector development unit, which is allowed to take equity stakes in and make non-guaranteed loans to private companies.

Other aid organizations also revised their approaches to the private sector. The Development Assistance Committee of the OECD, whose members are the major industrialized countries, produced a set of guidelines in the early 1990s for promoting private sector development. These include encouraging appropriate economic policies, improving the institutional environment that frames business decisions, and supporting activities like business training, microenterprise development, privatization, public enterprise reform, and foreign direct investment. The guidelines also call on the bilateral aid agencies of member nations to reorganize themselves and leverage scarce aid resources to achieve these ends (OECD 1994b: 9-10).

These changes in the international aid community reflected a new consensus about the central role of the private sector in development. The World Bank, so often the leader among aid organizations, moved more slowly than some of the bilateral institutions, including US AID, to reorient its activities to promote the private sector. Its size, financial independence, and well-entrenched organizational culture made it possible for the Bank to resist pressure from its largest member to change its approach well after a number of other aid agencies had become more active proponents of private sector development.

The role of the United States

The United States had long agitated for more direct Bank involvement with the private sector, but these efforts intensified in the 1980s. It is ironic that the United States came to serve as the leading proponent of the private sector at the World Bank. When the Bretton Woods institutions were being created, it was the US delegates who insisted that, in the words of Treasury Secretary Henry Morgenthau, the World Bank and IMF be "instrumentalities of sovereign governments and not of private financial interests" (Gardner 1956: 76).

An important factor behind the shift in US policy thirty years later was the ideological orientation of the Reagan and Bush administrations. The battle over the depth of the World Bank's commitment to the private sector was played out against the backdrop of the 1980s debt crisis, which was seen by many as the result of overreliance on the state as the engine of development; the emergence of alternative development models that emphasized a key role for the private sector; and the collapse of the Eastern bloc. Unlike the campaign to change the Bank's approach to environmental issues, US pressure on private sector development involved only minimal effort to seek international consensus. Also unlike the environmental effort, which enjoyed strong grassroots support and was initiated primarily by members of Congress at the urging of NGOs, the campaign to instill a private sector ethos at the Bank was led by the US Treasury Department. The result was a campaign to change the Bank that originated not as a response to societal demands but as a matter of ideological preferences.

A key early document in the dispute over the private sector (and US–World Bank relations more generally) was the report of an inter-agency review of the development banks, commissioned by the Reagan administration shortly after taking office (US Treasury, 1982). The newly elected administration was highly critical of the Bank and other multilateral institutions on ideological and political grounds; the Republican platform of 1980, in fact, had committed the party to reducing support for multilateral institutions in favor of bilateral assistance programs (Gwin 1994: 37). The report, *United States Participation in the Multilateral Development Banks in the 1980s*, presented a systematic assessment of US interests and how well they had been served by membership in the multilateral development banks. To the surprise of many in the administration, the report was generally positive, finding that participation had served US interests well. One of its major recommendations for improvement was that the development banks "increasingly emphasize attention to market signals and incentives, to private sector development and to greater financial participation by banks, private investors, and other sources of private financing" (US Treasury 1982: 7). The 1982 report provided the basis both for continued US support of the World Bank and for renewed agitation over what was considered inadequate Bank attention to the private sector.

With the onset of the debt crisis in 1982, the Reagan administration found that the Bank could serve as a valuable tool to promote neoliberal policy reform in the developing world. It was, after all, one of the only institutions that continued to lend money to debtor countries after Mexico's near-default and it was now attaching policy conditions to many of these loans. Administration support for the Bank grew as its help was enlisted in a variety of US plans to cushion the private banking system from debt-related shocks. The 1985 Baker Plan called on the World Bank to expand its lending to fifteen heavily indebted developing countries, making loans conditional on the adoption of market-oriented policy reforms. The 1989 Brady Plan proposed that the Bank guarantee bonds issued to facilitate debt reduction for countries that had met certain criteria.[9] But while successive Republican administrations found the Bank a useful ally in containing the consequences of the debt crisis, criticism of the institution's state-centered nature and seeming neglect of the private sector continued, especially from the many officials with backgrounds in business who staffed the highest levels of the Treasury Department under President George Bush.

In the late 1980s, the Bank took a series of measures to stem US criticism, including the creation of a unit to focus on the private sector, establishment of a task force on financial operations, and formation of a Private Sector Development Review Group made up of Bank staff and representatives of the business community. The findings of this group, approved by the board in 1988, resulted in an action program launched in 1989. A modest and piecemeal effort, it entailed few major changes in organization but laid out a set of priorities – improving the business environment, privatization, and financial sector reform – that continue to characterize the Bank's agenda today. These measures were considered unsatisfactory by the United States, which saw them as partial and half-hearted. At the same time, the Bank's other shareholders, while expressing support for the goal of private sector development, tended to be satisfied with the Bank's proposed policies and their implementation (Haralz 1992).

The specific event that triggered a harder US line was the request for a capital increase for the IFC, intended to be concluded in 1990. The United States, which had been lobbying the Bank's management for regular progress reports on what was being done to highlight private sector development at the Bank, decided to up the ante and "fight the battle on all fronts," in the words of E. Patrick Coady, the US executive director at the time and one of the Bush administration Treasury officials to come out of the investment banking world.[10] The United States would scrutinize every loan and look closely at the IFC, which it feared was being overshadowed by the Bank. Ultimately the Bank's largest member decided to link support for an IFC capital increase to the Bank's progress on private sector development. The message was clear: if the World Bank wanted its affiliate to receive the resources necessary to grow, the Bank would have to accommodate US concerns over its private sector efforts. The phrase heard most frequently in connection with this episode is that the United States "held hostage" the IFC capital increase for over a year while it pushed the Bank to reform its approach to the private sector.

The explicit trade-off proposed by the United States blindsided the Bank and infuriated management, along with many other member countries. As former Executive Vice President Ernie Stern put it, "People had thought they were doing the Lord's work" in promoting the private sector and were surprised to hear otherwise.[11] Representatives of other member countries, many of whom agreed with the substance of the US criticism, were angered by what they perceived as a unilateral and ideologically motivated attack. One executive director has said that the United States under the Reagan and Bush administrations tended to "hit everyone over the head" about its priorities, alienating even those on the board sympathetic to its views.[12] In the private sector development debate, only the Canadian executive director joined forces with the US representative, while Japan remained neutral. Most European members were put off by what they considered the strong-arm tactics of the US representative. Jonas Haralz, the Nordic executive director of the World Bank at the time, wrote later that:

> The US Treasury's attitude and actions regarding this whole issue was rooted in politics and ideology. It revealed an incomplete understanding of the character of the World Bank Group institutions and insensitivity to the different circumstances of the member countries and the views these circumstances gave rise to.
>
> (Haralz 1992: 37)

None the less, US pressure (and the leverage the United States enjoyed thanks to the badly needed IFC capital increase) forced an admission by the Bank that its private sector efforts were poorly coordinated and in need of retooling.

Institutional learning

Even as the US power play led the Bank to acknowledge that it could do more to support the private sector, internal developments brought Bank staff and management to much the same conclusion. By the early 1980s, the Bank had become convinced of the need for policy reform in most of its borrower countries. But as adjustment loans shifted from concern with macroeconomics to more sector-specific issues, it became clear to the Bank that in several areas it lacked the expertise necessary to advise member countries or structure the terms of such loans. An organization that had little hands-on experience with the private sector was now advocating that countries privatize many, if not most, of their state-owned enterprises. Financial sector reform was also becoming a priority as national banking systems faced growing strain as a result of the debt crisis. Yet few Bank staff members had spent any time working in the financial markets, either as participants or regulators. The Bank's existing private sector experts were scattered around the Bank and their efforts were not integrated into overall country lending strategies. These factors contributed to a growing recognition by management that the

Bank's bureaucratic structure and staff skills were not well suited to developing or overseeing important components of many adjustment loans.

While the Bank's organizational culture overall was not geared toward the private sector, some units within the institution were staffed by individuals with considerable knowledge of the private sector. The most obvious of these pockets of private sector expertise were those entities whose sole purpose was to work in partnership with private investors: the IFC, MIGA, and FIAS. At the time, however, these affiliates were tiny relative to the IBRD and IDA, and there was little cross-fertilization of ideas or knowledge. There were areas of expertise within the Bank as well, such as the Energy and Industry Department whose staff members served as internal consultants for the country units and were charged with bringing a private sector perspective to projects. It was here that the Bank's privatization experts were clustered. Another source of expertise was the group that ran the Bank's cofinancing programs with commercial banks. Finally, the Bank's treasury operation, responsible for raising and managing its funds, had extensive knowledge of international capital markets and private financial institutions and investors.

While staff members in these areas constituted a reservoir on which the Bank could draw, there were strong organizational barriers to making use of their knowledge. The units were small relative to the overall scale of World Bank operations; they were isolated from the mainstream of Bank work, which resided in the country operations units; and they were not connected to each other in any way (Purcell and Miller 1986). In acknowledging that it was behind the curve in responding to private sector needs, the World Bank faced the twin challenges of bringing into the organization more people with private sector experience and integrating those pockets of private sector knowledge that did exist into the mainstream of Bank operations.

Borrowers' policies

A final factor enabling the Bank to focus more closely on the private sector was widespread change in the governments and policies of many developing countries. In the 1980s many of the Bank's borrowers began to enact policies that called for greater private sector involvement in their economies. In the past, some of these countries had resisted the World Bank and IMF call for neoliberal reform. Now governments in Latin America and Asia were seeking help in privatizing state-owned enterprises, reforming their financial sectors, and attracting foreign investment. If the Bank was to be an effective partner, it would need to develop its skills in these areas.

At the same time, the bargaining power of some governments *vis-à-vis* the World Bank was declining, leaving them less equipped to resist the Bank's policy prescriptions. As governments, particularly those in sub-Saharan Africa, moved deeper into crisis, the Bank was able to intervene in more and more of their policy decisions. Once the Bank decided that the promotion of the private sector was one of the elements of reform required for its support, many of its poorest and weakest members had no choice but to agree.

In most of the countries to which it was lending, then, by the late 1980s the World Bank was well positioned to promote its private sector development agenda. In some cases this was because borrowers themselves had signed on to that agenda. In other cases it was because borrowers had become increasingly dependent on the support of multilateral lenders and were unable to oppose their policy prescriptions.

The Bank's response

The stand-off that developed in 1990 and 1991 between the United States and the World Bank over a capital increase for the IFC resulted in a compromise under which the Bank made changes in its private sector development activities while the US representative backed down at the urging of other members and Bank leaders. In June 1991, the United States finally agreed to discuss the capital increase provided its concerns were addressed. When the Bank's board opposed many of the points raised by the US Executive Director, the United States withdrew its support for the increase. A week later, as a result of direct negotiations between Bank President Barber Conable and US Treasury officials, the US representative accepted a compromise that was supported by other members of the board and agreed to the increase. "Overall," Catherine Gwin writes, "the US lack of analytic rigor and highhanded manner hindered its effectiveness in advancing what was, in fact, a timely and important issue for the Bank" (Gwin 1994: 53).

Although the compromise led to some significant changes, the Bank did not give the United States much of what it had asked for. In some respects the Bank resisted specific US demands, while in others it went beyond what the United States wanted.

- The United States had asked for a Bank study to examine changing the Articles of Agreement to permit direct, non-guaranteed lending to the private sector. Although such a study was eventually prepared by management, it was never delivered to the board, and the issue subsided with the election of the Clinton administration in 1992 and appointment of a new executive director.
- The United States had asked that a high-level committee be established to coordinate private sector development activities; such a committee met only a few times, then disbanded. Several years later, under President Wolfensohn, a new high-level group focusing on the private sector was constituted.
- The United States had wanted agreement on a target of 50 per cent of total Bank Group lending in support of the private sector by 1995, with precise conditions on what that meant. No such agreement was ever

reached and lending directed toward the private sector does not constitute anything close to that level today.

- The United States had asked that the Bank hire twenty new staff members with private sector expertise over the next year. The Bank went far beyond this, adding fifty within six months. Coady describes this as the Bank meeting US demands, but "on its own terms," recalling that the United States "could never win a battle directly on the first attack, but on the second attack, the Bank says they're already doing what's been asked."[13] Although overt US pressure on this issue evaporated when the Clinton administration took office, the Bank has significantly expanded its hiring of private sector experts.
- The United States had requested that a separate private sector department be created. Instead, the Bank dispersed responsibility among its country departments, with coordination provided within the Technical Department and policy issues handled in yet another division. By 1992, the Bank had become disenchanted with this high degree of decentralization and established a central vice presidency for Finance and Private Sector Development (FPD) as part of the Bank-wide reorganization that took place that year. A 1995 study by the Overseas Development Council concluded, "This organizational change, coming more than a year after the great private sector debate ended, seems to have been initiated within the Bank and without further donor pressure" (Richardson and Haralz 1995: 18).
- Finally, the United States wanted closer coordination between the World Bank and IFC. Repeated efforts in this direction fell short and tension between the two entities continued. In 1996, President Wolfensohn introduced a high-level strategy for coordinating the Bank's private sector resources, one with a greater chance of success than earlier initiatives.

The showdown with the United States contributed to the public perception that the Bank had changed its stance toward the private sector. In fact, there is a marked continuity between the Bank's private sector development agenda prior to 1991 and its approach after that date. The principles set forth in the 1989 action plan – that the Bank should act to improve the business environment, support privatization, and pursue financial sector reform – still guide the institution's activities. One of the executive directors involved in the debate, writing six months later, concluded that the US impact on Bank policies had been less than decisive: "The intense debate and clashes of opinions notwithstanding, there have been no dramatic changes in the Bank Group's policy and implementation regarding private sector development. Rather, there has been an evolution along already established lines" (Haralz 1992: 37–8). The lack of substantial changes in the shape of the private sector development agenda suggests that, despite the conflict with the United States, this agenda is one about which there was considerable consensus among the Bank's members and management, and one that remains relatively noncontroversial. These attributes set it apart from the other case studies examined here, both of which have been subject to far more ambiguity and evolution.

Assessing the importance of private sector development

The Bank's *Annual Report 1995* announced that "The private sector is now a recognized area of emphasis for the Bank, although there is not yet a formal, comprehensive policy other than the view that the Bank should complement, not displace or compete with, the private sector" (p. 17). The lack of a clear-cut policy has its costs. Staff members working on private sector development point out that it can be interpreted to cover almost everything the Bank does (except health, education, and other social sectors), making it difficult to disentangle the notion of "private sector development" from that of "development" in general. Like the other agendas addressed in this study, private sector development is not a functional category of Bank lending and the Bank provides no accounting of private-sector-related activities per se. Rather, certain sectors are identified as those that involve the private sector most closely and Bank activity in these areas is monitored. It is thus difficult to arrive at concrete measures of the Bank's private sector development activities.

What does the Bank mean when it claims to be supporting private sector development? The prominence of the issue is somewhat puzzling because the Bank's opportunities for direct interaction with the private sector are constrained in several ways. It cannot lend directly to private entities unless its charter is amended. It cannot become involved in private sector transactions without encroaching on the turf of the IFC. It has difficulty competing with private firms as a provider of technical assistance and fee-based services because its costs are high relative to smaller and more flexible organizations. Finally, growing private capital flows and the enthusiastic embrace of market-oriented policies by many developing country governments pose questions about whether the Bank's efforts in this area are necessary at all. Faced with the constraints of its Articles of Agreement, its affiliates, and the world outside its walls, what path has the Bank charted?

The Bank's private sector development effort focuses mainly on creating a policy environment within which a strong private sector can function. This has involved supporting changes in the policy, regulatory, and legal frameworks governing private sector activity; privatization and public enterprise restructuring; financial sector development; and support for private enterprises, such as microenterprises or export development assistance (although this support must be channeled through agencies that carry a government guarantee). The Bank pursues these goals through many avenues, including loans, guarantees, technical assistance, research, training, and policy dialogue.

Operational work

Private sector development is an explicit goal of many of the Bank's adjustment and investment loans.[14] Since the early 1980s, adjustment loans have supported fundamental reforms that affect the business environment, such as trade liberalization, tax reform, privatization, banking reform, and the streamlining of a country's regulatory and legal framework. Some loans are directed strictly toward policy reform, such as a $40 million loan to Senegal for policy reforms designed to improve the investment climate and enhance the country's competitiveness, or $150 million to Algeria for a broad program aimed at accelerating the transition to a market economy. Other loans combine an investment component with policy conditions, such as a $300 million loan to Brazil to improve the nation's main highway network, with the condition that road transport costs be reduced. Even pure investment loans (those that do not contain policy conditions) may represent a response to private sector needs; for example, the Bank has lent China $700 million for road construction to relieve traffic congestion and promote international trade and economic development in two rapidly growing regions.

An important component of the Bank's work on the private sector involves technical assistance designed to help borrowers carry out their own efforts to strengthen the private sector. Market-based economic reform in major Bank borrowers, including Argentina, Brazil, and Mexico, in the 1992–3 period, was furthered through technical assistance loans. More recent examples include $15 million in technical assistance to private enterprises in the Kyrgyz Republic, $3 million to help the West Bank and Gaza improve management skills and establish new recruitment processes in its finance ministries, and $30 million to Mexico for a pilot project demonstrating the suitability of rural financial markets for private sector participation. As part of its technical assistance loans, the Bank hires consultants, many of them from the private sector and many of them local, to work with governments to implement their agendas. The Bank's impact in this area is not easily captured by looking at the amount of technical assistance lending, in part because these loans tend to be small.

Guarantee activities represent a potentially important avenue through which the Bank can interact closely with the private sector. The extension of guarantees to private entities has always been allowed by the Bank's charter, but this capability was rarely used until recently. In the early 1980s, the Bank developed a series of cofinancing programs that were not used widely; these were abandoned in 1989 because of internal fears that the Bank would become involved in commercial bank debt negotiations. Efforts to create a more meaningful guarantee program were stepped up in 1994 when the Bank's board voted to "mainstream" the use of the guarantee instrument, broadening country eligibility, modifying the fees charged, and simplifying procedures. Because the goal of the guarantee program is to act as a catalyst for private financing, the Bank offers only partial guarantees. Guarantees may be used to mobilize financing for any investment project eligible for a Bank loan, but they are most often applied to infrastructure projects that require a substantial amount of long-term funding.

There are two types of Bank guarantees. The "partial risk" guarantee insures private investors against a change in government policies; for example, the Bank's guarantee would cover investors if a government did not maintain agreed-upon tariff formulas and regulatory frameworks, or if a project were delayed because of government action or political events. (Bank guarantees do not cover commercial risks, such as construction delays or weak consumer demand.) The second type is a "partial credit" guarantee that allows governments to extend the maturities of their borrowings beyond what creditors would normally accept. Government counterguarantees are required from the host government whenever the Bank provides a guarantee; this indemnifies the Bank for any payment it makes under its guarantee.[15]

Despite the publicity surrounding the mainstreaming of guarantees, progress has been slow. Only three such transactions, worth $420 million, were concluded in fiscal 1997 (*Annual Report* 1997: 2). None the less, the Bank has staked a great deal on the future of its guarantee program, seeing it as a way to pursue deeper private sector involvement within the parameters of the Articles of Agreement. (Of the guarantees issued in 1997, two supported private sector operations and one a public sector operation.) Senior Bank officials are examining ways in which the guarantee program could be used even more flexibly, and there are another fifty or so guarantee projects in the pipeline (*Annual Report* 1997: 33).

In addition to the Bank's guarantee programs, MIGA guarantees new foreign private equity and debt investments against major political risks. Most of MIGA's activity is in the financial, manufacturing, infrastructure, and mining sectors. MIGA issued seventy guarantee contracts in 1997 covering investments in 25 countries. In one transaction, MIGA insured a Turkish construction company against the risks of expropriation, war, and civil disturbance for its $25 million equity investment in the construction and leasing of an office building that is part of the new Russian Cultural Center in Moscow.

The IFC is the only member of the Bank Group that is allowed to lend to the private sector without a government guarantee and to make equity investments in private ventures. In 1997 the IFC approved 176 projects, committing $3.3 billion of its own funds and raising an additional $3.4 billion through loan syndications, underwriting, and private placements. There was a dramatic shift in the sectoral composition of IFC investments in the late 1980s and 1990s, away from capital and intermediate goods industries and toward the financial sector, infrastructure, and energy. IFC activities range broadly, from investments in hotels, hospitals, and manufacturing plants to the provision of credit lines, from acquiring ships to underwriting bonds. The IFC also offers technical assistance and advisory services to businesses and governments.

Non-project activities

In addition to making loans that support private sector development, the Bank has devoted considerable resources to what it calls Economic and Sector Work (ESW), that is, research and analysis of the role of the private sector in development. Some private-sector-related research is a response to queries from the Bank's executive directors, while other projects are the result of management requests or staff initiatives. The Bank's research effort in this field has been one of its most intensive. In the January 1996 index of Bank publications, for example, more than 100 reports are listed under private enterprise, private investment, and privatization, considerably more than the seventy-nine available under the poverty heading.

One category of ESW is the Private Sector Assessment (PSA), a comprehensive survey of the state of the private sector in a given borrowing country. PSAs were initiated after 1991 in response to US demands for closer coordination between the Bank and the IFC. The purpose of the PSA process is to draw a country's attention to the needs of its private sector; the reports are prepared following a mission to the country by Bank and IFC staff that includes substantial canvassing of private sector actors. Although there is no standardized format, PSAs generally include an overview of the role of the private sector in the economy, the constraints it faces, and implications for the overall country strategy being pursued by the Bank group. The PSA process varies in importance from country to country. Some countries are already sensitive to private sector needs; in others the private sector remains so underdeveloped that there is little to discuss. While pressure from the United States was the original motivation for the PSA process, that pressure has waned. PSAs are now seen less as a requirement to satisfy an important Bank member than as one route for engaging a borrower in dialogue about the private sector.[16] PSAs, along with other research reports, feed into the Country Assistance Strategy (CAS), since 1990 the key document setting forth the Bank's overall approach to a given borrower. Thirty-one PSAs were completed between 1992 and 1996, although only a dozen are available publicly.[17]

Another non-lending activity is training. The Bank's private sector experts have begun to offer seminars and short courses for staff from other areas of the Bank, an important element in the diffusion of the private sector development agenda throughout the institution. Seminars have also been held to acquaint the Bank's executive directors with its private-sector-related work and to bring together Bank staff, clients, and other private sector players.

Perhaps the most important influence exerted by the Bank on the private sector orientation of its borrowers has come through the content of its policy advice. Policy dialogue is the Bank's name for the range of discussions, both formal and informal, that take place between Bank representatives and government officials in borrowing countries. As part of the formulation of the CAS, during the negotiation of adjustment loans, and through the PSA process, Bank representatives consult with and advise policymakers in relevant government agencies. Through this dialogue, the Bank tries to influence countries to shift to a greater reliance on market forces, "often using the volume of lending as an incentive" (Shihata 1995: 6). Because these discussions are informal and off the record, there is little information available about them, but interviews and anecdotal evidence suggest that Bank officials exercise considerable influence by linking future Bank lending to the adoption or promotion of certain policies.[18] Prominent among these policies is the degree of support shown by the government toward the private sector.

Changes in Bank organization and policies

A series of organizational changes in the mid-1990s gave private sector development a prominent place within the Bank's bureaucracy. The Bank-wide reorganization announced in 1992 brought about the first major organizational change regarding private sector development at the World Bank after close to a decade of discussion. A new vice presidency for Finance and Private Sector Development (FPD) was established as one of three thematic vice presidencies designed to strengthen and centralize the Bank's functional capabilities. About 150 staff members were assigned to this new unit, some of them recruited from the private sector. By 1998 the FPD vice presidency had grown to 700 individuals, organized into four departments.[19]

Like the other central vice presidencies, the FPD group was structured to "sell" its services to the Bank's operational units, meaning that its budget was driven mainly by demand from the regions. It was also staffed differently from much of the rest of the Bank, relying on personnel with expertise in specific technical areas, such as legal reform or microenterprise development. The establishment of a vice presidency dedicated to the private sector symbolized the importance given to this area. Locating private sector-oriented activities in a highly visible department was considered necessary for both practical and political reasons: management felt that only with high-profile attention would the Bank's new emphasis on the private sector be convincing.[20]

A subsequent reorganization under President Wolfensohn in 1996–7 grouped all of the Bank's private sector experts into a network to facilitate information-sharing across the institution. The creation of networks was a Bank-wide initiative under which staff members working in the same field throughout the institution are linked to one another. The goal of this organizational change was to overcome the fragmentation of technical expertise and make it easier to share knowledge across the organization and with outside parties. Technical networks were formed for Finance, Private Sector and Infrastructure (FPSI) Development; Poverty Reduction and Economic Management; Human Development; and Environmentally and Socially Sustainable Development (ESSD). Of the three agendas examined in this book, only private sector development is the primary focus of a Bank-wide network. At the end of fiscal 1998, the FPSI network (which does not include

IFC or MIGA staff) encompassed 1700 individuals. By way of comparison, the ESSD network had 300 members at the end of fiscal 1997 (*Annual Report* 1997: 26).

Another important organizational development was the appointment in 1996 of Richard Frank as managing director with sole responsibility for coordinating the private sector activities of the Bank, the IFC, and MIGA. Frank had an ideal background to take on this task, having spent his career as a manager in both the Bank and IFC, a rare occurrence, as there had been no deliberate policy to prepare executives for joint Bank–IFC responsibility and little cross-fertilization between the institutions at the managerial level. As part of Frank's initiative, the heads of the three Bank Group agencies began to hold weekly meetings. Frank's department opened a Business Partnership Center designed to serve as a single point of entry and source of information for private investors. The most meaningful aspect of this innovation is that Frank was part of the Bank's top circle of decision-makers, giving him a great deal of leverage within the institution. When Frank left the organization in 1997, responsibility for the Bank's private sector initiative was assumed by President Wolfensohn.

Rhetoric and practice

Since the late 1980s, private sector development has been a consistent theme in Bank reports and in speeches given by its presidents. The Bank's private-sector-related activities have figured among the top five or six issues highlighted in annual reports dating back to 1988. Since 1994, private sector development has been featured as one of several major World Bank programs discussed in detail in the annual report. President Conable first began referring to the private sector in 1988. His successor, Lewis Preston, stressed the importance of the private sector in virtually all of his public addresses. In the position statement prepared on the occasion of the Bank's fiftieth anniversary and circulated widely, "Stimulating the Private Sector" was listed as one of five key development challenges facing the Bank (World Bank Group 1994). More recently, President Wolfensohn has identified the Bank's commitment to the private sector as one of his immediate priorities in his speeches at the IMF/World Bank annual meetings. The rhetorical shift is striking when one considers that Robert McNamara, in thirteen years as Bank president, never mentioned the private sector in any of his speeches.

Speeches, organizational changes, or even the commitment of resources cannot be equated with impact. At an institution like the World Bank, impact can be judged in two ways: first, by the content of the policy advice given to borrowers and the influence brought to bear in ensuring that it is followed, and, second, by the number and size of loans made, keeping in mind the measurement issues mentioned above.

It is difficult to assess the impact of the first factor, policy advice, because policy dialogue between the Bank and its borrowers is largely off the record.

Many of the Bank's loans also contain policy conditions that must be met if successive tranches of a loan are to be released, and these are publicly available. (Of course, the degree to which the Bank enforces compliance with its loan conditions and, perhaps more important, the overall effectiveness of adjustment lending, is the subject of intense debate.)[21] As for lending levels, it appears that the private-sector-related activities of the Bank Group are growing faster than its lending overall (which has been flat for several years). Most of this increase has come from the IFC and MIGA, which both showed strong growth in the 1990s. The IFC grew at an average rate of over 12 per cent annually for the 1988–97 period (Figure 3.1), although its investment activities leveled off in 1997 and 1998. In 1997, the IFC made investments of $3.3 billion in projects worth a total of $18 billion. This was more than four times the level of 1987, when the IFC invested $790 million in projects totalling $4.3 billion (IFC *Annual Report* 1996: 20). MIGA is also growing rapidly. In 1990, its first year of operation, MIGA issued four guarantees, for a maximum contingent liability outstanding of $132 million. Seven years later, in 1997, MIGA signed seventy guarantee contracts, and its outstanding contingent liabilities had risen to $2.5 billion (MIGA *Annual Report* 1997: 18).

IBRD lending to those areas where the private sector, by the Bank's own definition, is most deeply involved, held steady from 1988 to 1996 at about 30–40 per cent of total IBRD loans committed annually. This figure dropped to 22 per cent in 1997 (Figure 3.2).[22] Because IBRD lending was basically flat during the 1988–97 period, the actual amount of IBRD loans targeted toward the private sector has not increased in the decade since the Bank's initiative in this area was announced.

The IFC plays a key role in the Bank Group's overall private sector effort. Its $3.3 billion of investments in 1997 compares to $3.7 billion in Bank loans to those sectors with high private sector involvement, a striking number given that the Bank is almost eleven times larger than the IFC in terms of its loans outstanding overall (*IFC Annual Report* 1997: i; *World Bank Annual Report* 1997: 8). The gap between the Bank's private-sector-related lending and IFC operations is narrowing (Figure 3.3).

The IFC's growing importance makes the current initiative to coordinate its activities more closely with those of the Bank even more pressing. The other crucial element is the Bank's guarantee program, the expansion of which represents the most promising path for closer Bank–private sector collaboration.

Despite the high profile given to the Bank's various private sector initiatives, the sensibility embodied in the IFC, MIGA, and the Bank's private sector network has not permeated the Bank's operational apparatus. A 1995 Overseas Development Council study concluded, among other things, that "the private sector is still by no means an integral part of [the Bank's] operational culture" (Richardson and Haralz 1995: 23). The cultural gap between the Bank and the IFC is described in more detail below. There

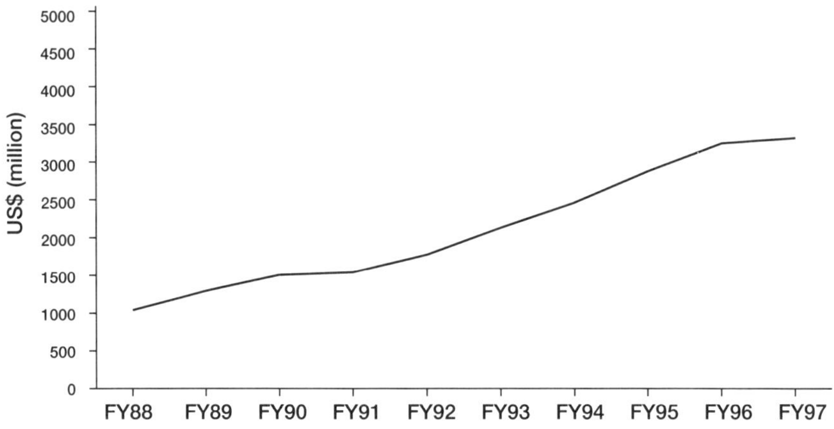

Figure 3.1 Growth of IFC (dollar amount of annual operations)
Source: IFC *Annual Report 1997*, p. 10

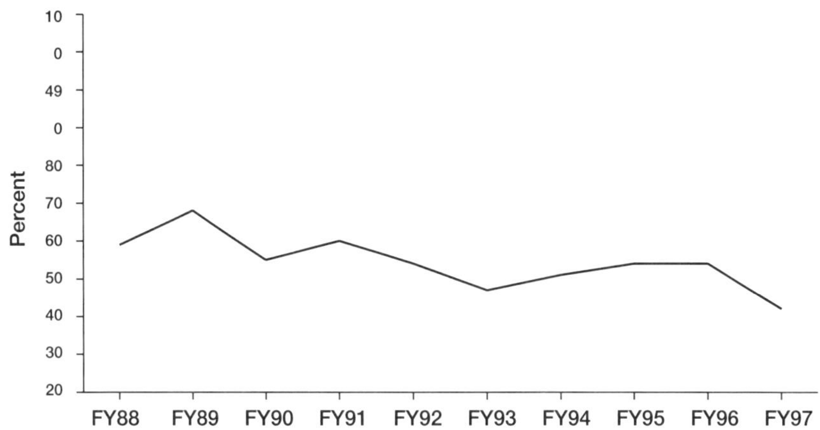

Figure 3.2 Private Sector Loans, IBRD (percentage of total IBRD loans)
Source: World Bank *Annual Report* 1997, Table 5-21; *Annual Report* 1996, Table 2-1; *Annual Report* 1993, Table 7-2; *Annual Report* 1990, Table 7-6

are cultural differences within the Bank as well, between, for example, those private sector experts who rely on demand for their services and the more entrenched regional operations units. But two factors have changed since the mid-1980s when pockets of private sector expertise existed throughout the Bank but had very little contact with operational units. There is now high-level support for a strong private sector emphasis at the Bank, and significant resources have been allocated to achieving this end. In addition, new policies have been designed to ensure that a private sector perspective is integrated into all the Bank's operations; for example, every Country Assistance Strategy (CAS) must address the status of the private sector in that country. No similar provision exists for addressing participation or governance in the CAS.

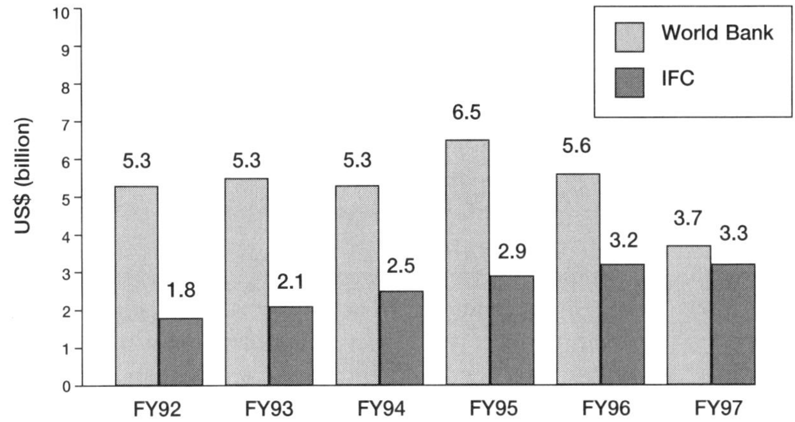

Figure 3.3 World Bank and IFC programs (resources to the private sector)
Source: World Bank and IFC annual reports

Private sector development and the Bank's organizational culture

Private sector development poses less of a challenge to the Bank's organizational culture than the other two agendas addressed in this book. Like traditional areas of Bank lending, private sector efforts can be quantified and a similar set of tools applied in different countries. It is relatively easy to identify projects as contributing to private sector development, count up the dollars the institution directs toward these projects, and assess how well the Bank is succeeding, or at least how much money it is moving, which until now has been the chief indicator of Bank effectiveness. More than participation or governance, efforts to improve the policy environment for the private sector rely on the kind of top-down, expert-oriented analysis that characterizes the Bank's organizational culture. Perhaps most important, promotion of the private sector fits well with the Bank's notion of development as a technical and apolitical process.

In his study of the Bank's poverty alleviation strategy under McNamara, William Ascher noted that the Bank's staff, dominated by economists, resisted adopting what it perceived to be the "softer" criteria associated with lending for poverty reduction (Ascher 1983). Lending to promote private sector development poses no such normative challenge. In addition, the cognitive orientation of the Bank's staff members and managers, instilled through similar education and training, much of it in the economics departments or business schools of US institutions, means that they are generally comfortable with a policy approach that calls for a dominant private sector role in the economy.

In many quarters, however, the Bank remains an institution that is more closely attuned to governments than to the private sector. Cultural gaps are evident between those staff members who specialize in private-sector-related issues and those concerned with a country's strategy overall. Similar divisions exist between private sector advocates and staff members who argue for paying closer attention to the political and social aspects of development. Organizational changes introduced by President Wolfensohn are intended in part to instill more of a private sector sensibility into the Bank, although thus far internal reorganizations have served mainly to dampen morale.

The "strategic compact" between the Bank and its member countries, approved in 1997, is the name given to Wolfensohn's plan for transforming the Bank into a more competitive, flexible, and results-oriented institution. Among the measures contributing to a cultural reorientation of the Bank are greater delegation of authority to staff members, some decentralization to offices located in developing countries, executive training for top management, exchange programs with the private sector, and the recruitment of staff with experience outside the institution. Even the language of the Bank has changed: President Wolfensohn speaks of "reengineering" instead of "reorganization," "business trips" rather than "missions." Responsiveness to clients and the delivery of better products and services is stressed, while new, more stringent performance indicators and evaluation mechanisms have been introduced for both Bank staff and Bank loans. The strategic compact calls for the Bank to "be run more like a modern business, rather than a bureaucracy" (World Bank 1997b: vi). Such an organization may be better able to operate on the borderline between business and government than the state-centered institution of the past.

Whatever the contradictions in its role, private sector development has emerged as a well-entrenched and dynamic area of activity at the World Bank. The general counsel writes that "Placing greater emphasis on private sector development and reliance on market forces have (*sic.*) probably been the most noticeable development in the Bank's operations since the initiation of adjustment lending in 1980" (Shihata 1995b: 6). While there were powerful internal reasons for the Bank's enthusiastic adoption of a strong pro-private-sector agenda, there are pressing external reasons as well. For one thing, the Bank relies on its new-found "market friendliness" to engage the support of the US Congress in battles over funding for the institution. It is the demands of member states for a more responsive and efficient institution that have largely driven Wolfensohn's effort to remake the Bank. The president understands that unless the World Bank can act as a cost-effective instrument for promoting the Western consensus for market-driven reform and private sector involvement in the economy, it may find itself marginalized within the international financial system, or even worse, out of business. While his reform plan is ambitious, two barriers stand in the way.

IFC–World Bank relations

Structural and cultural disparities between the World Bank and the IFC, and resulting problems of coordination, hinder institutional change and call into question the Bank's ability to contribute significantly to the development of the private sector in its borrowing countries. The tendency of the two agencies to work at cross-purposes was one of the factors cited by the United States in its decision to hold up the 1991 IFC capital increase. Even today, situations may arise where, for example, the Bank is lending money to a borrower for the rehabilitation of an unproductive state-owned enterprise, while at the same time the IFC is advising the country about privatizing that same firm.[23] The distinctions between the two agencies include marked differences in size, staffing, structure, mandate, clients, and culture.[24] A more integrated Bank Group approach to the private sector thus depends not only on better bureaucratic controls, but also on respect for each other's organizational culture and a sustained effort to cooperate.

Despite rapid growth, the IFC remains significantly smaller than the World Bank. In fiscal 1997, the IFC lent or invested $3.3 billion, bringing its disbursed loan and equity portfolio to $8.4 billion. By comparison, the World Bank committed $19.1 billion in loans and development credits, bringing total loans and development credits disbursed and outstanding to $182 billion. Even at its highest level to date (fiscal 1997), the IFC's annual investments amounted to only 17 per cent of World Bank lending, almost twice what they had been five years earlier, but still considerably smaller.

In terms of regular staff (excluding long-term consultants), the Bank is about six times larger than the IFC. The Bank had 5,443 regular employees at the end of fiscal 1997, compared to 880 at the IFC. (The IFC reported an additional 455 long-term consultants, temporary staff, and staff in overseas missions. The World Bank did not report a comparable figure in 1996 or 1997, but in 1995 there were 1,112 people in these categories.) Much of the IFC's staff is drawn from the private sector; the typical young staff member has an MBA, while an older staff member is likely to have worked at an investment bank or similar institution. In contrast, a World Bank staff member is more likely to hold a PhD in economics or to have experience in a technical field or in government.

The IFC's mandate is to mobilize domestic and foreign capital in order to promote growth in the private sector of developing countries; it does this without a government guarantee, providing loans and making equity investments in which it shares risk with its private sector partners. Like a private financial institution, it prices its services in line with the market and seeks to make a profit on its activities. This mandate has meant that the IFC is primarily a transaction-oriented agency, unlike the World Bank whose role is more strategic and policy-oriented. The average project cycle at the IFC is only 5–7 months, whereas it is 18–24 months at the World Bank. The IFC frequently becomes involved in a deal only after it is in the works, sometimes participating at the very end of the process to help put in place the final piece of needed funding. In contrast, the World Bank will work with governments to develop a project from the ground up, often over a period of several years.

The two agencies serve different clients. The Bank relates primarily to representatives of governments and government agencies, while the IFC deals with representatives of private sector firms and private investors.

Culturally, the IFC operates in a niche between the large, government-guaranteed projects of the World Bank and the more fluid, short-term flows of the private sector. Its goal of leveraging sources of private capital for risky but ultimately creditworthy endeavors means that it has a shorter time horizon than the World Bank and sees itself much more as an opportunity-seeking merchant bank than a development agency. In fact, the culture of the IFC most closely resembles that of an investment bank and IFC staff members frequently move to Wall Street firms or their equivalent upon leaving the organization.

Since its establishment, the IFC has played a decidedly junior role to the World Bank, but it has also enjoyed a great deal of autonomy. As Jonas Haralz writes for the World Bank History Project, the IFC:

> conducted its transactions without explicitly coordinating them with the Bank's general policies and country strategies, and its advisory activities had been largely confined to areas that at the time were of limited interest to the Bank . . . The Bank had tended to regard the IFC and its operations as irrelevant to its own activities, while the IFC had been satisfied to remain outside the Bank's sphere of attention.
>
> (Haralz 1997: 890)

With the emphasis on raising the prominence of the private sector within the World Bank Group, management began to focus on coordinating more closely the activities of the two organizations. Several earlier attempts to do this had failed because they were perceived by the IFC as encroaching on its autonomy or because Bank management did not carry through on its stated intentions. Early in his tenure, President Wolfensohn introduced his own initiative to overcome the problems of coordination that have long plagued the IFC–World Bank relationship.

Within a year of taking office, Wolfensohn appointed Richard Frank as a managing director and charged him with the task of bringing together all the institutions of the World Bank Group working on private sector development. To this end, Frank chaired a Private Sector Development Group in which senior managers from the IFC, MIGA, and the FPD vice presidency came together to coordinate their strategies and activities. (The contrast between this group and earlier efforts to coordinate Bank Group activities is revealing. The high-level Private Sector Development Committee, established in 1988 and reconstituted in 1991, was directed to meet at least once every three months, whereas Frank's group undertook to meet weekly with the head of each institution in attendance.)

The new group's goals were twofold. First, it was intended to harmonize policies among the World Bank, the IFC, and MIGA on issues such as the environment, social policy, and information disclosure, and to develop joint private sector approaches that would feed into the Bank's Country Assistance Strategies. Part of the unspoken agenda was to increase the sensitivity of IFC and MIGA staff and management to Bank policies in areas like the environment, participation, and gender. NGOs note that the IFC is not subject to the same accountability mechanisms as the World Bank; its operations are not governed by the Bank's disclosure policy, nor can claims about its projects be submitted to the independent Inspection Panel. (See Chapter 4). As a result, NGOs are beginning to turn their critical attention toward the IFC and MIGA, with the goal of bringing their operations into line with the more socially responsible policies already in place at the World Bank.

The second goal of the group was to create a focal point for outside clients. Borrowing countries seeking help with their private sector strategies and private firms interested in working with the Bank have complained that it is not clear which area of the Bank Group they should be dealing with; part of Frank's mandate was to provide "one-stop shopping" for these customers, something accomplished with the introduction of the Business Partnership Center in 1996. Frank's small staff organized working groups of mid-level managers and others from the Bank, the IFC, and MIGA to coordinate their activities on specific issues, such as the use of the Bank's guarantee authority. The staff also oversaw the Bank Group's work on specific projects involving two or more group institutions, several of which were approved by joint board sessions chaired by Frank.

This initiative seems to have had a greater impact than earlier efforts to coordinate Bank–IFC activities, for several reasons. First, it enjoys the full backing of the president and has been cited by him repeatedly as one of his top priorities. Second, one of the Bank's most senior officials was given the task of coordination as his sole mandate. Frank was one of five managing directors who with the president and vice president constituted the Bank's top leadership. Serving as the de facto spokesperson for the World Bank Group on private sector matters, he represented the president as a keynote speaker at some seventy international events. Third, the effort at coordination is led out of the Executive Office, which is perceived by the IFC as a fairly neutral bureaucratic location, rather than one that represents mainly Bank interests. Finally, the coordination team is small and non-threatening bureaucratically; its self-proclaimed function is to build on the work already going on at the Bank, the IFC, and MIGA, rather than reallocate tasks or consolidate the functions of different agencies. (Early rumors that the IFC would be subsumed by the World Bank – not surprisingly quite damaging to IFC staff morale – have subsided with repeated assurances by both agencies' leaders.)

In 1997, Frank left his position at the Bank to join a private investment firm. Uncertainty about who would succeed him was resolved when it was announced that President Wolfensohn would assume responsibility for leading the Private Sector Development Group. Some observers have questioned whether this is a good thing, noting the replacement of a highly competent and experienced official like Frank by an overworked and extended president. Others speculate that Frank left the organization precisely because coordination of the World Bank and IFC below the level of the president is simply impossible.

Whatever the change in personnel, Bank management appears to be serious about its initiative. A small but important indicator of the greater emphasis on coordination – and one that eventually may change how the two organizations relate to each in their day-to-day work – was the decision to locate many of the Bank's private sector experts in the IFC's new building. Plans call for Bank and IFC units that work on the same issues to be housed on the same floor; the power, telecommunications, and oil and gas sectors are among those where Bank and IFC staff members are now working side by side.

All these factors increase the likelihood that a more integrated approach to the private sector will be achieved. On the other hand, the adoption of such an all-out effort suggests the intractability of the problem. As the IFC seeks to preserve its niche between the rapidly growing investment activities of the private sector and greater assertiveness toward the private sector by the much larger World Bank, questions about the respective roles of the two agencies are growing. Several outside studies have called for a reapportioning of roles among the two organizations. An Overseas Development Council study recommended in 1995 that the IFC assume many of the private-sector-related functions of the World Bank (Richardson and Haralz 1995). The 1996–7 CSIS-sponsored Task Force on the United States and the Multilateral Development Banks proposed either that the IFC be expanded and assume responsibility for activities that currently reside within the World Bank (such as the private sector guarantee program) and that the appropriate World Bank staff be transferred to the IFC, or that the World Bank's Articles of Agreement be amended to permit lending without a government guarantee and the IFC and MIGA brought into a closer organizational relationship with an expanded World Bank private transactions unit (CSIS 1997: 38). Even if closer coordination can be achieved, the fundamental differences between the two agencies will not be erased. It is also unlikely that the IFC, operating in the faster-paced world of private transactions, will be able to respond seriously to NGO demands for greater sensitivity to the environmental and social implications of their activities. Bridging the structural and cultural gaps between the Bank and the IFC, and aligning their purpose, will require ongoing intervention and a sure hand.

The World Bank and private capital

The second major barrier confronting Wolfensohn's plan to keep the Bank center stage is well beyond his control. Surging private investment in developing countries, dating from the early 1990s, has made multilateral lending a much less important part of overall flows to the wealthier parts of the developing world. In the 1980s, the Third World debt crisis caused private lending to developing countries to dry up, meaning that official flows (bilateral and multilateral) took on greater importance, a development that increased the leverage of multilateral institutions like the World Bank over their borrowers' economic policies. As private capital flows resumed in the 1990s, official lenders were marginalized and their attendant policy influence declined. The World Bank and the IMF, of course, continue to play important roles in many areas and serve as valuable tools for addressing the geopolitical priorities of their member countries. Examples include IMF-led funding packages to assist Russia and contain financial crises in Mexico, Indonesia and Brazil, and the World Bank's contribution to post-conflict reconstruction in the West Bank and Gaza, Bosnia, and Haiti. But the middle-income developing countries that were the Bank's bread and butter in the 1980s have less need for its assistance in the late 1990s.

One of the most striking developments of the post-Cold War world was the resumption in private capital flows to developing countries, which grew from around $44 billion in 1990 to $244 billion in 1996.[25] Three-quarters of these funds have gone to only a dozen countries, with East Asia receiving most of the total. (China alone accounts for nearly a quarter.) Fifty countries, most of them very poor, receive virtually no private investment. At the same time, official development assistance from bilateral and multilateral lenders like the World Bank fell from $56 billion in 1990 to $41 billion in 1996, its lowest point in real terms since the early 1970s. Middle-income developing countries now have access to sources of capital apart from World Bank loans and are less willing to subject themselves to Bank conditionality in exchange for funds. Lower-income countries, such as those of sub-Saharan Africa, continue to depend on official lenders. The problem for the Bank's private sector development agenda is that the private sector remains very underdeveloped in this latter group of countries and the question of how to facilitate its growth is much more difficult.

The challenge of finding creditworthy investment opportunities involving the private sector that are not already being funded by private investors is particularly acute for the IFC. The bulk of IFC activity has occurred in its most developed member countries, which also receive large amounts of private capital. (Cumulative IFC commitments are highest in Brazil, Argentina, Mexico, India, and Turkey.) This has led to criticism in business circles that the IFC actually competes with, rather than stimulates private investment. At the same time (and for much the same reason) the IFC has been criticized by NGOs and others in the development field for failing to fulfill its development mandate. The "Extending IFC's Reach Initiative," announced in late 1996, represents an effort to address these concerns. Under the initiative, the IFC has begun work in sixteen countries or regions where it has not been active in the past, including Central and Western Africa, the

Caribbean, Bosnia and Herzegovina, the West Bank and Gaza, and some of the poorer republics of the former Soviet Union.[26] But the IFC must still find bankable projects in these countries and line up private investors behind them. As a result, the scope for extending its reach very far is distinctly limited.

While the IFC is likely to continue to expand gradually, the Bank's growth trajectory appears to be at an end. IBRD commitments have remained basically flat for the past ten fiscal years (Figure 3.4), while net disbursements (the net flow of capital from the Bank to developing countries) have declined markedly. (In fiscal 1994, net disbursements were actually negative, meaning that repayments of loans from borrowers to the Bank exceeded the amount of money disbursed by the Bank.) Some argue that the underlying trend in Bank lending peaked in 1980, while adjustment loans, the transition to market economies in Eastern Europe, and the move of China and India from IDA into the IBRD provided one-time "shots in the arm" that masked the decline. IDA lending has also shown almost no growth over the past six years (Figure 3.5).

Concern about the Bank's declining relevance in the face of resurgent private capital flows and lower demand from borrowers has given rise to proposals for a variety of new roles for the organization. Some continue to see the Bank as primarily a source of funds, albeit directed toward a smaller and more needy group of countries. Others advocate repositioning the Bank as a purveyor of financial advice and fee-based services; early in his tenure President Wolfensohn advocated such a role, saying that the Bank should become a provider of consulting services and technical assistance, rather than mainly a lender.[27] But there are questions about whether the Bank can compete on these terms, given its high costs relative to private sector firms. And many wonder whether the Bank will be an effective purveyor of policy advice without a large funding program to back up its recommendations.

In light of the challenges posed by the external environment and the difficulties of these alternative roles, it is possible that the Bank will simply continue as it is, becoming somewhat smaller and less relevant over time. Here, institutional impulses push in different directions. On the one hand, institutions have an imperative toward growth, constantly striving to become larger and more entrenched. Such a path would require that the Bank seek new roles for itself in order to maintain its central place in the international financial system. The Bank has done this throughout its history, beginning with its response to the introduction of the Marshall Plan in 1947, when it forfeited its role in post-World War II reconstruction and came to focus exclusively on the needs of the developing world. In the 1980s, when the IMF emerged to play a lead role in addressing the consequences of the debt crisis, the World Bank expanded its adjustment lending program in part as a way of remaining deeply involved in the important financial issues of the day. However, institutions also find it difficult to retool themselves in ways that require fundamental breaks with their organizational culture, as McNamara found during his long effort to boost the volume of Bank lending

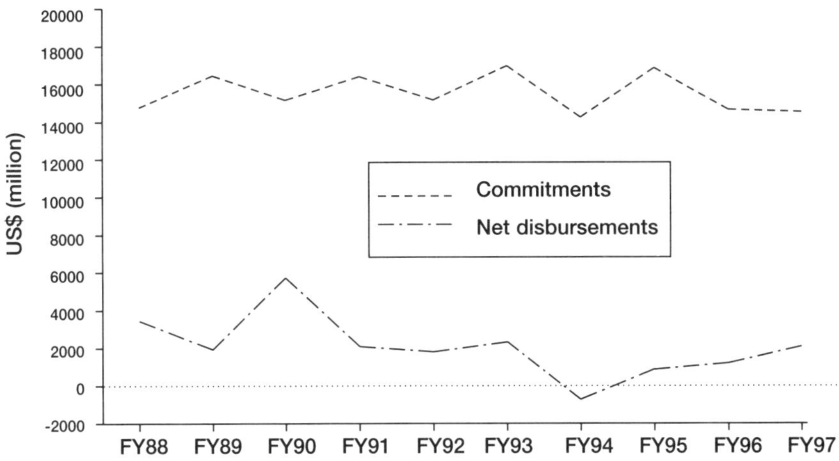

Figure 3.4 IBRD lending (dollar amount of loans)
Source: World Bank *Annual Reports* 1992, 1997

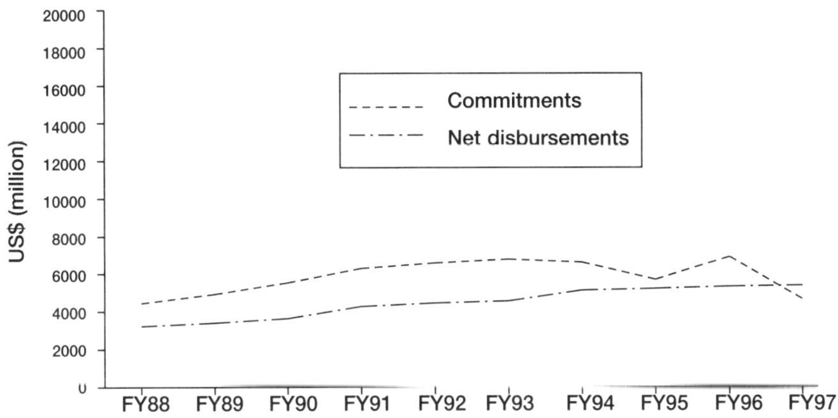

Figure 3.5 IDA operations (dollar amount of credits)
Source: World Bank *Annual Reports* 1992, 1997

and orient it toward the needs of the poor. Most of the new roles posited for the Bank today suggest the need for a new kind of institution, a transition that an organization with as well-defined a culture as the Bank will find it difficult to accomplish.

Conclusion

Contrary to popular wisdom, the Bank's private sector development agenda was not something imposed on the institution by its largest member. The real shift in the Bank's approach to the private sector began not in 1991 as a response to US pressure, but a decade earlier when the Bank, largely for its own reasons, began to make structural adjustment loans that promoted a policy environment conducive to a strong private sector. The United States was instrumental in pushing the Bank to raise the profile of its private sector agenda, but the Bank shaped its activities in line with its own priorities, needs, and experience.

Much more than a response to US demands, the private sector development agenda represented the Bank's efforts to adapt itself to a changing world. (In many ways, it also marked a return to the Bank's roots of forty years earlier after a lengthy detour.) In an environment where its borrowing governments are promoting markets at home, where global capital flows are surging, and where other lending institutions are reorienting their activities, the Bank faced the question of what it could do to maintain its central role in promoting economic development. One answer was to adopt a strong pro-private-sector agenda, while working around the legal limitations imposed by the Articles of Agreement and the Bank's cultural orientation as an agency that relates primarily to governments.

The private sector development agenda fits well with most aspects of the Bank's organizational culture, challenging neither its technical approach to development nor its insistence on remaining apolitical. As a result, private sector development is the most deeply institutionalized and least contested of the three agendas discussed in this book. It has received substantial new resources (even at a time of Bank downsizing), a prominent bureaucratic home, and high-level leadership. In addition, there has been remarkable continuity in how the Bank has defined its role *vis-à-vis* the private sector.

Some difficult issues remain. Achieving a unified and coherent approach to the private sector by the Bank Group's three organizations remains a challenge for their leaders. And the growing availability of private capital for investment in the developing world calls into question the Bank's future identity, not just in relation to the private sector but in general. More immediately, however, the prognosis is good for ongoing cultural change that will instill a private sector sensibility into the mainstream of Bank operations. The speed of this change depends not only on training and socialization, but also on staff turnover – traditionally low at the Bank, but increasing – which allows for the recruitment of individuals with appropriate skills. Pressure on the Bank's leadership to show results, and the Wolfensohn-era strategic compact designed to make the Bank more flexible and responsive to its clients, are also driving cultural change.

Unlike the participation agenda that requires the Bank to work closely with grassroots communities, or the governance agenda that involves it in the political affairs of its members, private sector development does not ask the Bank to redefine itself in any serious way. In this light it should not be surprising to find the promotion of the private sector at the heart of the Bank's operations and policy advice well into the twenty-first century.

Timeline of private-sector-related developments

1956	International Finance Corporation (IFC) founded.
1966	International Centre for Settlement of Investment Disputes (ICSID) established.
1968	Responsibility for industrial development and development finance corporations (DFCs) transferred from IFC to World Bank.
1983	First IBRD participation in a private loan syndicate.
1984	First IBRD guarantee of a private loan.
1987	Creation of a unit to focus on the private sector as part of Bank-wide reorganization.
1988	Multilateral Investment Guarantee Agency (MIGA) established.
1988	Private Sector Development Review Group convened; its recommendations are published in *Developing the Private Sector: A Challenge for the World Bank Group* (1989).
1989	Three-year action plan on private sector development (PSD) launched.
1989	Task Force on Financial Sector Operations meets, issues report.
1990	IFC requests capital increase.
1990–91	Ongoing negotiations between World Bank and United States over IFC capital increase.
April 1991	World Bank issues progress report on PSD action plan, published as *Developing the Private Sector: The World Bank's Experience and Approach* (1991).
June 1991	Compromise between United States and World Bank allows IFC capital increase.
January 1993	Central vice presidency for Finance and Private Sector Development (FPD), created as part of 1992 Bank reorganization, begins operations.
September 1994	World Bank Board of Executive Directors votes to "mainstream" guarantee program.
January 1996	Managing Director Richard Frank named to head Private Sector Development Group, as part of initiative by President Wolfensohn to increase coordination within World Bank Group on private sector development.
October 1996	Private sector development one of six top priorities addressed by President Wolfensohn in his speech to the Annual Meetings.

January 1997	Formation of network for Finance, Private Sector Development and Infrastructure.
May 1997	Richard Frank resigns from Bank; President Wolfensohn assumes responsibility for coordinating private sector development activities.

4 Approaching civil society
The participation agenda

> [World Bank] missions bring to the underdeveloped country a notion of what a developed country is like. They observe the underdeveloped country. They subtract the latter from the former. The difference is a program.
>
> Charles P. Kindleberger, *Review of Economics and Statistics*, 1952, p. 391.

> The Bank doesn't have any monopoly on ideas . . . [I]f we come and try and impose something, it doesn't work. What does work is participation.
>
> James D. Wolfensohn, Remarks at *Participation Sourcebook* Launch, 1996

The top-down, expert-oriented approach to lending criticized by Charles Kindleberger in the early 1950s has been a key feature of the Bank's organizational culture throughout its history. Development projects are generally formulated by Bank staff, most of them working out of the Bank's Washington headquarters, and then presented to representatives of the borrowing country government. The technical expertise needed to advise countries on these projects is believed to reside primarily within the Bank or among the host of consultants it hires. And the strategies advocated by the Bank, while not as "one size fits all" as in the past, embody fixed assumptions about the kind of policies a developing country should follow in order to advance.

Since the late 1980s, however, the Bank has begun to incorporate a wider range of perspectives in its approach to development. Increasingly, the Bank acknowledges that many parties – not just borrowing country governments – have a stake in its activities. Among the most important of these stakeholders are local communities whose involvement and support is necessary if Bank loans are to achieve their objectives. One way of improving the Bank's effectiveness, then, is to include grassroots organizations in the formulation and implementation of development projects. The Bank has also increased its interaction with non-governmental organizations (NGOs) based in industrialized countries, coming to consider many of them valuable repositories of technical expertise and appropriate partners for its activities.

The Bank's greater openness to participatory approaches was stimulated by advocates within and outside the Bank. Staff members seeking to work more closely with beneficiaries formed an alliance with representatives of NGOs, some of which were highly critical of the environmental and social consequences of Bank lending. The mere existence of this alliance, however, was not sufficient to convince a broader audience of the need for new approaches. Rather, organizational channels had to be created through which staff members could share knowledge and convey the benefits of NGO collaboration to their colleagues and managers. By working pragmatically and defining participation in narrow terms, internal advocates were able to shape their agenda to fit the Bank's norms and procedures and thus gain for it a high measure of acceptance.

While the value of participatory approaches has been accepted at the Bank's most senior levels, commitment to practicing them has not permeated the Bank's operations. The Bank now provides a more permissive environment and greater legitimacy for those seeking to work closely with NGOs and project beneficiaries, but there has not been the kind of large-scale cultural change required for such approaches to become a central premise of Bank activity.

The concept of participatory development is based on the simple idea that development agencies should pay closer attention to the individuals and groups affected by a development project and involve them in its design and implementation. While participation is ultimately something done by individuals, much of the Bank's work along these lines involves communities of individuals and the NGOs that represent them. The Bank's rationale for this new approach is largely pragmatic: "[to] improve the quality, effectiveness and sustainability of projects, and strengthen ownership and commitment of governments and stakeholders" (World Bank 1994c: i). In other words, by ensuring that its projects are not imposed from above but are responsive to the needs of the communities they affect, the Bank improves their prospects for success, and hence its own. The reliance on NGOs to facilitate community participation rests on the belief that they have greater local knowledge than the Bank; that, being closer to the poor, they are more responsive to their needs; that their small size makes them accountable to the groups they serve; and that they are able to adapt broad development approaches to local conditions (Cernea 1988).

Unlike the World Bank, some aid organizations advance a dual rationale for participation, seeing it not only as a means to better projects, but as an end in itself: one that is linked to democracy and human rights and that will bring about a stronger civil society and serve as a check on government. For example, the bilateral aid agencies of the industrialized nations have agreed that participatory development is essential not just because it enhances the sustainability of development programs, but also because "it strengthens civil society and the economy by empowering groups, communities and organisations to negotiate with institutions and bureaucracies, thus influencing public policy and providing a check on the power of government" (OECD 1994: 8). In its work on participation, the Bank has steered clear of these broader implications in order to avoid violating the provisions in its charter that it conduct itself without regard to politics.

Despite the fairly narrow construction of participation at the Bank, it is a radical concept in light of the institution's history and organizational culture. The paradigm that has guided Bank lending from the beginning emphasizes economic signals and technological development, the econocentric, technocentric, and commodocentric biases discussed in Chapter 1. Participatory approaches that require the Bank to focus on the people affected by its projects call into question this paradigm.

The Bank's basic approach to lending is built around a project cycle based on an engineering model and divided into stages of identification, preparation, appraisal, negotiation and board approval, implementation and supervision, and evaluation. Participatory projects, on the other hand, require what has been called a "learning-process approach," one that is more integrated and iterative (Korten 1984). A learning cycle centers on the needs of the borrower and beneficiary, not the requirements of the aid agency, and would consist of quite different stages that might vary from project to project. More flexible approaches to lending are beginning to be tried in projects with participatory components and in the areas of social development and governance, but the project cycle remains central to most of the Bank's work.[1]

Beyond their poor fit with the Bank's dominant paradigm and its standard approach to lending, participatory projects challenge other aspects of the Bank's organizational culture. They take more time and involve smaller amounts of money than infrastructure or adjustment loans, thereby undermining the Bank's ability to move large amounts of money quickly. They require a greater field presence, challenging the Bank's centralized organizational model in which the overwhelming proportion of Bank staff is located in Washington, not in the borrowing country. They require that the Bank work closely with leaders of grassroots organizations and other NGOs, challenging the Bank's usual practice of interacting primarily with governments. And they require knowledge of the culture and society of local populations, calling into question the Bank's reliance on quantitative indicators and the influence of economists on its staff.

Given these inevitable clashes between the Bank's organizational culture and the requirements of participatory development, how did the emphasis on participation come about? And how has the Bank's embrace of this new agenda been shaped by its institutional character?

The origins of participation

The same provisions in the Articles of Agreement that limit the Bank's work with the private sector – the requirement that loans be made to governments or carry a government guarantee – affect the nature of its collaboration with NGOs. But while the Bank has little flexibility in who signs for its loans, it has considerable leeway in how the projects and programs it supports are carried out. The Articles authorize the IBRD to "cooperate with any general international organization and with public international organizations having specialized responsibilities in related fields" (Article V, Section 8). The Bank's general counsel has interpreted this provision to include the possibility of working with NGOs, but only "in a manner consistent with the policies of those countries' governments towards NGOs and only with their full knowledge" (Shihata 1995: 238–9).[2] The Bank's relationship to its member governments supersedes its connection to any organization based in civil society. Thus, Bank–NGO collaboration is portrayed officially as part of a three-way relationship among Bank, borrower, and NGO. Formally, the government is charged with a project's implementation, while the Bank supports it with funding. This means that it is the government's responsibility, not the Bank's, to invite NGOs into a project. In practice, however, it is the Bank that usually takes the initiative in building NGO participation into its projects and programs, to which the government then signs on. The official relationship between Bank and borrower precludes the Bank from working with NGOs in countries where the government actively opposes their involvement.

During the first few decades of its history, NGOs played little part in the Bank's activities. The infrastructure projects that dominated Bank lending provided few opportunities for participation by organizations representing civil society. Although the building of dams and roads had as severe an impact then as it does now in terms of involuntary resettlement and environmental destruction, there was little public awareness of the environmental and social costs of industrialization and there were few groups in existence to represent affected populations. The NGO sector was also smaller and less active than it is today, and those NGOs that did exist were not necessarily interested in working with the Bank. As the Bank moved into lending for poverty alleviation in the 1970s, NGOs became involved in delivering services associated with Bank loans in fields like rural development, education, and health. Even then, however, the NGO role in Bank activities was marginal. A survey of Bank–NGO collaboration from 1973–88 found that only 6 per cent of Bank-financed projects involved NGOs. Most of the groups with which the Bank worked during this period were large international organizations, not local or grassroots entities. NGO involvement, usually confined to service delivery, was peripheral to most projects; there was no systematic reporting of collaboration; and Bank staff evinced widespread confusion over what even constituted an NGO (Salmen and Eaves 1991: 97–9).

The early 1980s saw the first initiatives to recognize formally the role of NGOs in Bank projects. The NGO–World Bank Committee was established in 1982 as the first institutionalized forum for discussions between Bank officials and NGO representatives. The committee is made up of senior Bank staff and twenty-six rotating NGO representatives from around the world, most of them from developing countries. (The NGOs on the committee select their own replacements, a process that some feel has made the committee a "closed club" to which newer and less established NGOs are unlikely to gain entry. Until the mid-1990s the committee met only once a year, limiting its impact. It now holds more frequent meetings, some of them in developing countries, and has been successful in eliciting greater participation from local NGOs.) At the same time, the Bank began issuing annual reports tracking the extent and nature of NGO–World Bank collaboration. In 1986, an NGO unit was created to oversee Bank–NGO relations. (Until 1993, this unit was part of the Bank's external relations area, distancing it from the more central operational and policy-making apparatus.) Discussions within the NGO–World Bank Committee in 1987–8 led to an effort to increase collaboration, including a request that staff members identify projects in which NGOs could be more closely involved. This marked the first time that such projects, and the staff associated with them, became a focus of managerial attention.

The emphasis on working with NGOs has grown steadily and rapidly since then as a result of several factors. The most important of these were the activities of NGOs outside the Bank and motivated staff members within it, assisted by pressure from a few member countries. The participation agenda was also facilitated by the attention of the Bank's recent leaders and a gradual process of learning within the organization about the effectiveness of its programs. Finally, broader changes in the developing world provided a supportive context for the new agenda. These factors, some internal to the Bank and others external, are examined below.

The role of non-governmental organizations (NGOs)

Beginning in the early 1980s, NGOs mounted a series of energetic and effective campaigns designed to focus public attention on the damaging environmental and social consequences of several large World Bank projects. In addition, NGOs pressed the Bank for greater openness and accountability in its operations and policy decisions. The following were three of the loans around which external criticism coalesced in the 1980s.[3]

- *The Northwest Region Development Program (Polonoroeste).* In 1981–3 the Bank lent more than half a billion dollars to Brazil for road construction and rural settlement in the Rondônia region, resulting in massive deforestation and violations of the rights of indigenous peoples.
- *The Sardar Sarovar (Narmada) Dam.* In 1985 the Bank lent India $450 million to support the construction of a huge dam. The forced resettlement of thousands of villagers led to a grassroots and transnational campaign against the Bank. In 1993, after a damaging independent review

of the project, the Bank withdrew from it at the request of the Indian Government and cancelled the remaining portion of its loan.

- *Indonesia Transmigration.* From 1976–86 the Bank lent Indonesia over $1 billion for what has been called the most ambitious resettlement project in history, designed to move 140 million people from the archipelago's overpopulated inner islands to the underpopulated, rainforest-covered outer islands. The result was deforestation of much of the remaining hardwood forests in Indonesia, and the impoverishment of many of the settlers.

By drawing attention to projects such as these, NGOs increased public awareness of the environmental and social costs of some of the Bank's highest-profile activities. Their grassroots campaign culminated in the "50 Years is Enough" coalition that in 1994 called for radical reform of the Bank and the International Monetary Fund (IMF).

Organization theorists identify cooptation as one strategy through which institutions buffer themselves from pressures arising in the environment. By incorporating alien and sometimes hostile elements into their decision-making structure, organizations are able to defuse external opposition to their activities. In this light, it is not surprising that the well-publicized attacks of NGOs on the World Bank coexisted with, and were to some degree the cause of, growing dialogue between the Bank and non-governmental groups. A central element of this dialogue was the need for the Bank to pay more attention to the individuals and communities affected by its programs, to enforce policies already in place on issues like involuntary resettlement, and to provide more information to NGOs at an earlier stage of the project cycle.

NGO pressure alone was not responsible for the Bank's growing interest in working with beneficiaries and cooperating with non-governmental groups. NGO efforts found a receptive audience among certain members of the Bank's staff, some of whom had already begun to pay greater attention to the social aspects of development and involve local organizations in their projects. These individuals played a crucial role in bringing participatory approaches to the fore within the Bank.

The role of internal advocates

In her research on people within organizations who serve as advocates for particular issues, Nüket Kardam finds that they are most successful when they understand the constraints that arise from organizational goals and procedures and shape their advocacy accordingly (Kardam 1993). She shows, for example, how those staff members who were interested in involving women more deeply in Bank projects framed the issue in terms of its economic benefits, rather than relying on social welfare or equity arguments, and thereby attracted broader support for their agenda (Kardam 1990, 1991). Kardam argues more generally that the ultimate incorporation of a new agenda depends both on its congruence with an organization's goals and procedures, and on the bargaining power of its internal advocates. The participation story suggests the importance of both factors: advocates shaped their agenda to fit with the broader needs of the Bank and increased their leverage by forming alliances with groups outside the organization that shared their agenda.

For most of those staff members who supported more participatory approaches in Bank lending, their involvement with NGOs and beneficiaries predated by many years the institutional innovations of the late 1980s. The extent of collaboration with NGOs depended in part on the sector in which an individual worked. In water and sanitation projects, for example, where the involvement of local groups and individuals is essential for a project's success, participatory approaches had been in use since the late 1970s. Rural and urban development are other areas where the need for working with beneficiaries had long been recognized.[4] Some advocates brought to the Bank an understanding of participation gained at other institutions. One staff member who joined the Bank after eleven years at the US Agency for International Development (AID) notes that AID was ahead of the Bank in using participatory approaches both because it has a stronger field presence than the Bank and because it is not required to lend only to governments.[5] Another staff member who works closely with NGOs spent ten years with OXFAM before joining the Bank. Collaboration with NGOs also depended on personal contacts between staff members and friends or colleagues – or even husbands or wives – in the NGO community. Informal networks were forged among advocates of participation within the Bank; one example is the sociology group instituted by the Bank's sociology adviser in the late 1970s (Kardam 1993: 1779). Another is the "Friday morning group" that began meeting in the early 1980s to discuss values and ethics, including the need to understand the cultures of the countries to which the Bank lends.

Specific areas and individuals within the Bank provided support for these informal networks. The Bank had appointed anthropologist Michael Cernea to a senior adviser post in 1974 and the number of sociologists and anthropologists on the staff had risen gradually since then. Greater emphasis on the environmental consequences of Bank lending, beginning in the late 1980s, had also introduced staff members with different skills into the institution. These non-economists, trained to focus on social issues, brought a new perspective to the Bank, one well-suited to participatory approaches. The NGO unit served as a focal point for those seeking to expand collaboration with NGOs. But it was not until an organizational channel was created through which advocates of participation could come together, share their knowledge, and bring managers and outsiders into the discussion that the participation agenda was articulated clearly. (This exercise, the Learning Group on Participatory Development, is discussed below.)

The role of member countries

The public awareness campaigns of the NGO community were directed not only at the Bank but also at the legislatures of member countries. Knowing that it is these countries that ultimately are responsible for Bank policy, environmental NGOs lobbied the US Congress strenuously in the 1980s, urging it to require changes in the policies of the multilateral development banks. This led to the somewhat curious sight of conservative Bush administration appointees pushing the Bank to improve its environmental policies. In 1992, congressional threats to cut the Bank's funding led to the implementation of a new and more open disclosure policy that made it easier for NGOs and others to obtain information about Bank projects. Members of the US Congress have continued to press the Bank on these issues; for example the US Congress's *Foreign Aid Conference Report* for the fiscal year 1998 called on the Bank:

> to systematically consult with local communities on the potential impact of loans as part of the normal lending process, and to expand the participation of affected peoples and NGOs in decisions on the selection, design and implementation of projects and economic reform programs.[6]

Other developed countries also encouraged the Bank to work more closely with NGOs, occasionally supporting initiatives through trust funds or other special contributions outside the Bank's regular budget process. For example, the Learning Group on Participatory Development was funded by the Swedish International Development Authority and Germany's bilateral aid agency.

Until the late 1980s, many of the Bank's developing member countries opposed more participatory approaches to Bank-funded projects. Closed societies, they resisted the extension of the Bank–government dialogue to NGOs within their countries. In some cases, individuals who understood the benefits of participation could be found within specific government agencies, allowing motivated Bank staff to build participatory components into some projects. But at the highest levels, most borrowers did not welcome the inclusion of NGOs in Bank projects. Democratization and growing ties between governments and civil society have led to a change in attitude on the part of many borrowers, creating a more permissive environment for the Bank to expand its work with NGOs.

Leadership and learning

Beginning with the presidency of Barber Conable in 1988, World Bank leaders have given rhetorical and sometimes material support to the cause of greater participation. Conable's successors, Lewis Preston and James Wolfensohn, have consistently highlighted the importance of participation in their speeches. The ability of these men, however, to raise this or any other single issue to great prominence is constrained by the Bank's increasingly complex agenda. In the 1970s, Robert McNamara could make poverty alleviation the central theme of his presidency because the Bank's agenda was fairly uncluttered. Today, the Bank is committed to supporting poverty reduction, environmental sustainability, appropriate macroeconomic policies, private sector development, social issues, and a host of other concerns. In such a congested environment, Bank leaders have many priorities to highlight and their influence is spread thin. But the vocal support of senior management for participation and President Wolfensohn's unbridled enthusiasm for Bank–NGO collaboration have created a climate in which bottom-up initiatives in these areas can claim greater legitimacy than in the past.

Also contributing to the acceptance of more participatory approaches was a gradual learning process about the factors underlying the success or failure of Bank programs. These lessons were first given voice at the Bank in the mid-1980s when members of its research staff began to publish studies that showed the importance of involving beneficiaries in Bank lending. Such involvement seemed to increase prospects for both the success and sustainability of many types of projects and reduce the negative environmental and social consequences of large infrastructure loans.

Growing intellectual conviction of the benefits of participation led to a series of operational policies made public in the late 1980s that called for beneficiary participation in Bank projects in a variety of areas, including involuntary resettlement, indigenous peoples, and the environment. The new policies, however, were often not translated into practice, in part because of the "pipeline" effect where projects already under way are not required to comply with new, more stringent guidelines, and in part because they were ignored or resisted by Bank staff. The Bank's policy on involuntary resettlement, for example, which had been in place since 1980, was the subject of scrutiny by an independent commission charged with evaluating the Sardar Sarovar dam project after vocal NGO criticism had pushed the Bank to take some action. The Morse Commission's 1991 report highlighted the project's "non-compliance with Bank resettlement and environmental requirements" (Morse and Berger 1992: xxiv) and recommended that the Bank step back from the project. These findings contributed to the Bank's decision to undertake a comprehensive internal review in 1993–4 of the Bank's resettlement policies.[7]

Another important source of institutional learning regarding participation was the conclusions of the task force on portfolio management as expressed in the 1992 Wapenhans Report (World Bank 1992b). The task force found that problems with the Bank's loan portfolio were on the rise. It attributed this mainly to the Bank's "pervasive preoccupation with new lending at the expense of effective implementation of the programs and projects that it financed" (*Annual Report 1993*: 62). Specifically, the report noted that the share of projects with "major problems" during implementation rose from 11 per cent in fiscal 1981 to 18 per cent in fiscal 1992, while the proportion of projects judged satisfactory in annual evaluations fell from 85 per cent in fiscal 1981 to 63 per cent in fiscal 1991. These findings triggered widespread alarm among management and member countries, and set off a series of initiatives designed to improve the quality of the Bank's portfolio. The report concluded, among other things, that "Successful implementation [of projects] requires commitment, built on stakeholder participation and local 'ownership'" (World Bank 1992b: ii).

The rhetorical support of Bank leaders, the findings of its researchers, and management's rising concern about the effectiveness of Bank lending program created a more responsive environment for the advocacy efforts of internal and external supporters of participation.

Contextual factors

The Bank's growing attention to participation took place against the backdrop of widespread political and social change in the developing world. The 1980s saw students, workers, religious groups, and others campaigning for greater democracy in Latin America and the Soviet bloc. Democratization, in turn, allowed new organizations to flourish; as a result, there was a burgeoning of institutions based in civil society in many developing countries. The greater prominence of Southern NGOs facilitated the building of alliances with Northern NGOs and the emergence of North–South non-governmental coalitions dedicated to environmental protection, poverty alleviation, and other social concerns.[8]

Another important international trend was the growing role of (mainly Northern) NGOs in providing financing for international development efforts. Between 1975 and 1985, annual disbursements for development by international NGOs rose in real terms by 185 per cent to $4 billion (Cernea 1988: 6); by 1993, this amount had more than doubled, as international NGOs contributed over $8.5 billion in aid to developing countries, or 14 per cent of total development assistance (World Bank 1996a: 1). Part of this growth came from official bilateral development agencies channelling some of their overseas aid through NGOs and pursuing greater cooperation with them. Among the organizations that began to work more closely with NGOs in the late 1980s were the British, Canadian, German, Swedish, and US bilateral development agencies. Unlike the World Bank, these agencies, along with the newly founded European Bank for Reconstruction and Development, adopted an explicit political program that links participatory development to broader questions of human rights and democratization. The World Bank's participation agenda has remained much more limited.

A third important factor was a growing body of academic research from outside the Bank also showing that development efforts are more likely to succeed when they involve beneficiaries.[9] These elements provided fertile ground for NGOs and internal advocates working to make the World Bank a more open and responsive institution.

The Bank's response

The alliance formed between internal advocates and external supporters of participatory development has led to significant changes in the way the Bank does business. While these changes fall short of the hopes of many advocates, even the Bank's staunchest critics admit that there has been an undeniable improvement in Bank policies toward NGOs. Activists are now focusing on whether these new policies are actually being implemented and, if so, what difference they make in terms of grassroots participation in development, ownership of programs, and project effectiveness.

Partly in response to the new policies, operational collaboration between the Bank and NGOs is on the rise. This growth began in the mid-1980s, accelerated in the late 1980s, and continued to expand in the 1990s. Almost half the projects approved in the 1994–7 fiscal years are classified by the Bank as including some form of NGO participation. Advocates are quick to point out that these numbers must be read with some caution. First, the criteria for classifying a project as involving NGOs are quite loose (including, for example, consultation with NGOs before a project begins, whether or not the groups' views are taken into account) and project manager claims are taken at face value. Second, if any part of a project involves collaboration of any kind, then the entire project is counted as one that involves NGOs. (For example, if a $100 million infrastructure loan includes a $1 million social fund in which NGOs help create jobs for people who are displaced by the project, then the entire project counts as one with NGO involvement.) While the upward trend in the numbers regarding collaboration is not disputed, some participation advocates believe that the volume and extent of the Bank's work with NGOs is greatly exaggerated in the official figures.

An important component of the Bank's response to those calling for closer collaboration with NGOs was a "program of action and learning on popular participation," initiated in 1991. The program had four goals:

- to implement effectively the community involvement provisions of the Bank's environmental assessment policy;
- to continue to involve NGOs in Bank-supported operations, especially in the planning stage;
- to review the Bank's operational directives on participation and evaluate the extent to which they are being implemented; and
- to initiate a learning process about how the Bank can support popular participation.

This learning process, described by one of its leaders as "a modest program" (Beckmann 1991: 151) turned out to have far-reaching implications, beginning with the establishment of a Bank-wide Learning Group on Participatory Development (LGPD). Under way from 1991–4, the LGPD became the chief mechanism through which internal advocates of participation joined forces with each other and with outside supporters.

The idea for the LGPD had emerged from discussions between NGO representatives and Bank managers in the NGO–World Bank Committee. A core group of staff members with a strong social and human development focus, many of whom were already experienced in participatory techniques, was nominated to lead the effort. Their tasks were to help develop and document twenty Bank projects with participatory elements, to accelerate Bank learning about participation, and to investigate whether the Bank might need to change its policies to further participation. An intensive research program, in which close to fifty papers were commissioned and produced, formed a part of the learning group's activities (World Bank 1994c, Annex III). From the beginning, the group made a conscious effort to work within the Bank's institutional constraints. As one member of the core group put it, "We recognized that the Bank is generally pragmatic and that task managers will integrate a new approach if it is shown to work."[10] The group was intent on keeping its activities from becoming marginalized; to that end, senior managers were invited to participate, some of whom have since become strong high-level advocates for participation within the Bank. The group also forged links with supporters outside the Bank; papers were commissioned from outside experts, including long-time critics of the institution, and the two workshops held by the LGPD brought together Bank staff with NGO representatives, academics, and others.

The group's report and an action plan endorsed by management was released in September 1994.[11] In a break with traditional Bank practice, the report included an addendum submitted by a group of individuals and NGOs critical of some aspects of its findings and recommendations. The Bank has never been known for acknowledging internal dissension or making transparent the deliberative process; the LGPD did, indeed, appear to signal a new openness.

Members of the core group say they never anticipated that the learning group's final report would be as forceful or concrete as it was. The 1994 action plan called for a variety of measures, several of which have been implemented in ways that have had an important impact. For example, an oversight committee of senior managers was created; it, in turn, decided that each region should prepare its own participation action plan, which has now been done. (Internal advocates point out that once participation becomes a tangible part of a country program mid-level managers must comply even if they are not necessarily believers.) A list of participation flagship projects was compiled and a report on their progress sent regularly to President Wolfensohn. (This initiative has since been discontinued.) Additional funds were made available for managers interested in building participatory components into their projects. *The World Bank Participation Sourcebook*, which includes "it can be done" testimonials from staff and "how to" case studies on working with NGOs was published in 1996 and has become a key reference document for those interested in participatory development.

Two separate initiatives coincided with the learning group's report and offered additional avenues for NGOs seeking greater accountability from the Bank. A new disclosure policy had been introduced in 1989 and extended in 1993, making it somewhat easier for NGOs to obtain information about Bank projects and policies. This led to the establishment of a Public Information Center (PIC) in 1994 from which a variety of Bank documents are available. (Interestingly, although NGOs were instrumental in bringing about the new policy, only 2 per cent of requests for information received by the PIC in 1995 came from NGOs (*Annual Report* 1995: 46), suggesting that they obtain much of their information through unofficial channels, such as informal contact with Bank staff.) While NGOs and others who support a more transparent Bank see the revised disclosure policy as a significant step, they note that only selected documents and only those dated after 1994 are required to be released by the PIC.[12] NGOs are particularly concerned about the lack of availability of the Country Assistance Strategies (CASs) that summarize the Bank's overall approach to a given borrower, especially now that the Bank is claiming to incorporate issues like participation into the CAS. (The Bank counters that CASs are actually the property of the country in question, not the Bank, and that it does not have the authority to release them.) NGO advocates also note that the Bank's field offices are far less forthcoming than the central PIC in providing information that is supposed to be publicly available.

The second development in the direction of greater accountability was the establishment of the World Bank Inspection Panel in 1994.[13] The three-member panel provides an independent forum for private citizens who believe their interests have been harmed by a Bank project. Groups of citizens, including local NGOs, may request an investigation of claims that the Bank failed to observe its operational policies in the design, appraisal, or implementation of a Bank-financed project. Only thirteen formal requests were received by the Inspection Panel in its first four years of operation. Advocates for developing country NGOs believe that there are several reasons why the Inspection Panel mechanism has not been used more widely. First, groups need to demonstrate that they have tried to get recourse through other channels. Second, while the process is accessible (for example, citizens can write to the panel in their own language), there is no mechanism for publicizing the existence of the panel to affected populations in developing countries. Finally, groups or individuals may face the threat of intimidation in their own countries if they submit a request to the panel.

In several cases, the Inspection Panel has determined that the request for inspection is inadmissible. In the cases that have been decided, the panel has generally ruled in favor of the Bank. In 1997, for example, the panel recommended that the Rondônia Natural Resources Management Project in Brazil, long a target of NGO opposition on environmental and social grounds, should continue. While noting that there had been only mixed progress in implementing a 1995 action plan put forth by the Bank, the panel concluded that local people affected by the project considered its continuation preferable to ending Bank involvement (*Annual Report* 1997: 127). The case with the highest profile, the Arun III Hydroelectric Project in Nepal, did not make it all the way through the Inspection Panel process. The request for review of this project was submitted by a citizen's group from Katmandu, as well as people living at the dam site, who believed that the project violated the Bank's policies on, among other things, involuntary resettlement, indigenous people, and environmental assessment. The panel's report, along with intense public opposition in Nepal and in developed countries, led President Wolfensohn to decide in August 1995 not to proceed with the project.[14] Although the decision to cancel Bank participation in this project was taken as a positive sign that the Bank may be becoming more responsive to NGO concerns, the decision says little conclusive about the effectiveness of the Inspection Panel process.

It is widely acknowledged, even by critics, that the Bank has made major changes in the way it interacts with NGOs, but there is less agreement on how deep these changes go. Do they signify a meaningful departure from past Bank practice or are they mainly window dressing? A third possibility is that members of the Bank's management and staff are genuinely committed to more participatory approaches, but are hindered from enacting them fully because of the Bank's organizational characteristics.

Assessing the importance of participation

One of the difficulties in assessing the importance of participation at the Bank is that most of the information available for such a task is produced by the Bank itself and provides only a partial picture of the extent and impact of participatory approaches. NGO activists point out that Bank figures showing increased collaboration with NGOs do not automatically mean that Bank-sponsored projects actually enjoy a high level of grassroots participation. Independent assessments of the results of Bank–NGO collaboration on the ground are needed, but efforts along these lines are fairly recent.[15]

The Bank reports on its cooperation with NGOs in annual progress reports available to the public. Issued since 1982, these include summary information about projects that involve NGOs, an analysis of the type of NGO and the type of participation, issues addressed in Bank–NGO dialogue, and special instances of collaboration. Progress on participation is also highlighted on occasion in the Bank's annual report. Other Bank publications, such as *The World Bank Participation Sourcebook* and *Working with NGOs*, provide material about specific cases and methods. Information about participation is also available from NGOs and generally provides a less rosy picture than that put forth by the Bank. Ongoing monitoring efforts, such as the Development Bank Watchers' Project at the Bread for the World Institute, are particularly helpful, as is the growing availability of information from advocacy organizations over the Internet. Finally, a number of more academic studies, including Paul Nelson's *The World Bank and NGOs: The limits of apolitical development* (1995), and Jonathan Fox and L. David Brown's edited volume, *The Struggle for Accountability: The World Bank, NGOs and grassroots movements* (1998), provide detailed analyses of different aspects of NGO involvement in the Bank's activities. From these disparate sources, an image emerges of the nature of Bank–NGO collaboration in the late 1990s.

The Bank's work with NGOs can be grouped into three categories: operational collaboration (the participation of NGOs in Bank-supported projects); economic and sector work (the involvement and commentary of NGOs in Bank research activities); and discussions between NGOs and the Bank over aspects of Bank policy.

Operational collaboration

The broad goal of increasing beneficiary participation in Bank-funded projects has been met chiefly by involving NGOs in one or more stages of a Bank loan. The Bank's work with NGOs has been tailored to fit existing approaches and technologies as much as possible. For example, opportunities for NGOs to collaborate with the Bank are structured around the Bank's project cycle, as indicated in Table 4.1.

The extent of NGO participation in Bank projects is rising (see Figure 4.1).[16] The first big increase came after 1988 when the Bank began to promote collaboration with NGOs. As noted earlier, from 1973–88 the proportion of Bank projects that included some form of NGO involvement averaged 6 per cent. During the 1991–3 period about one-third of Bank projects involved NGOs. (Some of this increase was accounted for by the identification and classification of projects already under way as involving NGOs, rather than new projects designed to incorporate an NGO role.) By 1994 almost half of Bank projects approved each year included some participatory component. This level has remained fairly steady. As greater numbers of projects with NGO involvement are approved, the proportion of such projects in the Bank's total portfolio is rising. At the end of the 1997 fiscal year, 38 per cent of all active World Bank projects involved NGOs in some way.

Perhaps more important, the nature of NGO involvement in Bank projects has changed. Historically, NGOs have been most active in implementing or operating projects that the Bank and borrowing country governments have designed. Critics of the Bank's work with NGOs have long maintained that NGO involvement at this stage does not constitute real participation; the important decisions have already been made and NGOs are relied upon only to carry them out. In recent years, NGOs have become increasingly involved in project design, a role that participation advocates find more promising. Figure 4.2 shows that prior to 1994, only 10–20 per cent of those Bank projects that involved NGOs included collaboration in project design, whereas after 1994, 40–60 per cent of Bank projects with NGO involvement included this form of collaboration.

Table 4.1 NGO roles in the project cycle

Identification	provide advice/information on local conditions participate in environmental and social assessments organize consultations with beneficiaries/affected parties transmit expressed needs/priorities of local communities to project staff act as a source, model or sponsor of project ideas implement pilot projects
Design	consult to the government, local communities, or the Bank assist in promoting a participatory approach to project design channel information to local populations
Financing	co-financier of a project component source of funds for activities complementary to the proposed Bank-financed project
Implementation	project contractor or manager (for delivery of services, training, construction, etc.) promote community participation in project activities financial intermediary role supplier of technical knowledge to local beneficiaries advisor to local communities on how to take advantage of project-financed goods or services implementor of complementary activities beneficiary of an NGO funding mechanism established by the project.
Monitoring and Evaluation	NGO contracted to monitor project progress or evaluate results facilitate participatory monitoring and evaluation independent/unsolicited monitoring and evaluation

Source: Malena (1995): 29

The Bank now works with different types of NGOs than in the earlier phases of collaboration, emphasizing local groups rather than large international organizations. In the 1973–88 period, 43 per cent of the NGOs collaborating with the Bank were international organizations, 31 per cent were indigenous or intermediary organizations (that is, groups located in the developing country that do not involve direct citizen participation), and 26 per cent were grassroots or community-based organizations. By 1997, international organizations were involved in only about 20 per cent of Bank–NGO projects, whereas grassroots organizations were involved in 80 per cent of such projects. Sixty per cent of Bank–NGO projects included the participation of both grassroots organizations and intermediary organizations with technical expertise in a relevant sector.

Regional patterns have also changed. In the 1990–2 period, about half of Bank projects involving NGOs were located in Africa. Instances of Bank–NGO collaboration are now found in all regions, with cooperation most pronounced in South Asia (where 84 per cent of projects have NGO

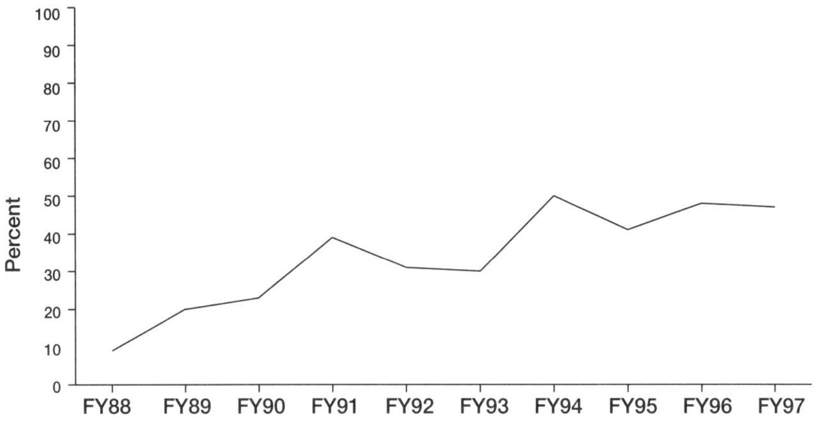

Figure 4.1 NGO–World Bank collaboration (percentage of all projects)
Source: World Bank Annual Progress Reports on World Bank–NGO Cooperation

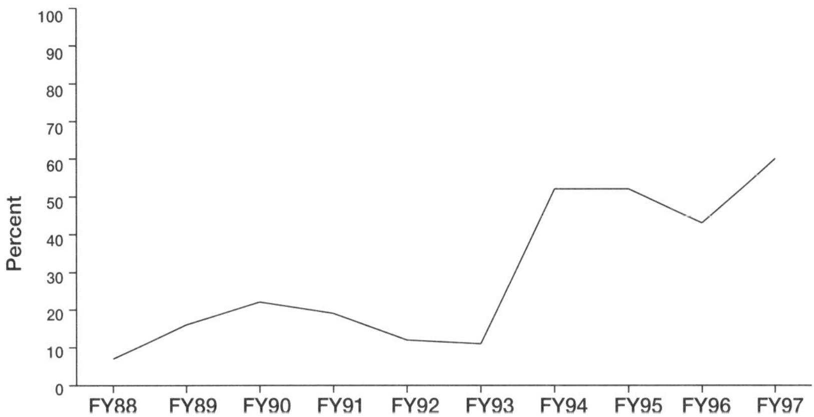

Figure 4.2 NGO role in project design (percentage of all collaborative projects)
Source: World Bank Annual Progress Reports on World Bank–NGO Cooperation

involvement), Africa (61 per cent), and Latin America (60 per cent). Sectoral patterns, on the other hand, have held steady. Eighty-one per cent of all Bank projects approved in 1997 in the agriculture and rural development sectors and all projects concerning the environment involved NGOs. NGO participation is also extensive in loans related to education; population, health, and nutrition; water supply and sanitation; and other social sectors (for instance, community development or employment creation).

In 1997 the Bank introduced two new lending instruments to overcome some of the rigidities of the existing project cycle. Both the Bank and the NGO community expect the new Adaptable Program Loans (APLs) and Learning and Innovation Loans (LILs) to be especially well-suited to participatory projects. These instruments allow a "grow-as-you-go" approach to lending in which solutions can be proposed and tested and, if successful, expanded. Part of the stimulus for developing the new loan types was to overcome the standard assumptions of the project cycle, namely, according to the Bread for the World Institute, "that a flawless 'blueprint' can be designed at project initiation and successfully implemented in a multi-year timeframe. Such an approach . . doesn't work for heuristic, participatory development involving constant learning and involvement of the affected stakeholders."[17] The first APL was approved in January 1998; over time, the Bank expects the demand for APLs to rise to about twenty per year, amounting to around 5 per cent of Bank lending. Demand for the smaller LILs is anticipated at about fifty per year for a total of $200 million, or 1 per cent of Bank lending.

Bank–NGO cooperation beyond projects

In addition to their involvement in projects, the World Bank cooperates with NGOs in other aspects of its work. The Bank spends substantial resources on what it calls economic and sector work (ESW), mainly research on development issues. NGOs are involved in ESW both as researchers/analysts and as stakeholders in the development process. The rationale for the first role is that an NGO may be in a better position than the Bank to conduct research that requires close consultation with beneficiaries. A stronger field presence and knowledge of local culture and conditions may also make NGOs more effective than the Bank in promoting consensus. Regarding the second role, the Bank has come to acknowledge that NGOs can provide an alternative perspective to the Bank's analysis and should be consulted as part of its research efforts, although the scope of this consultation remains more limited than many NGOs would like.

One example of Bank–NGO cooperation on ESW is the Bank's poverty assessment process. In fiscal 1996, twelve of the twenty-two poverty assessments conducted by the Bank were considered participatory, meaning that special attention was given to involving key groups of vulnerable people, such as women, members of indigenous communities, and racial and ethnic minorities, through a participatory research exercise in which NGOs were involved. All Bank projects that have a potentially significant environmental impact are required to include a full environmental assessment during which NGOs must be consulted. NGOs are also involved in social assessments, which have been prepared for selected Bank projects since 1994. The emphasis on participatory research is growing: for example, the Africa region now incorporates beneficiary consultation into all its activities.

Less progress has been made in ensuring that NGOs have input into the Bank's Country Assistance Strategies (CASs). NGOs may be consulted while the Bank is preparing a CAS or be asked to participate in discussion of a draft version. However, there is no requirement in the guidelines for preparation of a CAS that it address the issue of participation or the role of NGOs. In contrast, the role of the private sector must be taken into account in every CAS.

Another area of Bank–NGO interaction concerns the discussion and formulation of Bank policies on development. It is widely agreed that this aspect of NGO relations has proven most difficult for the Bank. For years, NGOs have criticized the Bank for its structural adjustment, environmental, and social policies. There has also been pressure on the Bank to make more information available to outside groups and to ensure that politically weak parties in borrowing countries have a voice in Bank decisions. In response, the Bank has increased the amount of contact it has with NGOs in both donor and borrowing countries by holding conferences and meetings that include NGO participants, by consulting with NGOs on some Bank reports, and by holding periodic meetings with NGOs on issues such as the environment.

One of the most important collaborative initiatives is a joint review of the Bank's structural adjustment lending. Announced in 1996, the Structural Adjustment Participatory Review Initiative (SAPRI) is the outcome of many years of demands by NGOs that the Bank include them in evaluating the impact of structural adjustment on the poor. One observer has called NGO efforts to change the Bank's structural adjustment policies a "remarkably unsuccessful decade-long campaign to challenge the legitimacy of the Bank's adjustment program" (Nelson 1995: 22). From the perspective of the NGO community, the joint review is one of the first signs of Bank responsiveness in this area. The initiative, which is financed by trust funds and special contributions, consists of a three-way study (among the Bank, governments, and NGOs) of the effects of structural adjustment policies in seven countries. The goal of the exercise is to draw into the debate members of civil society who can provide important information about the impact of adjustment on local communities. Contentious issues are being investigated by a civil society–Bank team through field work relying on participatory techniques. The exercise is significant for two reasons. First, the Bank's willingness to involve NGOs in an assessment of adjustment policies conveys a new level of openness on the part of the institution. (This topic has been among the most intractable aspects of Bank–NGO dialogue since the mid-1980s.) Second, the initiative may lead to changes in the way adjustment is planned in the future and make it a less disputed realm of Bank activity.

These examples of collaboration should not obscure the fact that much of the dialogue between the Bank and NGOs has been extremely antagonistic. The activities of the NGOs that comprised the "50 Years is Enough" coalition included strongly worded and well-publicized criticism of the Bank presented in full-page advertisements in major newspapers, anti-Bank posters plastered on walls around Washington, and dramatic public protests timed to coincide with the Bank's major meetings. Many within the Bank found what they call the "battering by NGOs" to be a traumatic experience. A Bank manager who worked in India at a time of intense NGO opposition to several Bank projects there observed that staff members had been trained to emphasize economic rationality and were genuinely motivated to help countries develop along the model they understood. NGO criticism came as a shock and led to disquiet and anxiety within the organization, and ultimately to some degree of cultural change in the direction of greater openness.

Bank–NGO tensions have eased further since 1995 for several reasons. First, President Wolfensohn has made clear the priority he places on meeting with and listening to NGOs. Second, the attacks on foreign aid and threats to funding launched by the Republican Congress elected in the United States in 1994 led to renewed support by US-based NGOs for the Bank's concessional lending activities. (As one former NGO staff member put it, "It's embarrassing to have (Senator) Jesse Helms' office asking you to join forces to gut the Bank.")[18] Third, the Bank's initiatives on participation have won over some of its former NGO critics. Relations are far from settled, though. Moderate critics recognize that Bank policies have improved, but cite the gap between rhetoric and practice in implementing these policies. Other groups continue to focus public attention on what they believe are environmentally or socially damaging projects. Some NGOs remain implacably opposed to the basic premises of the Bank's neoliberal development model, limiting the potential for better relations. One staff member with long experience of participatory projects believes that "many NGOs fundamentally misunderstand the Bank. 'Bank-bashing' is their raison d'être, how they raise money."[19] Clearly, however, more of the NGO community is now engaged in constructive policy dialogue with the Bank than was the case just a few years ago.

Changes in Bank organization and policies

As discussed in Chapter 3, the Bank's 1992 reorganization signaled the high priority given to private-sector-related activities. One of the three newly created central vice presidencies was devoted to private sector development and a private sector "czar" was named to coordinate all Bank activity in this area. The issue of participation was not granted a similarly high bureaucratic profile. Those responsible for working with NGOs and for leading the Bank's effort on participation could be found after 1992 in departments within the Bank's other two central vice presidencies. Several individuals had "functional responsibility" for participation and NGO relations, but no single department was created nor high-level leader named. In 1996–7, four networks were introduced that brought together staff working on particular issues across the entire Bank. One of these networks focuses exclusively on private sector development, while responsibility for participation and NGO relations resides within the "social development family" of the much broader Environmentally and Socially Sustainable Development network. The Bank's participation advocates continue to hope that their efforts will be rewarded with more institutional resources and stronger high-level leadership (although the president's outspoken support for participation has given them comfort in the absence of more formal mechanisms).

The oldest institutionalized forum for Bank–NGO discussion, the NGO–World Bank Committee, has tried in recent years to take a more active part in influencing Bank policy. For example, the idea for the participation learning group originated with committee members. In 1993 the committee commissioned several country-level studies of structural adjustment that contributed to the decision by the Bank to establish the joint review of structural adjustment mentioned above. Beginning in 1993, the committee started holding mid-year meetings at the regional level to allow for wider participation by local NGOs and to deepen its own links to civil society in developing regions.

The participation learning group represented an important organizational initiative, but one of limited duration. Its recommendations, however, have had some longer-term organizational effects, including the preparation of participation action plans by each region, now in place, and the tracking of participation flagship projects, which continued for several years. In addition, several training courses focusing specifically on participation were introduced in 1995.

A series of internal policy documents dating from 1989 to the present call for consultation or collaboration with NGOs. Operational Directive 14.70, introduced in 1989, states that "staff are encouraged whenever appropriate to involve NGOs, particularly local NGOs, in Bank-supported activities" (Section 10). Other operational policy statements with participatory components include those on indigenous people, involuntary resettlement, environmental assessments and action plans, dam and reservoir projects, agricultural pest management, forestry, gender, and poverty reduction. But despite the growing body of official pronouncements encouraging Bank–NGO collaboration, many within the Bank acknowledge that a gap remains between policy statements and actual implementation. This gap is not confined to the Bank's work on participation. For example, a review by the internal, but quasi-independent Operations Evaluation Department in 1996 produced a lengthy critique of the Bank's poverty assessment process, finding that:

> Bluntly put, a significant mismatch appears to exist between the ambition and specificity of [the operational directive] on the one hand, and the performance of the Bank and its borrowing member countries in delivering on its provisions on the other.[20]

In short, policy directives do not necessarily provide a meaningful barometer of institutional change. One way to determine more objectively the extent of the Bank's commitment to the participation agenda is to look at the resources it has received.

Resources supporting NGO–Bank collaboration

A characteristic of participatory projects is that they are more expensive and take longer to prepare than traditional Bank projects. One reason is that participatory approaches tend to require more staff time at an early stage in order to identify the appropriate NGOs to involve in the project or to consult with potential beneficiaries. Such projects also require a longer-term field presence than that provided by most Bank missions. Finally, participatory projects usually start small and then expand as they are shown to be successful; the flow of funds may slow as NGOs involved in the project take time to complete their component of it. All these factors translate into higher staff costs than those associated with the top-down approach of most Bank projects.

In recognition of these higher costs, the Bank established a number of small funding programs in line with the learning group's recommendations. Staff members could draw on this pool of money to supplement their own departmental budgets for projects with participatory elements. There is also money available for such projects through special trust funds provided by individual member countries. Some within the Bank argue that if the goal is to integrate participation into normal Bank activities, money should come from the regular budget. But others believe that the availability of special funds acts as a "carrot" for fence-sitters who are considering adding a participatory component to their project but are concerned about the additional cost.

One significant step in terms of the resources allocated to participation has been the addition of a staff person in many of the Bank's field offices to serve as NGO liaison for that country. By the end of fiscal 1997, all of the Bank's resident missions had in place a person responsible for relations with NGOs, although only about half of these were full-time NGO specialists (*Annual Report* 1997: 6).

As mentioned above, the World Bank is constrained by its charter from providing direct funding to NGOs, but some money is made available through special funds or other arrangements. The Small Grants Program, for example, provides institutions (including NGOs) in developing countries with funds to promote dialogue and dissemination of information about international development. In 1995 the Bank agreed to contribute up to $30 million in capital to a new Consultative Group to Assist the Poorest (CGAP), with additional funding from other donors. This is the first source of direct Bank funding for institutions and practitioners in the microfinance field, most of whom are NGOs. While other donors also participate in CGAP, its secretariat is housed at the World Bank and it is run by Bank staff. And, as part of its regular lending program, the Bank has helped create and finance social funds, either stand-alone or as components of projects, that are designed to mitigate the impact of adjustment for vulnerable groups. One of the explicit objectives of these funds is to provide financial support to local organizations well positioned to respond to the needs of the poor.

Rhetoric and practice

The Bank's relationship with NGOs underwent a sea change between 1985 and 1995. In 1985, the attention of the organization was focused on structural adjustment lending, which was accelerating in response to the debt crisis. The Bank's president at the time, A. W. (Tom) Clausen, was an apostle of trade liberalization and market-based economic reform who concerned himself with furthering this agenda among developing country governments and ensuring that the Bank's credit standing did not become tainted by its involvement in the debt crisis. NGOs were just beginning to publicize the negative environmental consequences of Bank lending and there was little dialogue between the Bank and the NGO community. The annual report for the year devoted only a few perfunctory paragraphs to the activities of the NGO–World Bank Committee and other dealings with NGOs.

A decade later, much had changed. The Bank had renewed its commitment to fighting poverty as the central feature of its mission.[21] Collaboration with NGOs had deepened, although much of the policy dialogue remained highly contentious. The *Annual Report* 1995 contained several discussions of participatory development (the first index entry for this subject had appeared the year before), and projects involving some form of stakeholder participation were identified as such in the summary of projects approved. The Bank's newly appointed president, James Wolfensohn, had come into office extolling the virtues of working with NGOs. Even the Bank's mission statement had changed, from helping to "raise standards of living in developing countries by channeling financial resources from developed countries to the developing world" (*Annual Report* 1985), to promoting "economic and social progress in developing nations by helping raise productivity so that their people may live a better and fuller life" (*Annual Report* 1995: 4).

Wolfensohn has continued to serve as a champion of the participation agenda. He has highlighted NGO relations in most of his speeches and spoken movingly of the individuals and community groups affected by Bank projects, as in the following remarks made a year and a half after taking office:

> I have visited over forty countries in these past sixteen months. I have met with governments, business and non-governmental groups. But it is the people – the poor and disadvantaged – who have made the biggest impression on me. I have learned that they do not want charity; they want opportunity. They do not want to be lectured to; they want to be listened to. They want partnership. Like all of us, they want a better life for themselves and for their children. What I have seen in country after country is that when they are given a chance, the results are truly remarkable.
>
> (Wolfensohn 1996: 1)

This emphasis on the human dimension of development has injected a sense of mission into the work of many at the Bank that had been lacking since the 1970s. Beyond rhetorical support, Wolfensohn has spent considerable time meeting with NGO representatives around the world and listening to their concerns. On a five-day visit to India early in his tenure, for example, almost one-third of the president's time was spent with NGOs; reportedly, a meeting with donor agencies was cut short so that Wolfensohn could extend his discussion with NGOs.[22] Wolfensohn estimates that in his visits to countries he spends only about a third of his time with governments and the rest in the field, a sharp break from the habits of earlier leaders.[23] The president's attention to the impact of Bank programs on individuals and communities has raised the profile of participation within the Bank and created a new set of positive incentives for staff interested in working with NGOs.

As is often the case with organizations, the signs from the top do not necessarily reflect the reality on the ground. Even the strongest leader cannot impose his priorities on a large bureaucracy like the World Bank, and Wolfensohn has many different agendas to promote. The incorporation of any new set of activities depends not on leaders' statements but on whether these activities are understood, accepted, and pursued by staff members working at all levels of the organization. In this sense, despite the change in official attitudes, the participation agenda is only partly institutionalized. On the one hand, the growth in the percentage of projects involving NGOs and the presence of NGO liaisons in the Bank's resident missions suggest that, to some degree, concern with beneficiary involvement extends across the institution. On the other hand, participation-related initiatives tend to be ad hoc and there is no high-level manager charged with furthering the agenda. Most of the funds for participatory activities come from special appropriations or trust funds, sending the message to some that participation is an "add-on," rather than a central feature of the Bank.

Representative comments from a range of staff members and outside observers made in 1997 suggest that participatory approaches are not integrated deeply into Bank operations.

- From a staff person involved in overseeing the Bank's participation activities: "The Bank has stopped short of mandating participation. There is more support for people who care [about it], but no pressure on those who don't . . . Staff doesn't 'live in fear' of ignoring participation," as it does regarding environmental considerations.
- From a member of the LGPD core group: "Awareness of participation is high everywhere, but this is not necessarily matched by a conviction of its importance."
- From a senior staff member overseeing the Bank's change process: "Participation is now on the map, but [it] is not integrated into operations."
- From a long-time Bank advocate of participation: "Participation is a 'buzzword' that is sometimes put into projects to make them more appealing, but is not well understood."
- From an NGO representative involved in environmental policy: "Space has been created at the Bank within which entrepreneurs and advocates can work. But environmental and social practices have not become 'business as usual'."

- From a former NGO representative, currently overseeing the Bank's NGO-related activities: "The term 'participation' is often misused – the participation of communities is still in its infancy at the Bank."

Despite the ambivalence reflected in these comments, there are a plethora of participation-related initiatives under way at the Bank. Individual advocates have joined together in formal and informal networks and created institutional channels through which consultation with beneficiaries has become officially sanctioned. And staff members can now claim high-level backing for their interest in working with beneficiaries.

The ultimate evaluation of the status of the participation agenda at the Bank depends in part on how it is defined. If participation is thought to involve working more closely with NGOs in a variety of capacities, there has been undeniable progress and trends point in the right direction. If, however, one is seeking evidence that these initiatives translate into the actual participation of beneficiaries and results on the ground, the outcome of Bank efforts is much murkier. An evaluation of the success of Bank–NGO collaboration also depends on whether one takes the view that the glass is half full or half empty. Even those who acknowledge that the Bank has made significant progress in approaching civil society believe much more can be done. For example, one NGO representative says she would like to see the Bank "push the envelope" and pursue participation not only where it is easy but also where it is difficult.[24]

A crucial variable in how far the participation agenda can advance is the attitude of developing country governments. Bank staff cannot promote a more active role for NGOs without at least the tacit support of the borrower. The Bank's recently retired senior adviser on social policy, Michael Cernea, believes that the Bank has come a long way toward embracing participatory development but that the remainder of the journey will be more difficult, in large part because of continued resistance by some borrowers.[25] Outside advocates recognize the importance of borrower support and believe the Bank should do more to encourage developing country governments to adopt participatory approaches. As one long-time observer of the Bank puts it, "In the long run, citizens in borrowing countries are better served by participatory governments than by a participatory World Bank" (Alexander 1998: 5).

Participation and the Bank's organizational culture

Staff members who work with NGOs are well aware of the poor fit between basic tenets of the Bank's organizational culture and the participation agenda. Noting that "organizations tend to replicate externally the styles of operations that prevail internally" (Bhatnagar and Williams 1992: 8), participants in the 1992 learning group workshop pointed out that the Bank is closed, hierarchical, and resistant to sharing information. It prefers "easily quantifiable, supply-driven projects over those that are demand-driven and hard to appraise in advance" (ibid.: 8). Writing about the development community more generally, a Swedish aid official argues that "The efficiency criteria and incentives of development agencies tend to favor easily quantifiable goals, such as planted areas and annual yields, over the vaguer accomplishments of participation" (ibid.: 47). Staff face the well-known pressures to conclude loan agreements and disburse funds. Overall, "the Bank's culture and structure of incentives [are] remarkably unconducive to innovative and creative project identification and risk taking" (ibid.: 76).

The privileged position of economists within the organization is also frequently identified as problematic for the integration of participation into Bank activities. Robert Picciotto writes of the "intellectual tension" that flared between economists and other development professionals at the 1992 workshop (Picciotto 1992). Discussions of participation usually highlight the need to change the Bank's skills mix and add more non-economists to the staff. An internal task group on social development, reporting in 1996, acknowledged the importance of adding new staff, but stressed that the social dimensions of development must "be regarded by the entire Bank staff as an essential part of the Bank's daily work"; to that end, it is not just a question of staffing, but "also one of changing values and attitudes" (World Bank 1996c: 27).

The 1992 workshop discussed several ways of encouraging participation-related activities among existing staff: the introduction of new incentive systems to maximize the visibility of those working on participatory projects; taking into account participatory field experience in decisions about promotion; reorienting Bank training to provide appropriate professional and personal skills; and the creation of exchange programs between the Bank and NGOs. The 1994 report of the learning group picked up on some of these ideas, advocating stronger incentives, selective recruitment, and focused training to "encourage a culture of participation and strengthen the requisite skills of Bank staff" (World Bank 1994c: 35). Modest steps have been taken to develop exchange and training programs, but the Bank's technical orientation and emphasis on economic and financial analysis hinder its ability to accord social development the same priority it does economic development.

To the extent that the constraints imposed by the Bank's organizational culture have been overcome, it is in large part because participation has been construed in fairly narrow terms. Unlike other development agencies, for which participation is part of a package of political and social concerns that includes democratization and human rights, the Bank has adopted a more limited definition. Yet Bank officials are aware that participation has the potential to lead the organization down the slippery slope to political reform. To avoid this course, the general counsel has clarified the Bank's stance as follows:

> *The Bank's advocacy of participatory development is laudable and may be further encouraged to ensure grassroots development. This does not, however, mean that the Bank has a role in the general political reform of borrowing countries.* The participation advocated by the Bank is meant to allow the people affected

> by a Bank-financed project to participate effectively in its design and implementation. This is a lesson drawn from the experience of development effectiveness, not a political direction based on a mandate for the Bank to ensure the democratization of every country to which it lends.
>
> (Shihata 1995b: 24; emphasis in original)

Such a view of participation allows staff to move forward with this agenda without challenging the claim that the Bank's work is apolitical.

Not everyone within the Bank, however, accepts this compartmentalization. From the beginning, participation was viewed by many as part of a broader "good governance" agenda that emerged within the Bank around the same time. (See Chapter 5.) There has been considerable overlap among staff members and managers involved in the Bank's governance and participation initiatives, and certain institutional exercises have addressed the issues together. Some supporters of the two agendas believe that their separation weakened both of them, stripping them of content and slowing the Bank's momentum toward being able to grapple with the political and social problems that hinder development in many of its borrowers.

Others have stressed the link between participation and human rights, noting that NGOs and community leaders occasionally come under political pressure as a result of their work on Bank projects. "A commitment to participation brings the Bank a concomitant responsibility to play an advocacy role for the people placed at risk in these conflicts, on the platform of international human rights," (Bhatnagar and Williams 1992: 159) reads the proceedings of the 1992 workshop. But the learning group emphasized in its report that the Bank's work on participation must not challenge its primary relationship with governments: "[T]he Bank should not, indeed cannot, be perceived as trying to circumvent governments, or attempt to intermediate between governments and the governed" (World Bank 1994c: 4). Thus, the Bank's chief role should be to encourage governments to increase their attention to participation, not to push them in the direction of political reform or greater support for human rights.

Another way in which the participation agenda has been shaped by the Bank's organizational culture is that working with NGOs has not been presented as an end in itself, but as a means through which the Bank can improve the quality of its projects. The emphasis has been on achieving greater development effectiveness, rather than on strengthening civil society within borrower countries. Coming as it did at a time of management and shareholder concern about the Bank's performance (highlighted by the findings of the Wapenhans Report in 1992), the participation agenda was seized on by those seeking ways to improve the performance of the Bank's lending program. Participation thus helped fill an institutional need that had arisen quite independently of the other factors that gave birth to the agenda.

Finally, instead of conceiving of participation as a "soft" approach that relies mainly on interpersonal communication and an understanding of other cultures, the Bank has emphasized the development of tools and methods for pursuing participation and has structured its work with NGOs around the existing project cycle. This "how to" emphasis has allowed the development of participation strategies that fit comfortably with the Bank's technical orientation.

Fostering a more authentic culture of participation may require the kind of large-scale organizational change that the Bank is simply not prepared to make. The concentration of staff at headquarters and limited field presence hinders the Bank's ability to promote participation. Some decentralization is under way and more is expected, but the vast majority of staff members will remain at headquarters for years to come. In addition, the policy of regular staff rotation under which individuals move from region to region every few years leads to a lack of continuity that is particularly damaging to participatory projects that require a longer lead time than traditional projects. And the absence of a strong, high-level organizational home for the Bank's work on participation hinders its dissemination throughout the institution.

These cultural and organizational issues provide the most serious barrier to the full incorporation of the participation agenda into the Bank's activities. A longtime advocate of participation on the Bank's staff, Lawrence Salmen, has written that one element of participatory research, the beneficiary assessment, runs counter to what has always been the Bank's dominant culture. His comparison of the two approaches summarizes the cultural challenge facing the Bank in this area. (See Table 4.2.)

The first step to reorienting the Bank's culture may be to recognize how collaborating with NGOs poses a challenge to it. In many quarters, this step has been taken. But institutional change will not be consolidated unless people with training in the skills needed for participation come to account for a larger share of the institution's staff, and organizational changes take place that make working with beneficiaries part of the Bank's business as usual.

Conclusion

Unlike the private sector development agenda, which marked a response by the Bank to outside developments, including pressure from the United States, the participation initiative bubbled up from the Bank's own grassroots. Staff members working in certain fields came to recognize that involving beneficiaries in Bank projects and working more closely with NGOs was essential to the success of their efforts. These internal advocates formed alliances with NGOs interested in a more responsive World Bank. Together, they developed organizational channels through which the issue of participation was brought to the attention of management and others within the Bank. Despite external pressure to widen the agenda – and whatever their personal beliefs about the normative value of greater participation – internal advocates approached their task pragmatically. Casting participation in narrow terms, they framed the agenda in ways that fit readily with the Bank's

Table 4.2 Traditional Bank approaches and participatory approaches

Traditional Bank approaches	*Participatory approaches*
deductive	inductive
top-down	bottom-up
economic	socio-cultural
quantitative	qualitative
impact	process
abstract	grounded
theoretical	practical

Source: adapted from Salmen 1995a: 14

concerns about its effectiveness and with international trends, thereby attracting high-level support.

The participation agenda remains fraught with contradictions. The involvement of local stakeholders in Bank activities has become a prominent feature in the work of some departments and in the rhetoric of the Bank overall, but it is not integrated into the mainstream of operations. Despite the existence of an operational policy on collaboration with NGOs, the use of participatory approaches is not mandated; to paraphrase a staff member quoted earlier, while there is greater support for people who care about participation, there is no pressure on those who don't. While almost everyone, including the president, speaks of the importance of participatory approaches, commitment to using them has not percolated out to the majority of Bank staff. And there is real uncertainty about whether closer Bank–NGO collaboration translates into the actual involvement of local beneficiaries in Bank projects, with improved results not just for the Bank but for the lives of individuals and their communities.

Finally, the participation agenda may have unintended consequences. Some scholars argue that greater responsiveness by the Bank to NGOs has paradoxically served to tighten a country's accountability to the Bank, rather than to its own civil society. Paul Nelson offers the example of the Bank's new-found emphasis on environmental protection. Bank efforts to incorporate the concerns of environmental critics into its policies toward borrowers has in some cases resulted in diminished national control over policymaking: "What began as a NGO effort to check the lending by the Bank for environmentally destructive projects has become a source of influence for the Bank over borrowers" (Nelson 1996: 631). A shifting of accountability from national policymakers to the Bank may be one of the unforeseen results of closer Bank–NGO collaboration.

Bank–NGO collaboration has come as far as it has because its advocates have tailored it to fit the Bank's organizational culture as closely as possible. Rather than framing cooperation as an end in itself, supporters cast it in more technical terms as an important element in the sustainability – and hence, success – of Bank projects. Participation thus fits well with efforts to improve the Bank's portfolio and change its culture to one that emphasizes results. Even narrowly formulated, however, participation violates key tenets of the Bank's organizational culture. Its emphasis on learning from beneficiaries challenges the Bank's expert stance, participatory approaches fit only awkwardly with the Bank's project cycle, and the skills needed for working effectively with local groups are not those possessed by the majority of Bank staff. Without changes in the Bank's organizational culture, the relationship between the Bank and NGOs will remain constrained and the participation agenda only partially realized.

Timeline of participation-related developments

1982	Establishment of NGO–World Bank Committee.
1986	NGO Unit formed.
1988	President Barber Conable mentions NGO collaboration in his speeches.
1988	Bank begins systematic effort to increase collaboration with NGOs by asking staff to identify projects that have the potential for greater NGO involvement.
1989	Operational Directive 14.70 on collaboration with NGOs issued.
1991	Three-year learning process on participation begins. Learning Group on Participatory Development formed.
February 1992	First International Workshop on Popular Participation, organized by Learning Group.
August 1992	Interim Report of Learning Group submitted to management.
October 1992	*Participatory Development and the World Bank* published; proceedings of the first workshop.
October 1992	Portfolio Management Task Force releases its report (Wapenhans Report).
1993	New, more open disclosure policy approved.
January 1994	Bank's Public Information Center opens its doors.
1994	World Bank Inspection Panel established.
1994	Second Working Conference on Participatory Development, convened by learning group.
August 1994	Policy Review Committee supports and adopts learning group's recommendations to management.
September 1994	*The World Bank and Participation* released. Contains report of learning group and management-approved action plan.

August 1995	President Wolfensohn cancels Bank loans to controversial Arun III Hydroelectric Project in Nepal, following NGO criticism and negative report by Inspection Panel.
February 1996	Formal publication of *The World Bank Participation Sourcebook.*
July 1996	Annual Report announces that NGO specialists are in place in more than half of the Bank's resident missions.
July 1997	First Global Forum held to launch the Structural Adjustment Participatory Review Initiative (SAPRI).
November 1997	Bank introduces two new lending instruments – Adaptable Program Loans and Learning and Innovation Loans – that allow more experimentation and greater flexibility than traditional loans.

5 Approaching politics

The governance agenda

By governance is meant the exercise of political power to manage a nation's affairs.

The World Bank, *Sub-Saharan Africa: from crisis to sustainable growth, a long-term perspective study*, 1989, p. 60

Governance is defined as the manner in which power is exercised in the management of a country's economic and social resources for development.

The World Bank, *Governance and Development*, 1992, p. 1

The World Bank's reputation is built on the premise that it is a technically competent institution that conducts its business without regard for politics. This identity has allowed the Bank to operate for most of its history with maximum freedom in a polarized world. Shortly after the Bank began operations, the Cold War divided nations into East and West. Developing countries chose sides or struggled to remain nonaligned. In the midst of these divisions, the Bank stood for a future in which those countries would become incorporated into the liberal international economic order supported and led by the United States. Only by emphasizing its technical and apolitical identity could the Bank gain sufficient legitimacy to lend to governments of many different political complexions, including those that were not committed to this future.[1]

As the 1980s drew to a close, it appeared for a brief time as though the Bank's identity might change. Economic and political transitions were beginning in the Eastern bloc. Democratization was under way in Latin America, Africa, and Asia. Developing countries around the globe had accepted the notion, long promoted by the Bank, that their economic future lay with liberalization and integration into a capitalist world. The geopolitical constraints that had shaped the Bank, essentially from birth, were lifted and the institution's shareholders and staff, along with the rest of the development community, felt a new sense of possibility.

This was the context within which the Bank's governance agenda emerged. As with the other agendas examined in this book, there were both external and internal reasons why this new set of concerns came to be articulated. But, unlike the participation and private sector development agendas, governance has remained a constrained and ambivalent area of activity. One reason is the Bank's charter, which prohibits its involvement in politics and is cited by leaders arguing that the Bank must tread a fine line in its governance work. A more important reason is that governance concerns are difficult for any lender to address and are particularly ill suited to elements of the Bank's organizational culture.

In 1989, a World Bank publication on sub-Saharan Africa announced that a "crisis of governance" plagued many of the Bank's borrowers. Governance was defined broadly and the remedies proposed included political pluralism, respect for the rule of law, and protection of human rights (World Bank 1989b: 60). Over the next few years, the Bank explored the implications of these findings for its work through, among other activities, a Bank-wide task force. The task force arrived at a more limited definition of governance that focuses exclusively on a country's capacity to manage its economic and social resources (World Bank 1992c).

The recognition and progressive narrowing of the governance agenda reflected the intersection of three elements: the end of the Cold War, the Bank's experience with structural adjustment lending, and the contours of the Bank's organizational culture. These elements account for the Bank's initial attention to governance writ large and the subsequent focus of its activities in a more technical direction.

The shift in the policies of many developing countries in the 1980s toward market-oriented reform and democratization led to a general view in the development community that "all good things go together," or should. As the 1980s drew to a close and the Cold War wound down, bilateral aid agencies sought a new mission. They found it in a commitment to promote democracy, market-based economic policies, human rights, and strong civil societies. The European Bank for Reconstruction and Development (EBRD) was established in 1990 with an explicit mandate to lend only to democracies. The World Bank's Articles of Agreement prohibited it from addressing political factors formally in its work, but the attention of the broader development community stimulated the Bank to examine how it could participate in the sweeping political changes taking place.

At the same time, the Bank's concern over its own effectiveness was growing. Structural adjustment lending had been under way for close to a decade, with disappointing results in many cases. Governments made commitments to ambitious reform programs, which they then found themselves unable to implement. The emphasis on promoting market forces had left public sector institutions weak and demoralized, lacking the will and capacity to carry out many of the provisions of Bank loans. Corruption continued to siphon resources away from productive purposes in many developing countries. Conviction was growing within the Bank that, in many countries, political rather than economic factors constituted the main obstacles to progress.

The Bank's attention to governance was prompted by these two realizations: that the potential scope of its activity had widened to encompass the realm of politics, and that it was precisely this realm that was responsible for some of the shortcomings of Bank programs. But a third factor – the Bank's organizational culture – had an equally important influence, acting as a filter through which governance concerns passed.

An explicit focus on the political dimensions of development calls into question key elements of the Bank's identity. Chief among these is the provision in its charter that, "The Bank and its officers shall not interfere in the political affairs of any member; nor shall they be influenced in their decisions by the political character of the member or members concerned" (Article IV, Section 10). This has led the Bank to focus throughout its history on improving borrowers' economic performance while paying little attention to the functioning of their political institutions. In part as a result, the Bank is not well versed in techniques for improving governance. Unlike traditional Bank lending for discrete projects like bridges or health clinics, loans that aim to strengthen institutions take many years to bear fruit and their impact is not easy to measure, especially with the quantitative tools the Bank has at hand. Loans to improve governance, which generally do not require large amounts of money and rely more heavily on technical assistance, contribute little to sustaining the Bank's lending levels. Such loans take considerable time to prepare and are difficult to monitor, and thus are at odds with an approval culture that focuses on getting projects through the Bank's board and paying little attention to them thereafter. Strengthening public institutions requires hands-on experience in public administration, a field historically undervalued by the development community and within the Bank. Finally, the Bank's traditional approach to its borrowers – handing out expert advice along with loans structured according to a standard project cycle – is ill suited for projects that seek to improve a nation's ability to govern itself.

The governance agenda that has emerged from these institutional constraints is a narrow, technical one that emphasizes issues of state capacity and accountability. Observers have drawn a distinction between the "liberal democratic" governance agenda of many bilateral aid agencies that links democratic institutions, market-oriented economic policies and respect for human rights, and the more limited "process of government" agenda pursued by the World Bank that eschews mention of the form of political regime in a borrowing country (Moore 1993). In fact, the need to distinguish between these two agendas is one reason why the term governance, after an initial upsurge of attention, has gone out of vogue at the Bank. Bank officials fear that the word itself carries political overtones and confuses the efforts of the Bank with those of other lenders that are pursuing better governance through the promotion of electoral reform and political democracy.

Governance is officially defined by the Bank as "the manner in which power is exercised in the management of a country's economic and social resources for development" (World Bank 1992c: 1). As the Bank's research points out, this definition:

> excludes any normative content, and any attribute of specific political regimes from the conception of governance; that is, the term does not refer to the substance of rules, the design of institutions, or the nature of conflict-solving mechanisms. The very existence of such systems of rules, institutions and mechanisms, as long as they are universal and predictable, defines governance capacity in the modern state.
>
> (Frischtak 1994: 15)

The amorphous nature of the governance concept has given rise to widely varying interpretations of the Bank's underlying goals. For some staff members, poor governance is simply the explanation they resort to when projects don't work: "In the absence of explicit definitions, governance often is used as an 'umbrella concept' under which elusive and ill-defined political processes and concerns, as well as desirable goals and value preferences, can be subsumed" (Frischtak 1994: 1). For a number of the Bank's critics on the left, attention to governance represents a new form of blaming the victim, a way for the Bank to shift accountability for failed and misguided projects from the institution to recipient governments (George and Sabelli 1994: 160–1). Other NGOs criticize the Bank's work on governance as partial and one-sided, concerned mainly with the creation of a favorable investment climate and driven by the needs and concerns of private sector actors, rather than civil society as a whole (Hunter 1996: 66). As for the Bank's members, some developed countries have urged it to consider expanding the definition of governance to cover issues like democracy and human rights. At the same time, some borrowing countries have resisted the governance agenda, claiming that it represents a new form of conditionality that imposes Western models of government in an echo of colonialism.

Despite these ambiguities, the Bank's governance agenda springs from real institutional needs. The failure of many Bank programs to meet their intended aims has given rise to a new emphasis on stakeholder involvement, greater government ownership of projects, careful implementation, and sustainability. These principles are embedded in the Bank's work on both participation and governance. Governance is also related to private sector development. Reliance on the private sector as the engine of growth has made clear the need for a system of governance that can provide a regulatory framework in which markets can operate smoothly, transparency in the application of laws, and an end to corruption. The three agendas covered in this study – private sector development, participation, and governance – are thus linked. But whereas the Bank's efforts regarding the first two areas have intensified since they were first introduced, progress on governance has been more halting. The initial surge of interest has not been sustained and the content of the governance agenda has been altered over time.

The newest element among the Bank's governance concerns is its willingness to tackle corruption. The corruption initiative suggests both how far the Bank has come and the limits of its approach. The Bank has long been concerned about fraud or misprocurement in the projects it finances and has had systems in place to detect it. But concern with corruption more generally was off limits until very recently. As late as 1990, when the Bank's resident representative in Kenya, Peter Eigen, proposed that the Bank join forces with governments and multinational companies to develop a code of conduct to reduce corruption, he was ordered by senior Bank officials to stop his work amid claims that battling corruption went beyond the Bank's mandate.[2] Eigen's decision to take early retirement after a twenty-five-year career followed shortly thereafter and in 1993 he established Transparency International, an NGO devoted to tracking and combating corruption. In a few short years, the Bank's position changed considerably, to the point where the Bank is now required to take the level of corruption into account as a factor in its lending strategy and refrain from lending in serious cases of corruption when the government is not willing to address the issue satisfactorily.[3]

The story of how governance issues were first raised at the Bank and how they have been translated into practice suggests that, despite global political change, the Bank's identity as a technical and apolitical institution has remained basically intact.

The origins of governance

The official requirement that the World Bank focus on economic issues alone is rooted in the conditions surrounding its establishment. When the Bank was founded, it needed to be able to lend to a wide variety of countries and build confidence in its impartiality. The Bank also had to establish its standing as a conservative financial institution and maintain the support of the capital markets; it did this in part by making clear that its lending would not be driven by the vagaries of national politics. Nevertheless, political considerations have never been absent from the Bank's work, even in its earliest days. A 1954 book noted that, "Although the Bank is precluded by its charter from making or denying loans to achieve political objectives, it cannot ignore conditions of political instability or uncertainty which may affect the economic and financial prospects of the borrower" (IBRD 1954: 61). Political factors that could harm a country's ability to repay its loans from the Bank were thus clearly within the realm of its attention. But the Bank's political activity and influence went further, as suggested by several dispute settlement efforts in the 1950s and 1960s. For example, in mediating the dispute between India and Pakistan that resulted in the Indus River Treaty of 1960, the Bank was able to reformulate what was a political problem into a technical issue, serve as mediator, and then invest considerable sums to secure the outcome, thereby "demonstrat[ing] H Street's unforeseen powers as a peacemaker" (Morris 1963: 219). And, unlike the United Nations, which had no tangible means of enforcing its decisions, the World Bank could bring to bear a powerful weapon: its money.

In recent years, too, the Bank has taken a series of actions that on the surface appear to be driven by political logic; these included the suspension of loans to China in the immediate aftermath of the Tiananmen Square massacre in 1989 and the cancellation of IFC participation in a project in Nigeria following the execution of environmentalist Ken Saro-Wiwa in 1995. Within days of the Tiananmen Square attack, the World Bank announced that it would delay discussions of two loans to China.[4] After Saro-Wiwa's execution, along with those of eight other human rights activists, the IFC announced that it had decided against participating in a $3 billion liquefied natural gas project that had been opposed by Saro-Wiwa. The IFC attributed its decision primarily to economic reasons, but noted that it could proceed only "if we felt we had the support of our member country shareholders," and that opposition had been voiced by many major countries because of the death sentences.[5] In both cases, the Bank presented its decision as rooted not in normative concerns for democracy or human rights, but in fear that events had undermined each country's stability to the point of calling into question the viability of Bank lending. In neither case, of course, was the stability of the government in question, but the Bank's reasoning served to preserve the organizational myth that its decisions are made on technical, rather than political grounds.

Upholding the apolitical ideal has become increasingly difficult as the line between the political sphere and the economic sphere blurs. Many of the areas the Bank now considers ripe for its attention would even a decade ago have been thought inappropriate. Issues such as gender, environmental sustainability, participation, military expenditures, and corruption are currently treated as acceptable areas for Bank activity, whereas in the very recent past they would have been off limits because of their political implications (Blackden 1996: 3). The borderline between the economic and the political will probably continue to shift as an increasing number of factors are found to affect a country's development prospects.

As the concept of development has evolved, the range of activities pursued by the Bank has grown. It is in this context that specific events both outside and inside the Bank served to bring the organization as close as it has ever come to addressing political issues explicitly in its work.

Contextual factors

Democratic transitions throughout the Third World and the Eastern bloc, epitomized by the fall of the Berlin Wall in 1989, altered the context in which most industrialized countries made decisions about granting overseas aid. Aid policies designed to shore up political allies or prevent the spread of communism lost their purpose. As donors searched for a new rationale on which to base their foreign aid programs, the promotion of democracy emerged as one prominent goal. Western leaders and bilateral aid agencies stressed the importance of democracy and governance issues more generally in their speeches and reports. The United States was among these donors, reorienting the work of AID (the Agency for Information Development) to support democratic regimes and market-based economies and appointing the head of the National Democratic Institute to lead it. A new multilateral development bank, the EBRD, was established with the provision that it lend only to democracies. Foundations and other NGOs also turned their attention to the promotion of democracy abroad.

This liberal democratic governance agenda was precipitated not only by geopolitical change, but also by academic research on the link between political and economic reform.[6] The dominant development paradigm of the 1980s, structural adjustment, had been conceived initially as a set of short-term, macroeconomic measures that would lead to the resumption of growth. Close to a decade later, the experience of international development agencies with structural adjustment was discouraging. In most cases, policies agreed to by developing country governments had been implemented unevenly, private investment had not materialized, and growth had not resumed. The reforms called for in adjustment loans were encountering political resistance that was too strong for many governments to overcome; thus, "institutional reforms came to be included in the adjustment agenda in an effort to equip governments to meet this resistance and stay the course of adjustment" (Frischtak 1994: 6). A consensus emerged that the political environment was a major source of obstacles to sustained economic change. In addition, earlier beliefs that authoritarian regimes were better than democracies at managing economic reform had given way to agnosticism on the subject.[7]

An equally influential body of academic research came from the field of economics, where institutional analysis had taken on a new importance in the 1980s with the work of Oliver Williamson, Douglass North, and others. The World Bank, which casts itself as an organization of ideas and a leader in the field of development thinking, is in reality often a follower of fashion, and the preeminence of institutional economics outside the Bank led to an increase in the number of researchers within the Bank who began to practice it themselves. The result was growing attention by the Bank's research apparatus to how the institutional environment affected the prospects for economic reform and development in borrowing countries.

Institutional learning

Essential to the emergence of the governance agenda at the World Bank was a process of institutional learning through which Bank staff and management became convinced of the importance of political factors in their work. These lessons emerged from concern about the poor results of the Bank's structural adjustment programs, particularly in sub-Saharan Africa but also in Latin America.

The Bank had begun making structural adjustment loans to Africa in the early 1980s as a way of providing fast-disbursing, balance of payments support in exchange for policy reforms. The 1981 Berg Report had provided the analytical justification for this type of lending (World Bank 1981). After examining the relative roles of external factors (such as declining commodity prices) and domestic factors, the report concluded that domestic policy failures and poor economic management were chiefly responsible for Africa's economic problems. The findings of the Berg Report were extremely controversial, in part because of what one Bank official now admits was its "stern schoolmaster tone" (Madavo 1997). African leaders even drafted a resolution in a meeting of the heads of state of the Organization of African Unity to censure the Bank for the report (Agarwala and Schwartz 1994: 2). Although the draft resolution was later dropped, resentment over the report continued to charge the relationship between African leaders and the Bank.

Several subsequent reports on Africa were prepared by the Bank, including *Towards Sustained Development in Sub-Saharan Africa: A joint program for action* in 1984. This report presented a more balanced view than the Berg Report about the relative importance of economic liberalization and social development, and proposed a program for fast-disbursing assistance in the context of famine in Africa. Shortly after its publication, the Bank and bilateral donors established a $2 billion Special Facility for Africa. An important feature of the fund was that not every poor country was entitled to assistance from it, but only those that the Bank and donors had deemed as having appropriate economic policies.

In an atmosphere of donor fatigue and concern that repeated programs for Africa had met with only minimal success, the Bank decided to look at the longer-term prospects for social development and growth, and plans for the Long-Term Perspective Study (LTPS) were born. During the LTPS process (described below), Africans and others involved in assessing the continent's prospects expressed doubts about the effectiveness of Bank-sponsored adjustment programs, while the Bank's own monitoring of African economies showed only very uncertain results. One scholar maintains that, "The Bank's concerns about governance arose from one major source: the failure of its structural adjustment programmes to produce a definitive success on the African mainland" (Lancaster 1993: 9). The inability of sub-Saharan African nations to improve their economic performance, even when complying with Bank programs and receiving high levels of aid, suggested that deeper factors, such as a lack of government capacity to enact reform, were at the root of their problems. But concern about the effectiveness of adjustment lending was not confined to Africa. Most of the Bank's largest adjustment loans were to Latin American countries and here, too, with the exception of Mexico, the results of many Bank-supported programs had been disappointing. It was becoming clear that privatizing state-owned industry and shrinking the size of the public sector would not lead automatically to the resumption of growth. In fact, the dismantling of the state had left Latin

American governments without the institutional capacity to carry through on central elements of their economic reform plans.

From its beginning, adjustment lending had required the Bank's staff to pay close attention to the details of government policy and had drawn the Bank into new forms of policy-related conditionality. Some see the broadening of the reform agenda from economic to political issues as "a natural consequence of the momentum of structural adjustment itself" (Gwin 1995: 13). One of the chief lessons of the failure of adjustment loans to achieve their intended results was the importance of the recipient country government "owning" its adjustment program. According to the Bank's periodic reports on the topic, adjustment lending is most successful when it is supported actively by the borrower country; the finding that "ownership helps explain the success or failure of past adjustment loans" brought to the Bank's attention the crucial role of government intentions and capabilities in shaping an adjustment program (World Bank 1992a: 22).

This finding was reinforced when the Wapenhans Report was published in 1992. As noted in Chapter 4, the Bank's task force on portfolio management had found that almost 20 per cent of Bank projects had major problems in their implementation – a sizeable increase over previous years – and highlighted the dangers of an approval culture that focused on new lending at the expense of effective implementation. The report stressed the importance of borrower ownership of projects and the need for the Bank to judge a government's commitment to implementing Bank-funded programs. Coming shortly after the task force on governance had concluded its work, the Wapenhans Report underscored the relevance of governance concerns for the Bank's ongoing financial health.

Another aspect of institutional learning concerns the Bank's acknowledgment that it has a role to play in strengthening the public sector. The swing of the pendulum from a state-centered development paradigm in the 1960s and 1970s, to an emphasis on freeing markets in the 1980s, moderated in the 1990s. The clearest articulation of the Bank's new acceptance of the role of the state came in the *World Development Report 1997: The state in a changing world*, which made the case that:

> An effective state is vital for the provision of the goods and services – and the rules and institutions – that allow markets to flourish and people to lead healthier, happier lives. Without it, sustainable development, both economic and social, is impossible.
>
> (World Bank 1997c: 1)

This is a far cry from the pronouncement in the 1991 *World Development Report* that the policy should be to "let markets work unless it is demonstrably better to step in" (p. 5). Avoiding the extremes of the past – development must be state-led; development depends on freeing markets – the 1997 report steered a middle course, focusing on how to match the state's role to its capability and how to increase state capability by reinvigorating public institutions. It also reflected a more nuanced view of what the Bank can contribute to this process. Rather than putting forth a new "Washington consensus" on what policies should be followed, the 1997 report provided a framework for thinking about the role of the state informed by the recognition that there are several successful models and that historical and cultural differences among states must be kept in mind.

The role of member countries and NGOs

Outside actors played less of a role in bringing governance to the fore at the Bank than they did in the cases of private sector development and participation. The contribution of developed member countries was largely indirect. The United States believes that by promoting the private sector and the environment, it contributed to putting governance on the Bank's agenda. The US rationale goes as follows: in order for the private sector to function effectively, countries need a clear regulatory framework and a government capable of enforcing the rule of law. US efforts to promote the private sector thus translated into support for these attributes of governance. Similarly, US support for environmental protection furthered Bank efforts to promote greater transparency in borrower countries and ensure that governments are accountable to civil society. Other developed member countries, especially the Nordic countries, Germany, and the Netherlands, have been strong advocates of the Bank's work on governance. Eveline Herfkens, the outspoken executive director from the Netherlands from 1991 to 1996, was among those who provided leadership on this issue within the board.

A divide in the ranks of the Bank's borrowers also facilitated the emergence of the governance agenda. As many developing countries democratized, they became more open to Bank efforts in this area. Their representatives on the Bank's board could join representatives of developed countries in support of Bank efforts to pay closer attention to issues of institutional capacity and management. Other countries, particularly some in Asia, resisted the introduction of a focus on governance into Bank activities. (The financial crisis that hit many Asian economies in 1997 underscored weaknesses in some of their fundamental institutions, such as those governing the financial system. In part as a result, few countries have the same resistance to discussing governance issues with multilateral lenders as they did before the crisis struck.)

Many NGOs have urged the Bank to pay greater attention to governance in the context of an integrated agenda that also supports strengthening civil society and protecting human rights.[8] While the Bank has resisted efforts to add what it calls "political" human rights concerns to its mission, good progress has been made on participation. (See Chapter 4.)[9] Some NGOs, suspicious of the Bank's private sector emphasis to begin with, are wary of governance approaches that seem to be driven by the needs of the private sector. A 1996 report sponsored by a broad range of NGOs found that:

> All components of good governance are not treated equally by the Bank . . . Noneconomic governance issues are typically not supported or considered . . . {while} the Bank readily embraces those governance issues that it deems necessary for a positive and stable investment climate.
>
> (Hunter 1996: 66)

NGOs have urged the Bank to ensure that efforts to improve governance focus as much on the needs of poor and disenfranchised members of society as on those of the private sector.

The role of internal advocates

In contrast to the situation regarding participation, there was no group of individuals at the Bank already experienced in addressing issues of governance. There was, however, awareness that many Bank programs faced serious institutional and political barriers to success. For example, the goal of reducing public sector expenditures contained in an adjustment loan might fall short due to resistance from within the government bureaucracy, or the absence of a transparent accounting system might make it difficult for the Bank to track how its funds were being used and audit government expenditures. Such issues, especially the ever-present concern about corruption, transcended the Bank's traditional focus on economic and financial factors and attracted the attention of many Bank staff members.

The Public Sector Management Symposium, an annual meeting of interested staff that had begun in the 1980s, became one gathering place for people within the Bank interested in expanding the purview of the Bank's public sector management activities. Managers of the public sector teams working in the Bank's African, Latin America, and Europe/Middle East/North Africa regions played an important role in fostering these discussions. Other pockets of interest and expertise also formed. In the early 1990s, discussions began between Bank staff members and Peter Eigen, leading to formal cooperation between the Bank and Transparency International. The occasional "brown bag" discussion on corruption reportedly drew overflow crowds. These connections among Bank staff and budding networks with outside organizations were less extensive than in the case of the participation agenda, but they provided a base of support as the Bank began to pay greater attention to issues of governance.

The Bank's response

A key event in the development of the Bank's governance agenda was the publication in 1989 of *Sub-Saharan Africa: from crisis to sustainable growth, a long-term perspective study* (LTPS). From the beginning, the preparation of the

LTPS was conceived as a project that would involve African and other development experts drawn from outside the World Bank. These participants had an important effect on the final shape of the report. A draft of the report was completed in late 1988 and circulated within the Bank. Some of those who saw the draft were troubled by its failure to address problems of corruption or governance, but it was finalized despite their criticism. The report was then presented to development experts, government officials, and others at a series of workshops in Africa designed to serve as a sounding board before official publication. The African response to the report was highly critical for the same reasons flagged by internal critics. The negative reaction by African experts, however, was taken more seriously by Bank management and led to a reshuffling of the LTPS team, appointment of a new head, and redrafting of the report. The result was a substantially different report, with new chapters and a more candid tone.[10] In retrospect, staff members feel that the Bank's initial error was one of excess caution in not recognizing the extent to which Africans themselves were prepared to discuss governance and their eagerness to have the Bank do so as well.

The LTPS found that "Underlying the litany of Africa's development problems is a crisis of governance" (World Bank 1989b: 60). It argued that private sector initiative and market mechanisms are not sufficient for economic growth, but must be accompanied by an efficient public service, a reliable judicial system, and an accountable public administration (ibid.: xii). And it advocated "a systematic effort to build a pluralistic institutional structure, a determination to respect the rule of law, and vigorous protection of the freedom of the press and human rights" (ibid.: 61). While the more overtly political features of the report did not find their way into the Bank's ultimate formulation of its governance agenda, the LTPS opened up new areas of discussion and brought previously off-limits subjects into the light.

Around the same time the LTPS was published, Bank staff in the Africa region began to apply some of the principles addressed in the report in their dealings with borrowers. Frequently, governance concerns were raised in the context of discussions between the borrower and consultative groups of bilateral aid donors that were chaired by the Bank, but the Bank also took some actions itself. In 1989, the Bank suspended disbursements of its structural adjustment loan to Benin, saying that it could not continue payments until the government had secured popular consent for its reform programs. The Bank's position gave support to those calling for a national conference and subsequent elections. (Similar conferences in other Francophone African countries contributed to political liberalization in the region in the early 1990s.) Beginning in 1990, Bank officials joined donor countries in pressing for political reforms in Kenya, Malawi, and Tanzania directed at improving public accountability and transparency, and building a broader political consensus.[11]

In response to the issues raised in the LTPS and the sensitive areas being touched on in discussions with borrowers, the Board of Executive Directors requested clarification of the nature of the Bank's work on governance. In response, an internal task force was appointed in the fall of 1990 to explore how the Bank might address governance in its activities. The first act of the task force organizers was to ask for a legal opinion outlining the parameters of Bank work in this area.[12] In his opinion, General Counsel Ibrahim Shihata carefully drew a line between "aspects of governance that are relevant to the Bank's work and may therefore defensibly fall within its mandate," and "aspects that are clearly political considerations that cannot be taken into account without breaching the Bank's Articles" (Shihata 1991: 81).

The general counsel concluded that the Bank is prohibited from allowing its decisions to be influenced by a country's political ideology, interfering in partisan politics, or using its position as coordinator of foreign assistance for a given country to act on behalf of donor countries to influence the recipient's political orientation or behavior. Among activities thought to be consistent with the Articles of Agreement are those related to the stability and predictability of government actions and the rule of law, such as support for civil service reform, legal reform, accountability for public funds, and budgetary discipline. The opinion also distinguished between Bank support for participatory approaches in its lending (acceptable), and "popular participation as a general requirement" (unacceptable) (Shihata 1991: 92). In sum, "Technical considerations of economy and efficiency, rather than ideological and political preferences, should guide the Bank's work at all times" (ibid.: 95). This legal document has had a profound effect on the governance agenda.

The task force began its work early in 1991. By all accounts, it was an intellectually ambitious and nonbureaucratic exercise. Those involved in formulating its agenda cast the issue broadly, then put their ideas through what one leader called a "tight grid" by asking what they meant for the Bank operationally. The task force commissioned a series of research papers that explored topics such as the intellectual roots of the relationship between governance and development (Brautigam 1991) and ways to increase public participation in improving governance (Paul 1991). Successive drafts of the task force report were circulated to the Bank's regional managers with the goal of clarifying how the issues it raised could be applied in each region. Ongoing negotiations with the Legal Department also ensured that the task force's recommendations fit within the parameters of the earlier legal opinion. The group's report was discussed by the board in July 1991 and published as *Governance and Development* the following spring.

The report claimed that, for the World Bank, "good governance is synonymous with sound development management," (World Bank 1992c: 1) and went on to examine Bank experience and "best practice" in those areas of governance consistent with the Bank's mandate. The broad political concerns raised in the LTPS were absent. A progress report on Bank work in the area was provided two years later in *Governance: The World Bank's experience.* While initial plans to track the Bank's governance activities called for reports to the board to be prepared every two years, management has backed away from this position. The progress report on governance planned for fiscal 1996 was cancelled and the next official assessment of the Bank's activities in this area is scheduled for fiscal 1999. Competing explanations have been offered for the change in plans. Some say the Bank is simply trying to cut down on the number of reports the board is called upon to review. A more political explanation was offered by one staff member involved in the issue, who claimed that every time the issue is discussed by the board, pressure emerges for the Bank to do more, a signal that governance remains a controversial and ill-defined area of Bank activity. It is also possible that efforts to track governance activity have been eclipsed by the attention given to those aspects of the agenda that are relatively easy to define, such as legal reform or strengthening public sector management.

While the work of the task force was under way, the World Bank annual conference on development economics, held in April 1991, took as two of its major themes governance and the reduction of military expenditures. Robert McNamara's presentation on the need for developing countries to cut their military spending was taken as an important signal by Bank staff members of the legitimacy of including this issue within the scope of their work. McNamara argued that financial assistance be made conditional on progress toward "optimal levels" of military expenditure and stated that "International organizations, including the World Bank, can catalyze this process" (McNamara 1992: 95).

Concurrent with the task force, the Africa region was engaged in its own institutional exercise exploring how to apply the governance issues that had been raised in the LTPS. A thematic team on governance, participation, and human rights was established, which, as its name suggests, took a broader view of the issue than the governance task force. The group held a series of workshops between 1990 and 1995 with the dual goal of increasing awareness of governance issues and understanding better how governance might affect the department's operational work. While several discussions were held on human rights, this issue dropped out of the work of the thematic team early on. The participation thread was picked up by the Learning Group on Participatory Development, while the focus on governance contributed to a reorganization of the Africa Technical Department to create a capacity-building unit and a rethinking of how best to pursue civil service reform in the region (Dia 1993, 1996).

Two subsequent initiatives suggest that the Bank's work on governance has continued to move away from broad political concerns and in a more technical direction. The first was a research program launched in 1992, called Africa's Management in the 1990s, which focused on building institutional capacity in sub-Saharan Africa. The second is the Partnership for Capacity Building in Africa undertaken in 1995-6 at the instigation of the Bank's African member countries. Its report, based on studies, assessments, and working groups carried out across the region, acknowledges that the Bank has given thought to the problem of capacity deficiencies in Africa, but claims that Bank rhetoric has not been translated into practice and that these ideas have not been mainstreamed. To this end, the report calls for changes in incentives for Bank staff, establishment of a capacity-building secretariat, and the creation of a trust fund to support capacity-building initiatives at the Bank.[13] The emphasis on capacity-building, an activity viewed by the Bank as encompassing many aspects of institutional reform, can also be interpreted as a narrowing of the governance agenda and a way of avoiding its more political elements. For example, Carol Lancaster, a longtime observer of the World Bank in Africa, maintains that while building capacity is important, it may be a diversion from even more pressing issues, such as the politicization of government agencies or the problem of patronage: "If you don't have the right policies, improving capacity won't help matters."[14]

Assessing the importance of the governance agenda

The Bank's work on governance has adhered to the guidelines set forth in the general counsel's 1990 memorandum and the report of the 1991 task force. The four areas of governance that were identified as consistent with the Bank's mandate are public sector management, accountability, the legal framework for development, and information and transparency (World Bank 1992c: 2).

The rationale for public sector management activities relates to the need to have in place a well-functioning government to carry out Bank-financed projects and create an "enabling environment" for the private sector. Until the 1980s, the Bank's work on public sector management focused on improving the performance of those agencies responsible for implementing Bank-financed projects (for example, by making a loan to strengthen the technical capabilities of a transportation ministry charged with overseeing the construction of a Bank-financed road). With the advent of adjustment lending, public sector management took on a broader focus, encompassing the management of public expenditures, civil service reform, and support for privatization. Governance lending addresses all these areas, with the goals of increasing government capacity to implement public policy, making public programs more effective, and strengthening public institutions.

While public sector management represent a continuation of a traditional area of Bank lending, supporting accountability, the rule of law, and transparency require new approaches altogether, as well as the articulation of a rationale linking these areas to economic development. The goal of accountability-related loans is to make it easier to hold governments responsible for their actions. In this area, the Bank has supported the decentralization of governing activities and greater NGO participation in government decision-making. The Bank also supports technical work, like the development of better auditing and accounting capabilities, to strengthen governments' financial accountability. The Bank's anti-corruption initiative also falls into the category of making governments more accountable.

Combating corruption is one of the more promising – and most delicate – areas of Bank action on governance. The Bank has worked with Transparency International (TI) since its establishment in 1993; in fact, one can argue that the Bank's support for TI, first informal and then formal, helped create the kind of NGO that would help the Bank pursue an anti-corruption agenda. President Wolfensohn has made opposition to corruption a central theme of his presidency, speaking about it frequently and, in 1996, establishing an internal task force to develop a strategy for the Bank's anti-corruption activities. The task force report, presented to the board and published in 1997 as *Helping Countries Combat Corruption: The role of the World Bank*, provides the first systematic framework for the Bank's work in this area. Explicitly locating the fight against corruption within the broader governance agenda, the report calls for the Bank to place a concern for corruption in the mainstream of its operational work and research. This includes ensuring that its own projects meet the highest standards of accountability; raising the impact of corruption in its dialogue with borrowers; addressing corruption more explicitly in Country Assistance Strategy (CAS) documents and project design; filling critical skills gaps within the Bank; and working in partnership with NGOs and international organizations to combat corruption.

Activities related to the legal framework for development center mainly on supporting the construction of laws and legal institutions appropriate for the functioning of a market economy. The rationale, again, is to provide an enabling environment for private sector actors and contribute to market-led economic development. In this area, too, a strong awareness of the limitations of Bank activity is evident, as in the legal department's finding that, "the Bank may not be involved in financing legal reform activities that do not have a direct and obvious link to economic development" (World Bank 1995d: ii).[15] Loans to improve the legal framework might include support for government efforts to communicate laws more effectively; support for reform of a country's regulatory framework, such as laws governing financial institutions or securities markets; or legal training and technical assistance to improve countries' judicial systems and support conflict resolution capabilities. In addition, a small amount of grant funding for legal technical assistance is available through the Bank's Institutional Development Fund. Occasionally, Bank projects provide technical advice with no money attached, although countries are reluctant to borrow for legal technical assistance, especially through the IBRD, in part because they may receive such assistance from other donors free of charge (World Bank 1995d: 18). The Bank has been particularly active in supporting legal reform in Russia, Eastern Europe, and Central Asia where the basic institutional framework necessary for a market economy is lacking.[16]

Activities related to information and transparency are harder to characterize. The Bank states that "the themes of transparency and information pervade good governance and reinforce accountability" (World Bank 1992c: 29), and concludes that information is essential to the functioning of a market economy. Transparency is also necessary for combating corruption. Bank work in this area centers mainly on encouraging countries to make budget information and financial reporting more transparent and raising issues of information availability in policy dialogue with governments. Some Bank publications have mentioned the importance of media freedom, and the Bank's training arm, the Economic Development Institute (EDI), carries out some programs for journalists in borrowing countries.

The nature of governance activities varies widely from region to region. In Africa, the lack of state capacity has led the Bank to focus on civil service reform and institutional reform more generally. In Latin America, where economic reform is more advanced, the Bank has targeted improvements in public sector management achieved through changing budget laws, modernizing accounting systems, computerizing financial information systems, and so on. In the transitional economies of Europe and Central Asia, Bank-supported projects seek to define the role of the state in the economy, addressing issues like privatization, the clarification of property rights, and the development of market-based financial systems.

There are some special difficulties in assessing the importance of governance at the Bank. First, many loans that predated the Bank's governance initiative have been reclassified as governance loans, making it difficult to determine the degree to which governance is really something new or whether it is just a new name given to ongoing activities. Second, information tracking Bank work in this area is in short supply. There is no vocal external constituency for the Bank's governance-related activities; thus, there has been no demand for the kind of periodic reporting that has been done on Bank–NGO collaboration or the environment. Perhaps for the same reason, the list of projects presented each year in the Bank's annual report denotes, among other things, whether a project involves NGO collaboration or the participation of affected stakeholders, but not whether it addresses governance concerns.

Bank staff and officials have sent out contradictory messages about what they believe governance to mean. On the one hand, there is the careful deliberation and cautious wording found in the general counsel's legal statements on the topic, which are generally taken as efforts to rein in those members of the staff and Bank shareholders who are pushing to expand the range of acceptable Bank activity. On the other hand, there is the kind of broad assertion made in the Bank's first governance progress report that, "In short, there are governance components in all projects" (World Bank 1994b: xv). An assessment of how the Bank pursues governance operationally reveals a more modest yet still substantial set of activities, many of them a continuation and deepening of earlier Bank work on the public sector.

Operational work

Governance itself is not a category of Bank lending. (Neither is private sector development or participation.) Rather, loans or technical assistance for purposes of civil service reform, legal and judicial reform, and regulatory reform, all of which aim to improve the performance of borrowers' public institutions, fall under the governance rubric. Projects in the financial sector, as well as in the multi-sectoral category where many of the Bank's adjustment loans are clustered, also contain governance provisions. The following loans, approved in fiscal 1997, convey a sense of the variety of activities included in the governance agenda (*Annual Report* 1997: 92–112):

- $300 million IBRD loan to Argentina for a provincial pension fund reform program.
- $125 million IDA credit to Tanzania for reforms in public expenditure, social services, privatization, and the banking and petroleum sectors.
- $29 million IDA credit to Pakistan to improve public sector accounting standards and reporting systems.
- $22 million IBRD loan to Russia to build the institutional capacity for sound economic analysis in support of market-oriented structural reforms.
- $16 million IBRD loan to Indonesia to enhance the capabilities of the country's supreme audit board.
- $12 million IDA credit to Haiti to improve tax and customs administration, public expenditure and human resources management, and to modernize and reorient the role of the state.
- $10 million IBRD loan to Kazakhstan to support a pilot real estate registration system.
- $10 million IBRD loan to Ecuador for judicial reform aimed at improving the efficiency of the judicial system and making decision-making more predictable.

In one of the Bank's few attempts at measurement in this area, the following data was presented covering 455 projects in three regions during the 1991–3 fiscal years. (While details of the study are not reported, the regions chosen were presumably those where the Bank is most active in governance.) The study found that most of the projects in these regions contained governance elements related to capacity-building and decentralization; almost half the projects surveyed contained provisions to improve economic management; about one-third involved reform of state-owned enterprises or the participation of stakeholders; and a small fraction involved some aspect of legal reform. (See Table 5.1.) A separate review of projects in the Latin America and Caribbean region found that some 90 per cent of current or pending operations were expected to have an impact on governance, half of them a major one (1994b: xv).

A more systematic measure of the importance of governance is provided by

Table 5.1 Proportion of selected operations with governance content, 1991–3

Operation	*Governance content* %
Capacity building	68
Decentralization	68
Economic management	49
State-owned enterprises reform	33
Participation	30
Legal framework	6

Source: World Bank 1994b: xv

tracking the Bank's work on public sector management, a functional classification of Bank lending that forms a central part of the governance agenda. Figure 5.1 shows a moderate increase in public sector management lending operations for the Bank overall during the 1990s. Figure 5.2 shows more pronounced trends in the three regions where the Bank's governance initiative has been the most advanced: Latin America and the Caribbean, Africa, and Europe and Central Asia. In all three cases, public sector management activities expanded significantly over the decade, reaching a high point in fiscal 1996 when they amounted to close to a quarter of Bank lending in Africa and somewhat less in the other two regions.

Figure 5.3 shows the regional distribution of cumulative Bank loans for public sector management, indicating which regions have received the bulk of Bank financing in this area, which is the largest component of governance-related lending.

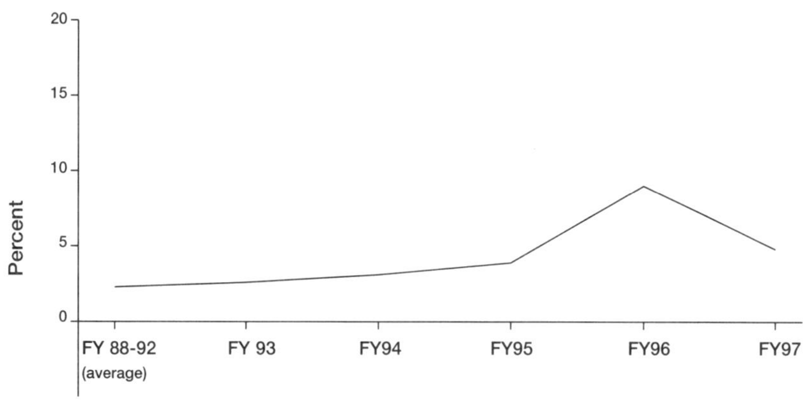

Figure 5.1 Public Sector Management Operations (percentage of total IBRD/IDA *loans)*

Source: World Bank *Annual Report* 1990, Table 7-6; *Annual Report* 1993, Table 7-1; *Annual Report* 1997, Table 4-1.

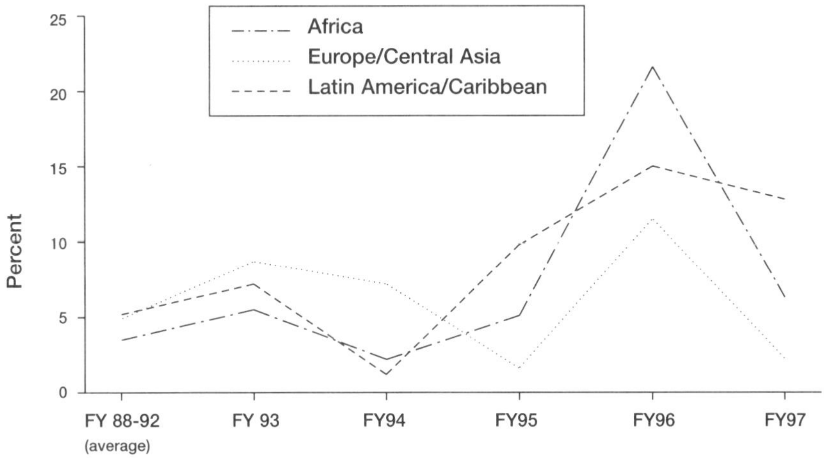

Figure 5.2 Public Sector Management, Regional Trends (percentage of total IBRD/IDA loans to region)
Source: World Bank *Annual Report* 1997, Tables 3-1, 3-10, 3-13, 4-1

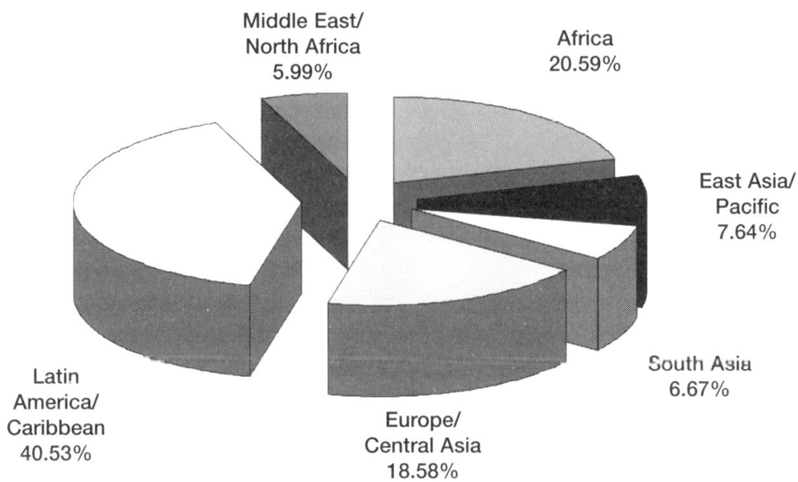

Figure 5.3 Public Sector Management, Regional Distribution (percentage of cumulative loans as of 6/30/97)
Source: World Bank *Annual Report* 1997, pp. 168-69

Non-project activities

In addition to lending, the Bank addresses governance in its research program. The private sector assessments mentioned in Chapter 3 cover, among other topics, the legal and regulatory framework in which the private sector operates. Governance concerns are also supposed to be addressed in the Country Assistance Strategy (CAS) document that guides overall Bank policy in a given country. The Bank's best-practice guide requires the CAS to assess "any governance issues related to the government's willingness and capacity to carry out needed reforms" (World Bank 1994b: 61, note 8). But an internal analysis of a sample of forty CASs showed that their coverage of governance focused almost exclusively on public sector management and that other concerns, such as transparency, accountability, and the rule of law, were addressed only rarely (World Bank 1994b: 38–9). Bank staff speculate as to why this is the case, offering three possible reasons: the subject matter of governance is so sensitive that staff members may be reluctant to commit their views to paper; governance is not well understood and staff are thus uncomfortable writing about it; or the raising of certain governance issues involves treading near the murky boundary between economics and politics delineated in the Articles of Agreement. A fourth possibility is simply that governance has not joined the ranks of those issues to which staff members know they must pay attention in order to be viewed as having done their jobs well. The Bank's 1997 report on helping countries combat corruption recognizes that this issue has rarely been dealt with in the CAS, but says that future CASs "will discuss any serious effect that corruption has on a country's development prospects and, in turn, define ways in which the Bank could help mitigate the problem, consistent with the Bank's mandate" (World Bank 1997a: 50).

The Economic Development Institute (EDI) continues to work in the governance area, usually in collaboration with other donors. While EDI was for many years viewed as something of a backwater within the Bank, it has come to be seen as less bound by bureaucratic rules than the Bank itself and has attracted some dynamic young staff members. Because EDI has always worked in partnership with other organizations, it is well positioned to play a leading role in the Wolfensohn era, which encourages partnerships and the leveraging of resources. One example of EDI's governance activities is its support, along with the Canadian government, for an International Conference on Governance Innovations in 1996 that drew 300 people from thirty countries to Manila. The conference launched a longer-term process of research, learning, and pilot activities that seek to adapt governance innovations to local governments in Southeast Asian countries. EDI also offers courses for leaders in developing countries on building institutions, strengthening the judiciary, and fighting corruption.

Governance concerns are frequently addressed in policy dialogue between the Bank and borrower. Policy dialogue occurs at several levels: in ongoing interactions that take place through the Bank's field office or resident mission; in the periodic exchange of ideas between the Bank's country staff members and their counterparts in the government; and in discussions between senior Bank officials and political leaders. The last mechanism is the most meaningful when it comes to raising politically sensitive issues, such as military expenditures or corruption. Another avenue for high-level dialogue on these topics are the consultative group meetings of bilateral donors and aid recipients chaired by the Bank. By the Bank's account, between October 1990 and January 1993, forty-five consultative group meetings were held for twenty-nine countries. The issues, and the number of countries where they were discussed, included military expenditures (12), transparency (13), human rights and democracy (18), accountability (21), the legal framework for development (22), and public sector management (28) (World Bank 1994b: 43). Bank officials stress that in these meetings it is the views of donor countries that are being discussed, not its own. While separating the message from the messenger helps preserve the Bank's apolitical character, the fact that these issues are raised at meetings chaired by the Bank adds to the weight of donor concerns.

Because Bank–government dialogue is informal and off the record, it is difficult to evaluate the seriousness with which Bank staff and management address governance concerns in their own discussions with borrowers. In its assessment, the Bank claims that:

> The issue of military expenditures has been discussed with a number of African and Asian governments. Aspects of human rights that have an impact on the effectiveness of the Bank's assistance have also been raised in this way, and in a number of countries, public sector corruption and its implications for continued Bank lending have been part of the dialogue agenda.
>
> (World Bank 1994b: 41)

President Wolfensohn's emphasis on fighting corruption raises the possibility that the Bank may begin to present its concerns about this last issue in a more forceful and public manner. But here, too, the Bank has been careful to emphasize the technical rationale for its anti-corruption program, saying that corruption should be viewed "not in moral terms but as a constraint to development. The more corruption can be presented in terms of its effect on the outcomes of government policies, programs, and projects, the more constructive the dialogue is likely to be" (World Bank 1997a: 50).

Changes in Bank organization and policies

Governance has not received the same level of organizational attention as that given to either the Bank's private sector development or participation initiative. The 1992 reorganization that created the central vice presidency for private sector development treated governance much the same way as participation: a small unit led by the Bank's public sector management adviser was given responsibility for tracking the Bank's governance work from the center. An Africa region study concluded, "The recent reorganization (1992/1993) did not enhance the role to be played by [public sector management] staff on the issues of capacity building, institutional development, or improved governance" (Adamolekun and Bryant 1994: 23). And whereas participation and NGO collaboration are supported by NGO liaisons in the Bank's field offices, governance-related activities do not have this sort of broad reach.

On the other hand, there are public sector management specialists in each of the Bank's regional divisions, including a large presence in Latin America where virtually all member countries are committed to modernizing their public sectors. The Africa region also has an active group of staff members working on capacity-building initiatives. There is a small group that covers both the Europe/Central Asia and Middle East/North Africa regions, and another small group that covers South and East Asia. (The size of these units reflects the fact that demand for their services is low from member countries in these parts of the world.) The technical networks established in 1996–7 to manage the sharing of knowledge across regions located public sector management in the Poverty Reduction and Economic Management network. A Public Sector Group was established within the network to give impetus to the public sector reform agenda set out in the 1997 *World Development Report*. While the resources of this group will need to be expanded if it is to play an effective role, one of its principals notes that "the pendulum is swinging back from the low point" of a few years ago.[17]

In addition to personnel, a few training courses have been added that address governance-related issues, including a training workshop on corruption, first offered in February 1997. The latest call for additional resources comes from the corruption task force, which found the Bank's staffing in this area inadequate and called for an increase in the number of financial management specialists, procurement specialists, and experts in public sector reform (World Bank 1997a).

Many of the Bank's governance-related initiatives have been short-term, one-time affairs, such as the 1991 task force on governance, the partnership for capacity-building in Africa, and the working group on corruption. None of these efforts has led to any significant organizational change, and the restructuring of the Bank that has taken place under President Wolfensohn has not raised the profile of those working on governance issues. Yet clearly evident in official speeches and public pronouncements is a shift in the Bank's attitude toward public sector reform and a new willingness at least to talk about the political dimensions of development.

Rhetoric and practice

Bank publications have addressed governance issues since 1990, when the annual report mentioned the Long-Term Perspective Study and its findings about the role of poor governance in Africa's economic crisis. The 1991 *World Development Report*, while setting forth the Bank's market-oriented development strategy, noted that governments should have a greater capacity to step in where they need to play the role of regulator. It also mentioned the issue of corruption and the importance of building strong public sector institutions. The *Annual Report* 1994 summarized the Bank's review of its governance activities published that year, but without mentioning corruption. Subsequent annual reports have highlighted civil service reform and capacity-building in their discussions of Bank work in Africa, but have offered no further assessments of Bank progress on governance in general. In the position statement prepared for the Bank's fiftieth anniversary, "reorienting government" was identified as one of the Bank's five major challenges for the coming years. The Bank defined this challenge as, "Reorienting government so that the public sector can complement private-sector activity and efficiently undertake essential tasks such as human resource development, environmental protection, provision of social safety nets, and legal and regulatory frameworks" (World Bank Group 1994: 8).

Recent Bank presidents have also given voice to concerns about governance. Barber Conable mentioned governance as a prospective issue for the Bank in a speech to its African governors in 1990, saying, "Allow me to be blunt: the political uncertainty and arbitrariness evident in so many parts of sub-Saharan Africa are major constraints on the region's development" (Quoted in Lancaster 1993: 10). (Reportedly, the board's request for a staff report on governance was stimulated in part by this speech.) Lewis Preston usually paired his comments about the importance of a vibrant private sector with remarks about the need for effective government, saying "governments should do less where markets work well and more where markets alone cannot be relied upon" (World Bank 1995b: 22). President Wolfensohn in his first two speeches at the World Bank/IMF annual meetings cited corruption as "a major barrier to sound and equitable development" and committed the Bank to fighting it. In his comments, Wolfensohn has carefully avoided violating the Bank's charter, while pushing outward the scope for Bank action:

> [T]he Bank Group will help any of our member countries to implement national programs that discourage corrupt practices . . . The Bank Group cannot intervene in the political affairs of our member countries. But we can give advice, encouragement and support to governments that wish to fight corruption.
>
> (Wolfensohn 1996: 11)

Turning from rhetoric to practice, it becomes clear that governance concerns are less integrated into the Bank's operational work than the other two agendas covered in this study. A sampling of comments from Bank staff members and others working in the area suggests the ambiguous status of the governance agenda:

- From a member of the core group involved in the governance task force: "The tough question with governance is how to operationalize these concepts. You need to keep in mind that countries borrow from the Bank.

It's difficult to get them to borrow to improve something that they may believe is not the purview of the Bank."

- From a close observer of the Bank's recent history: "Governance has been an utter failure. The reason is we don't know how to do it. There is a big difference between whether the issue is important or has merit and whether the World Bank has the wherewithal to affect it. The Bank is great at analysis but not as good about implementation."
- From a task manager of an innovative governance project who has since left the Bank: "The real issues have to do with governance in the broader sense, not institutional development more narrowly."
- From a member of the thematic team: "Governance has been subsumed under public sector management and capacity building, and its political content removed."
- From one of the Bank's governance experts who has since moved to another division: "There is no organizational entity with the mandate for pushing governance. The governance staff is small, dispersed, and has to work on many different issues."
- From a former member of the Bank's research division: "Risk-taking is needed, especially in research on governance. But the Bank's incentive structure discourages risk-taking. A typical pattern at the Bank is that someone is brought in to try something new, but when he does he is marginalized."

While many of the Bank's activities relate to governance in some way, the average project manager will not list improving governance or fighting corruption among his or her first tier of concerns. Issues like the environment, the role of women in development, and even participation are more prominent in the day-to-day discourse of the organization. In part, the low profile of governance concerns is due to a lack of well-developed and documented techniques for improving institutional performance. It is thus not surprising that governance has been narrowed to discrete areas of activity, especially those where the Bank already has a track record, such as reducing public sector expenditures or reforming the civil service. Another factor contributing to the marginalization of governance concerns is the absence of signals from management that the issue is of central importance. Staff members speak repeatedly of the role of incentives in shaping their behavior: unless the signals are clear and incentives are in place to reward staff effort on a given issue, it will not receive much attention in the daily work of the institution. This has been the fate of governance thus far within the Bank.

This is not to say, however, that the Bank's governance agenda has not had an impact. Salvatore Schiavo-Campo, formerly a public sector group manager at the World Bank now at the Asian Development Bank, points out that the impact of the Bank's initiative cannot be judged fairly by looking only at its own activities:

> Just as the *Governance and Development* paper provided an "enabling environment" for World Bank staff who knew quite well the importance of governance factors but couldn't openly tackle them, so the World Bank entry into this area opened the door for other international institutions. The IMF, the Asian Development Bank, the Inter-American and the African Development Bank found comfort, a measure of political cover and encouragement from the World Bank's opening of the dialogue.[18]

In 1997 the IMF made a line of credit to the Argentine government dependent on such evidence of "good governance" as overhauling the tax system, improving judicial practices, and opening the government's books.[19] And the Asian Development Bank is the first international institution to have a formally approved board policy on governance. In short, by acknowledging the importance of political factors in development, the Bank furthered the governance agendas of other organizations, while opening up previously off-limits topics for discussion, debate, and analysis among its own staff.

Governance and the Bank's organizational culture

The governance agenda fits poorly with important elements of the Bank's organizational culture. The apolitical ideal embodied in the Articles of Agreement is the most obvious constraint, but governance also poses challenges to the project cycle, the expert-oriented approach to lending, the emphasis on quantitative measures of success, a Bank staff dominated by economists and financial experts, and the structure of incentives faced by that staff.

The project cycle was designed for "brick and mortar" projects. Loans to help countries improve public sector management, strengthen the legal system, or reduce corruption are far more complex than those made to build a road or even fund an innovative education program. It will take several years before the results of such loans can be seen and even longer for them to be judged a success. It is almost impossible to determine a rate of return for a loan intended to improve institutional capacity. These difficulties are increasingly recognized within the Bank, to the point that social projects and those related to institutional reform are not subject to the same kind of rate of return analysis and unfold along the lines of a modified project cycle.

The Bank's expert stance is also problematic. Loans to improve government capacity simply cannot be designed within the Bank and then presented to a borrower because the key ingredient in their success is the commitment of the government. Callisto Madavo, vice president for the Africa region, acknowledges the difficulty, saying it is only recently that the Bank in its relations with Africa has begun to "provide that which Africa required rather than that which the Bank thought was good for Africa" (Madavo 1997).

The Bank lacks tried and true techniques for governance lending, although it has begun to develop new tools. One example is the institutional environment assessment methodology (Pinto 1994). This technique, which relies on workshops, surveys, and other forms of participatory research, allows the Bank to diagnose the "missing" institutional capacity needed for effective civil service reform. While new tools are welcome, the Bank's technocratic approach serves to narrow the governance agenda to specific problems that are amenable to the application of such techniques.

The Bank also lacks appropriate staffing to be able to work effectively on governance issues. Governance lending requires staff with a different set of skills than those readily available at the Bank. In especially short supply are people with hands-on public administration experience in developing countries that have undergone public sector reform. (The Bank's principal public sector management specialist points out that a majority of Bank staff involved in public sector management have no government work experience at all.)[20] In the words of the authors of the World Bank history project:

> What makes institutions tick is an amorphous area to begin with, and an understanding of public bureaucracies was not the Bank's strongest suit. In part, the discipline of public administration ranked low in the intellectual hierarchy in the "development" field, and the Bank was no exception. More than any other part of the Bank's activities, it was an area where one would assume that experience would be especially prized. Notwithstanding endless incantations about "institution building" in reports and analysis, the internal organizational culture of the Bank was inimical to individuals with deep-rooted external experience.
>
> (Kapur *et al.*, 1997: 758)

Like advocates of private sector development and participation, supporters of an active governance agenda have called for changes in the Bank's recruitment patterns to bring into the Bank more people with relevant experience. The Africa region's 1994 progress report on governance advocates "increasing staff capacities in the field of management (e.g. either those with formal training in the field of management, doctorates, MBA, degrees in law, etc., and/or proven management experience in organizations of some size)." It also calls for public sector management specialists to be recruited as part of the Bank's Young Professionals program and for the (public sector management) capacity of selected resident missions to be strengthened (Adamolekun and Bryant 1994: 22). But hiring remains biased toward individuals trained in economics and finance.

Finally, governance lending is at odds with the Bank's approval culture, a structure of incentives that encourages staff members to develop projects and have them approved by the board, but that provides almost no sanctions if those projects then turn sour. Salvatore Schiavo-Campo, a former Bank manager involved in its governance efforts, summarizes the situation as follows:

> If as a lasting hangover from the McNamara years the objective function of the institution was to maximize lending volumes, the real incentive framework was naturally consistent with that function. It is thus not surprising that staff have downplayed governance considerations. Attention to governance issues is seen as an impediment, because it slows down the process; and governance assistance itself carries a low weight – because you can lend much less than through financing bridges, or hospitals, or a million school books.[21]

The Bank's organizational culture has exercised a strong influence on the evolution of the governance agenda. In the decade after the authors of the LTPS first noted the crisis of governance in sub-Saharan Africa, various institutional exercises narrowed the scope of governance concerns to those that do not clash with the deeply held belief that the Bank's work is apolitical and that can be addressed with the tools the Bank has at hand. Even a limited engagement with governance issues, however, poses dilemmas for the Bank. The most difficult of these stems from the sometimes delicate relationship between the Bank and its members.

Some governments have resisted any foray by the Bank into their internal workings, charging that it represents an overstepping of the Bank's mandate and a violation of their sovereignty. Other governments object to the imposition of what they perceive as Western models of governance on their indigenous cultures. The Bank Information Center, which monitored the 1996 World Bank/IMF annual meetings on behalf of NGOs, reports the negative reaction of the G-24 group of developing countries to the emphasis on corruption in President Wolfensohn's speech. Representatives of the G-24 claimed that, by imposing political conditionality on Bank loans, the Bank would be encroaching on its members' national sovereignty and extending its power beyond the parameters of the Articles of Agreement. They called the initiative "an extension of [the Bank's] mandate by stealth" and warned of a backlash against such efforts.[22] The result of these concerns, again, has been a narrowing of the governance agenda to technical considerations and an avoidance of its broader political content.

Officials point out that the Bank is a development finance institution, not a world government, and should not operate as a self-appointed reformer of its borrower countries. But in many spheres the Bank has taken upon itself the mantle of reformer and far outstepped the boundaries of its original development finance role. The question is where the line is drawn between those factors that affect development (legitimate for Bank involvement) and those that do not (off limits to the Bank). Since it is the Bank, with the tacit approval of its members, that draws this line for itself, its protestations of the limits on its activities rings somewhat hollow.

There is another reason why the Bank has kept its governance activities tightly focused on issues of technical capacity and institutional development. It is not just that a broader agenda – one that included factors like pluralism, elections, freedom of association, or protection of human rights – would contravene the Bank's apolitical ethos. Such an agenda would also undercut its ability to incorporate governance criteria into some of its largest lending programs. The case of China, currently the Bank's largest borrower, comes to mind. In many ways China, by virtue of its size, is more important to the Bank than the Bank is to China. Nancy Alexander, a long-time observer of the Bank, recounts the story of a junior Bank official on a mission to China who asked his senior colleague whether the Bank was pressuring China to permit greater levels of grassroots participation in development. "The senior official replied, 'We are fortunate that China is allowing the World Bank to participate in its development efforts'" (Alexander 1998). Strict adherence to a governance agenda with strong political content would impair World Bank lending to large borrowers like Brazil, China, India, Indonesia, and (until recently) Mexico and hurt the Bank's ability to keep lending levels steady.

The problem for the Bank is made more acute by growing private capital flows that are concentrated in the largest and fastest-growing developing countries. As Alexander observes, "Big borrowers with alternative sources of credit . . . are senior partners in relationship to the Bank" (Alexander 1998). In lending to these countries, the Bank is competing with private capital and is loath to add more conditions to its loans. It is the poorest and weakest of the Bank's borrowers, those still dependent on it as a source of finance, that are most subject to the Bank conditionality to improve governance or reduce corruption. And, not surprisingly, it in is these countries, with their underdeveloped and often corrupt political systems, that it is most difficult to bring about these improvements.

The narrowness of the Bank's official definition of governance obscures what many believe to be a broader agenda that the Bank cannot address formally, but to which it none the less is committed. The Bank identifies three components of governance – "the form of political regime; the process by which authority is exercised in the management of a country's economic and social resources for development; and the capacity of governments to design, formulate and implement policies and discharge functions" (World Bank 1994b: xiv) – while confining its work to the latter two areas. Some of the Bank's statements on governance reflect ambivalence over this procedural and substantive distinction. Whereas the Bank's 1992 report noted that "a country's form of government and traditions of political participation and public debate . . . are beyond the World Bank's purview" (World Bank 1992c: 40), the 1994 report made explicit the Bank's concern with "freedom of the media, of which a free press is especially important" (World Bank 1994b: 30). In a paper prepared for the World Bank annual conference on development economics in 1991, two senior Bank staff members suggest a minimum core of characteristics for good governance that includes a "well-defined open process of public choice such as elections," freedom of association, a sound judicial system, and freedom of information and expression (Landell-Mills/Serageldin 1992: 306). While acknowledging that the Bank's statutes rule out political considerations and that "actions must focus on the technical aspects of governance" (ibid.: 316), these officials locate the World Bank's governance agenda within a broader context. They suggest that the Bank's governance agenda comes not simply from concern with good development management, but is part of a trend among aid donors to promote good governance in both the political and economic spheres. As Carol Lancaster has noted, the official focus of the Bank's governance approach "underestimates the real scope of the Bank's interest in governance, a scope that extends by implication to political participation, to open political debate, and to establishment of political legitimacy" (Lancaster 1993: 10).

The Bank's definition of governance, which has shifted over time, remains contested within and outside the institution and is likely to continue to evolve in the coming years. Despite the technical bent of much of the Bank's governance-related work, there is pressure on the institution to consider expanding the scope of its activities in this area. This pressure comes from some developed member countries, acting either through their executive directors or their legislatures, as well as from the NGO community. In 1995, for example, the Parliamentary Assembly of the Council of Europe and a committee of the Canadian House of Commons both suggested that the Bank's members consider amending its Articles of Agreement to allow the Bank to become more involved in the promotion of human rights and democratization.[23] A 1997 task force on the United States and the multilateral development banks concluded that governments are not likely to succeed in poverty reduction "unless they have the incentive of some form of representative government under which popular support matters" (CSIS 1997: 25), and that the development banks should see this as a matter of their legitimate concern and consistent with their charters. In addition, some of the more activist executive directors have called on the Bank to deepen its governance activities, especially those related to participation, although they stop short of suggesting that the Bank adopt an explicit human rights/democracy agenda. The argument in favor of a human rights agenda is made by some NGOs, such as the Lawyers Committee for Human Rights. They argue that the distinction drawn by the Bank between economic/social rights and civil/political rights is artificial and unfounded, and that respect for human rights, construed broadly, is essential for sustainable development.

In response to these concerns, senior managers have made a series of public statements clarifying the institution's position on a range of political issues, including governance, human rights, and participatory development (Shihata 1995a, Shihata 1995b, de Capitani 1994). Shihata, in his role as guardian of the Articles of Agreement, issued an internal legal opinion on governance in July 1995 at the request of the Bank's executive directors. This document restates many of the views presented by the general counsel in his influential December 1990 legal memorandum on the boundaries the Bank should observe in making political judgments or issuing political statements about borrowing countries.[24]

- Bank staff cannot establish relationships with opposition political parties without government approval. In other words, staff may not support reformists when they are out of power, even if the staff feels that their success is crucial to a country's economic recovery.
- As chair of consultative group meetings and coordinator of foreign assistance, the Bank should not act as the agent of donor countries (many of which are committed to the liberal democratic agenda outlined above) in influencing the political behavior of the recipient country. The Bank's coordinating role should be guided "only by considerations of aid effectiveness and efficiency" (Shihata 1995b: 23).
- The legitimacy of Bank efforts to promote participatory development does not mean that the Bank has a role in the general political reform of borrowing countries.

The reiteration of these guidelines flags some of the areas where management feels that Bank staff may have overstepped the institution's rules.

In his 1995 opinion, Shihata restates the distinction between economic/social and political/civil human rights and identifies two areas where human rights concerns may legitimately be addressed by the Bank (Shihata 1995b: 29–30):

- Because participation by affected groups [in the design and implementation of projects] requires a reasonable measure of free expression and assembly, the Bank would be acting within proper limits if it asked that this freedom be guaranteed for these purposes. If such freedom were restricted, the Bank would be within its rights to deny a loan for which participation was required.
- An extensive and pervasive violation of political rights, if it had significant economic effects or if it led to the breach of international obligations relevant to the Bank (such as those created under binding decisions of the UN Security Council), can be taken into account in the Bank's lending decisions.

These provisions create some space within which the Bank can pursue the protection of human rights through its work on participation. One observer notes that the general counsel's opinions generally have combined a negative tone with a wide set of openings, such as those that led to the Bank's energetic stance on corruption.[25] Others decry the continued focus on limits. A longtime advocate of Bank attention to human rights notes, "It's easier for the Bank to hide behind the veil of its political prohibition and say that human rights is not part of its mandate than it is to explore what positive can be done within that mandate."[26] Currently, though, whatever the legal climate, there is neither the managerial will nor the staff capacity to expand the Bank's definition of governance in the direction of including support for human rights.

The dilemmas outlined above point to the tension inherent in Bank efforts to carve out an appropriate role for itself in the pursuit of good governance. The Bank has been careful to support only those activities that can be tied directly to questions of efficiency and governmental processes, separating its concerns from those of the larger development community, which extend to democracy and human rights. This has led to calls from some quarters for the Bank to widen its definition. At the same time, the Bank's governance work represents a break with the economic and financial focus of past lending and an extension of its mandate to issues of institutional capacity and political management. This has generated resistance from some developing country members who see such efforts as impinging on their national sovereignty. The Bank is in a difficult position. Only when governance concerns are presented as development-related issues that can be addressed technically do they fit comfortably with the Bank's organizational culture. Yet, by their very nature, questions of governance spill over from the technical realm into the broader political arena. Ambivalence over the Bank's role and conflicting signals from management and member countries have transformed the sense of possibility that existed in 1989 to a sense of the limits the Bank faces in seeking to address the political dimensions of development.

Conclusion

The Bank's concern with governance emerged naturally from its experience with adjustment lending in the 1980s. Frustrated with the poor results of such loans, particularly in sub-Saharan Africa, the Bank came to acknowledge that the main obstacles to development in many countries lay in their political environments more than in their economic policies. Bank thinking was facilitated by the end of the Cold War and the reorientation of many aid programs toward promoting good governance as part of a package of support for democracy and human rights. Although the Bank's charter and deeply held belief that its work is apolitical precluded it from joining in this larger agenda, in the early 1990s governance concerns came to occupy the attention of some members of the Bank's staff and several institutional initiatives emerged.

Work on governance, however, has been marked by shifting definitions and a poor fit with the Bank's organizational culture. Governance-related initiatives have tended to be one-time affairs that result in little organizational change and no allocation of additional resources. The Bank's approach to public sector management has evolved in light of governance concerns, and legal reform is now an established area of Bank lending, but governance has not been elevated to a first-tier issue that commands the attention and commitment of staff throughout the institution. Over the years, the broad agenda raised in the LTPS has become progressively narrower and more technical, as it has been shaped by the Bank's organizational needs and character.

The fate of the nascent anti-corruption agenda will provide an interesting test of how far the Bank is willing to go in seeking better governance. Reducing corruption is necessary for the Bank to achieve its chief goals of creating an enabling environment for the private sector, promoting efficient government institutions, and alleviating poverty. This suggests that there is room for an aggressive approach on this issue. But corruption is also a sensitive subject for developing countries and a strong anti-corruption stance by the Bank may lead to charges that it is violating national sovereignty. The Bank may also avoid raising corruption concerns with those large borrowers that account for most of its lending and that increasingly have access to alternative sources of financing. The seriousness with which the Bank proceeds in its anti-corruption campaign will provide a good indicator of the degree to which the dilemmas highlighted above constitute serious barriers to institutional change.

Timeline of governance-related developments

1989	World Bank publishes *Sub-Saharan Africa: From Crisis to Sustainable Growth.* First Bank publication to mention the "crisis of governance" in some borrowing countries.
October 1990	Board of Executive Directors convenes Task Force on Governance to explore how to operationalize governance at the Bank.
December 1990	General counsel issues legal memorandum, "Issues of 'Governance' in Borrowing Members: The extent of their relevance under the Bank's Articles of Agreement," to clarify the legitimate scope of Bank activity on governance.
1991	Thematic team on Governance, Participation, and Human Rights, convened by Africa Technical Department, holds first workshops. Workshops continue through mid-1995.
1991	World Bank Annual Conference on Development Economics includes focus on governance.
1991	Learning Group on Participatory Development formed. Meetings continue through 1994 and result in an action plan to create a "culture of participation." (See Chapter 4.)
June 1991	"Managing Development: The Governance Dimension – Discussion Paper" prepared by the Bank staff for executive directors.
April 1992	World Bank publishes task force report as *Governance and Development*.
October 1992	Portfolio Management Task Force releases its report (Wapenhans Report).

May 1994	World Bank publishes progress report on governance agenda, *Governance: the World Bank's Experience.*
1994	"Reorienting government" listed as one of Bank's five major challenges on occasion of fiftieth anniversary. Governance receives special attention in annual report.
July 1995	General counsel issues legal opinion on "Prohibition of Political Activities in the Bank's Work."
Fall 1996	Internal working group on corruption established.
October 1996	President Wolfensohn highlights issue of corruption in his annual meetings address.
January 1997	Initial report of working group on corruption goes to management.
February 1997	Bank offers first training workshop on corruption.
July 1997	*World Development Report 1997, The State in a Changing World,* published.
September 1997	*Helping Countries Combat Corruption: The Role of the World Bank* approved by the board and subsequently published.

6 Effecting change

The challenge of organizational transformation

> The Founders of the World Bank created what turned out to be an enduring *institution* – which is to say, an organization of some staying power whose character could not be conveyed simply by adding up its functional elements. There was a corporate identity that, for the institution, was roughly comparable to what personality is to a person. The identity expressed itself both in internal characteristics and behaviors and external relations, and it evolved . . . Yet, arguably, the most noteworthy feature of the institution was its continuity, the hardiness of a set of characteristics it acquired in its very early years.
>
> Kapur et al., *The World Bank*, 1997, p. 1161

The World Bank's institutional character, forged in the years immediately following World War II, allowed it to secure from its environment the resources it would need to operate effectively. Chief among these were the confidence of the capital markets and the support of a broad range of member countries – hence, the Bank's identity as a technical and apolitical institution. Four decades later, the world changed dramatically and the Bank responded. Yet the Bank was constrained in its response by both its formal character and its organizational culture.

Is the World Bank imprisoned by its past? Will it be able to reshape itself to meet the needs of a changing world? The cases of private sector development, participation, and governance examined in the previous chapters cast light on these questions. This chapter draws on the Bank's experience in these areas to reach some conclusions about the balance between stability and change, the strictness of the parameters imposed by the Bank's institutional character, and the prospects for its future evolution.

New agendas, old rules

In pursuing closer relations with the private sector and NGOs, and becoming more deeply involved in issues of governance, the World Bank has had to work around the limits imposed by its Articles of Agreement. The Articles prohibit the Bank from lending to the private sector without a government guarantee, so activities in this area have focused on getting governments to improve the climate for business. The task of financing the private sector directly has fallen to the IFC. The Bank's charter also provides limited avenues through which it can interact directly with NGOs. And the requirement that the Bank operate without regard to political considerations has complicated efforts to improve the governance of borrowers and brought about a constant checking of boundaries on the part of Bank management to ensure that the apolitical provision is not being violated.

None the less, the Bank's charter has proven flexible enough to accommodate significant changes in its activities. In part this is because the charter is a minimal document that focuses on issues of process rather than purpose.[1] In larger part it is because responsibility for interpreting the charter falls to the Bank itself, giving its leaders the freedom to pursue any number of paths provided the Bank's fundamental rules are left intact.

A more important set of constraints in the pursuit of new agendas arises from informal aspects of the Bank's organizational culture. The habit of interacting with government officials and lack of familiarity with private sector needs makes it difficult for the Bank to pursue private sector development seriously, and the structural and cultural gaps between the Bank and the IFC make coordination a major undertaking. The top-down, expert-oriented approach to project design is incompatible with efforts to involve beneficiaries in Bank programs. Participatory approaches also require the leadership of staff members with a deep knowledge of local cultures and an interest in social development – commodities that are in short supply in an organization dominated by economists and other technical experts. The apolitical orientation of the Bank's staff and management makes it difficult to address head-on issues of governance and the development field's bias against individuals with experience in public administration further hinders these efforts. Finally, both participation and governance activities fit poorly with an incentive system that rewards staff members who can move large projects quickly through the approval process.

In spite of these limitations, in the 1990s the Bank made significant changes in its approach to business, civil society, and politics. How and why did these changes come about? In particular, what was the balance between external and internal sources of change and how did they interact in these three areas?

The case of private sector development demonstrates that the United States was able to bring about a shift in the image the Bank presented to the world once US policymakers became willing to expend considerable political resources to do so. The United States pushed a stronger private sector agenda on the Bank for close to a decade with little effect. Only when the United States ratcheted up its pressure by holding the proposed IFC capital increase hostage to changes in the Bank's private-sector-related activities did it meet with a meaningful response. By its unilateral action, however, the United

States complicated its relationship with other member countries and Bank management, and undermined the credibility of its commitment to multilateral approaches. Even then, the actions ultimately taken by the Bank were in line with its own organizational priorities, not the preferences of the United States, and marked a basic continuity with earlier decisions. The Bank's enthusiasm for the private sector is due as much to an internal recognition of its importance and broader changes in the international context as it is to the direct pressure of the United States.

Unlike private sector development, which in some respects was imposed on the Bank from the top down, the participation agenda bubbled up from within the Bank. Staff members working in certain sectors had come to recognize that involving beneficiaries in Bank projects was essential to the success of their efforts. In part through the institutional forum provided by the NGO–World Bank Committee they formed alliances with external advocates of greater participation, including NGO representatives, development experts, and supportive member countries. Together, these groups developed organizational channels through which the issue of participation could be brought to the attention of management and others within the Bank. Despite external pressure to widen the agenda – and whatever their personal beliefs about the normative value of greater participation – internal advocates approached their task pragmatically. Casting participation in narrow terms, as a means to greater success for Bank projects rather than an end in itself, they framed the agenda in ways that fit readily with the Bank's concerns about its effectiveness, thereby attracting high-level support for participatory approaches.

Even more than participation, the governance agenda grew out of the Bank's own institutional experience, facilitated by a more permissive environment internationally. Governance enjoyed no strong external sponsors among either member countries or NGOs. Instead, greater awareness of the importance of governance issues was related to frustration with the results of Bank lending for policy reform and a growing conviction that institutional and political factors lay behind this poor performance. At the same time, other development agencies were reaching the same conclusion and adopting governance agendas that went beyond process issues to include support for democratization and human rights. The Bank could not embrace this wider political agenda because of resistance from many of its developing country members and concern about violating its charter provisions. As their political regimes have become more open, developing country members have shown greater willingness to have the Bank address governance issues. But the Articles of Agreement and its identity as a technical and apolitical institution have continued to restrain the Bank from delving too deeply into issues of political reform.

This brief summary suggests that there are a variety of paths through which a new agenda can be introduced at the World Bank. In all three of the cases examined here, forces within and outside the Bank interacted to bring new issues into focus. Although the balance between external and internal factors varied, in no instance were external preferences translated smoothly into institutional change. Often, changes in the international context were as important as direct external pressure, causing Bank staff and management to question their traditional approaches and altering the internal balance of forces in favor of change. Some agendas originated mainly as a result of institutional factors, such as lessons learned from Bank experience or the presence of internal advocates. Internal–external linkages were important, as internal advocates formed networks with external supporters to push forward the pace of change.

The Bank's activities in the areas of private sector development, participation, and governance have progressed along very different lines since they were introduced. What accounts for the variable treatment of these new agendas? How important a role has the Bank's organizational culture played in shaping their evolution?

Private sector development is the most deeply institutionalized of the three agendas studied here. Private sector concerns have been integrated into the Bank's key strategy documents, given a prominent bureaucratic location and high-level leadership, and allocated substantial new resources. At one level, the new attention dedicated to the private sector violates the Bank's traditional way of doing business, especially its primary connection to governments and lack of direct relationship with private sector entities. It also challenges the Bank's reputation as a slow-moving bureaucracy that is poorly suited to interacting with a dynamic private sector. At a more meaningful level, however, the private sector development agenda is in line with the Bank's organizational culture. Creating favorable conditions for business can be accomplished through the Bank's basic technology of the project cycle and does not challenge its expert stance. While some new, specialized skills are needed in areas like financial sector reform or privatization, the economic and financial training of most Bank staff provides an appropriate background for understanding the importance of the private sector. In addition, a more pronounced role for the private sector in borrowing countries is broadly in line with the Bank's dominant neoliberal ideology. In short, the private sector agenda fits well with the Bank's technical and apolitical rules and the values and beliefs of its management and staff.

Participation is a prominent feature in the work of some departments and in the rhetoric of the Bank overall, but it is not integrated into the mainstream of operations. Despite the existence of an operational policy on collaboration with NGOs, the use of participatory approaches is not mandated; to paraphrase a staff member quoted in Chapter 4, while there is greater support for people who care about participation, there is no pressure on those who do not. The participation agenda has come as far as it has because its advocates have shaped it to fit the Bank's organizational culture. Rather than framing participation as an end in itself, supporters have cast it as a means to more sustainable – hence, more successful – Bank projects. Participation thus fits well with current efforts to improve the Bank's portfolio and shift its culture to greater concern with results. Even in its narrower conception, however, participation violates key tenets of the Bank's organizational culture: its emphasis on learning from beneficiaries challenges the Bank's top-down, expert stance; participatory approaches require a different kind of project cycle; and the skills needed for working effectively with beneficiaries and NGOs are not those possessed by the majority of Bank staff. These factors have hindered the full incorporation of participatory approaches into Bank operations.

The governance agenda is even less institutionalized. Few new resources have been allocated to it and no operational policies guide its implementation. The concept of governance has been progressively narrowed from the initial concerns raised in the Long-Term Perspective Study, which included political factors, to the current focus on capacity-building and corruption. Bank staff and managers have identified improved governance as essential to the success of Bank-supported programs, yet it is difficult to translate this recognition into operational activities in a way that does not violate the Bank's technical and apolitical orientation. As a result, much of the Bank's work in the area consists of traditional public sector management activities going by a new name. The rest of the agenda has been cast in terms of economic efficiency: reducing military expenditures is necessary to bring budgets under control; corruption must be eliminated because it hinders the smooth functioning of the private sector. While a willingness to address the quality of governance represents an important departure for the Bank, its efforts are constrained by its charter and organizational culture. Governance loans take many years to yield results, do not fit the Bank's project cycle, and require skills that are not in ready supply among staff. Relations with members are another difficult issue. Although the governance agenda has been presented in a technical light, some borrowers still view elements of it as an infringement of national sovereignty. It is extremely unlikely that the Bank will make effective governance a precondition for its lending; at a time when the Bank is striving to become more responsive to its clients and keep its lending volume stable, Bank efforts to improve governance will be pursued only in those countries that are already moving in this direction or that are too poor to resist the Bank's prescriptions.

In general, the fate of private sector development, participation, and governance at the World Bank has had little to do with the preferences or power of external actors. Perhaps more surprising, there is no guarantee that a new agenda will become institutionalized even when it has been deemed essential by the Bank to the success of its work. Instead, the Bank's organizational culture has acted as a filter, enabling some concerns to be addressed more thoroughly than others and shaping how new issues are defined. Private sector development, participation, and governance have become incorporated into the Bank's day-to-day activities to the degree that they conform (or can be shaped to conform) to its core technology, technical and apolitical norms, and the values and beliefs of management and staff. An issue that does not fit well with the Bank's organizational culture may be able to find a home within the institution, but it will be small, precarious, and not in the Bank's best neighborhood.

Patterns of change

The new agendas studied here emerged not as the result of either outside pressure or World Bank initiatives alone, but from the interplay of internal and external factors. Do other instances of change at the World Bank fit this pattern?

Several of the Bank's major shifts in mission were stimulated by institutional factors alone, but they required outside support to grow. The basic human needs agenda of the 1970s was largely the product of presidential entrepreneurship. Robert McNamara, eager to put his stamp on the institution, used the overarching goal of poverty alleviation to legitimize a much more active role for the Bank in transferring resources from North to South, eventually gaining the acquiescence of member countries and the financial community.[2] Policy adjustment lending was devised by the Bank in the early 1980s as a way to address the shortcomings of its project-based loans, then accelerated when it came to be seen by the United States as helpful in containing the consequences of the debt crisis.[3] This is an example of how an agenda that originated internally was subsequently embraced by a strong external actor and given a higher profile as a result. The opposite pattern prevailed when the Bank began to pay greater attention to the environmental consequences of its lending in the late 1980s.[4] In this case, change was urged on the Bank initially by external groups (mainly environmental NGOs), while the presence of internal supporters made the Bank's response faster and more meaningful.

In the cases examined in detail in this book, the World Bank's organizational culture acted as a filter for the incorporation of new agendas. This pattern also helps make sense of the Bank's past evolution. The Bank has acted throughout its history to preserve the technical and apolitical norms that were necessary for its credibility when first founded. The persistence of these institutional norms means not only that some agendas have been incorporated more quickly and easily into Bank practice than others, but also that proponents of new agendas have been most successful when they have shaped them to fit the Bank's culture. A cursory look at the cases of poverty-based lending, adjustment lending, and the environment bears this out.

When first introduced, the poverty agenda posed a challenge to the Bank's organizational culture in that the Bank's economists resisted adopting what they considered the "softer" criteria necessary for lending in social sectors (Ascher 1983). McNamara overcame this resistance through two strategies. First, opposition was diluted by the addition of departments dedicated to new areas of lending and a rapid increase in loan volume. (The first major policy objective announced by McNamara was to double Bank lending within five years. He succeeded, but did not stop there; during his tenure, annual lending rose from just under $2 billion in 1969 to over $12 billion in 1981 (*Annual Reports* 1978, *1982*).) As staff members came to understand that they would be evaluated based on the number of loans concluded, they made loans in spite of discomfort with the new criteria. Second, the poverty alleviation agenda was shaped to accord with the Bank's culture: techniques were developed for measuring poverty loans quantitatively and lending was tailored to fit the project cycle. In part as a result, poverty-oriented loans did not necessarily go to the poorest segments of society; for example, larger farmers, not subsistence farmers, were the ones to benefit from the Bank's emphasis on rural development.[5] In short, what Barbara Crane and Jason Finkle (1981: 518) observed about population lending held true more generally: the task was shaped to fit the organization, instead of the organization being changed to fit the task.

Adjustment lending was incorporated more easily than poverty-based work into the Bank's activities, in large part because it fit well with the organizational culture. The neoliberal policy prescriptions underlying adjustment loans were closely in line with the values and beliefs of Bank staff, and the ability to move large amounts of money quickly served the institutional imperative of keeping lending levels high. Admittedly, adjustment loans required the Bank to intervene more deeply in the policy decisions of its borrowers in a way that could be interpreted as violating the Bank's apolitical norm. But the Bank paid careful attention to delineating those economic policy questions that were considered appropriate for its intervention, from the more political issues that were off limits.[6] In addition, the fact that most borrowers were desperate for financial flows of any sort during the debt crisis of the 1980s gave the Bank added leverage in expanding what it considered to be its legitimate sphere of influence.

Environmental considerations have come to occupy a central place in the Bank's activities in part because they can be addressed technically. Once the Bank had signed on to the environmental agenda, it was able to extend its traditional analytic approaches to this new area. The Bank has pushed accounting reform so that natural resources can be treated as economic assets. It has extended its work on the negative externalities of subsidies to the environmental field, showing, for example, how government-subsidized pesticides entail hidden costs. It has developed complex and innovative financial instruments, such as debt-for-nature swaps, that contribute to environmental preservation. In all these endeavors, the Bank's emphasis on development as a technical and apolitical process has been preserved.

There is no single explanation for the emergence of new agendas at the World Bank or their subsequent evolution. But the detailed investigation of three cases of change in the 1990s and a brief look at a few other important agendas underscore the persistence of the Bank's technical and apolitical identity. An understanding of the parameters imposed by this identity can be useful to those interested in tracking or furthering institutional change, whether from inside or outside the Bank.

Strategies for change

Lessons for the United States

The World Bank was created under strong US leadership in the years after World War II as part of a broader multilateral framework designed to secure a stable, liberal international economic order. From the beginning, US policymakers have been sensitive to charges that a commitment to multilateralism entails some sacrifice of US independence. This critique became especially pronounced when a Republican-majority Congress took office in 1995 amid claims that the national interest was being compromised by US participation in multilateral institutions. In recent years, Congress has taken aim at US foreign aid more generally, contending that it represents a misdirection of scarce financial resources.[7] In order to assess the value of membership in international organizations, policymakers need to have an accurate understanding of how and when these organizations respond to US preferences and what other factors might account for their policies.

The agendas studied here suggest that US efforts to impose its ideas unilaterally (as in the case of private sector development) require the expenditure of political capital, generate resentment among other member countries, and call into question the US commitment to multilateralism. (One observer decries the "ill-concealed proclivity to exercise unilateral control over the affairs of the institution at a time when the United States must depend increasingly on other donors to provide the financial support the bank needs" (Mistry 1989: 140)). In addition, growing US arrears in the contributions it has pledged to IDA and efforts to secure special benefits in exchange for these contributions are not without cost. For example, in the 1996 IDA replenishment negotiations, the United States opted to spend the first year of the three-year replenishment cycle paying its arrears to IDA without contributing any new resources. Much to the displeasure of the US business community, other members insisted that, as a result, US firms would not receive the benefits of any IDA procurement activity during the period in which the United States was making no new contributions.[8] This stance marked a new assertiveness by other member countries no longer willing to allow the United States to retain the prerogatives of leadership while failing to provide a matching level of resources. Future battles of this sort are to be expected unless the United States agrees either to commit the resources necessary to maintain its leadership or to accept a diminished role within the World Bank and other international organizations.

In deciding these issues, US policymakers should be aware that, throughout its history, the World Bank has acted broadly in line with US priorities and has represented an extremely cost-effective way for the United States to disseminate its values throughout the developing world. In the 1950s and 1960s, membership in the Bank served to integrate newly decolonized countries into the liberal economic order by facilitating trade and investment relations with the West. In the 1980s, the Bank helped maintain the stability of the international financial system by channelling funds to debtor countries and encouraging the neoliberal policy reforms favored by the US government. More recently, the World Bank has participated in US-led campaigns to inject capital into the struggling economies of newly democratic countries in Eastern Europe and the former Soviet Union; helped rebuild post-conflict economies in Haiti, Bosnia, and the West Bank and Gaza; and joined with the IMF in assisting a crisis-ridden Mexico following the 1994–5 peso crash and the faltering Asian tigers in 1997 and 1998. (One observer notes that "the approval culture was at its worst and most evident in the early years of Bank assistance to the former Soviet Union, when the objective was to maximize the transfer of resources or even – the more cynical say – the appearance of the transfer of resources."[9] This objective, of course, had been urged on the Bank by its largest member.)

US leverage over Bank policies is naturally more constrained than over its own bilateral aid programs, both because of the need to compromise with other member countries and because of the Bank's considerable institutional autonomy. But the World Bank represents an efficient mechanism through which the United States can facilitate the flow of capital to the developing world and exert influence over how it is used. The callable/paid-in capital structure of the Bank, which allows for a sizeable flow of funds with only small budgetary appropriations, has meant that over the years the United States has received excellent value for its investment.[10]

The relationship between the United States and the Bank has not been trouble-free but, on balance, the Bank has served US interests well and has done so at very little direct cost to the US taxpayer. Multilateral lending institutions represent especially useful tools for the United States at a time when it appears increasingly unwilling to commit the budgetary resources needed for an effective bilateral aid program. As the willingness of the United States to support the Bank financially declines, so will its leverage over the institution. But as the international consensus in favor of market-oriented economic policies, a leading role for the private sector, and environmentally sustainable development has deepened, there is less need than ever for the United States to act unilaterally in pursuit of these objectives. It would be a shame if the United States were to abandon its creation at a time when the World Bank's goals, and those of most of its members, are more closely aligned with US interests than ever before.

Effecting change

The analysis presented here yields four models of how new agendas have emerged at the Bank. Each suggests strategies for Bank leaders and outside advocates working to reshape the organization in line with their priorities. The factors contributing to the evolution of the World Bank in the 1990s have included:

- Changes in the international context, such as democratization, a growing consensus in favor of market-oriented policies, and stronger civil societies in developing countries.
- Shifts in the views of development experts about the necessary conditions for sustainable development, such as a growing emphasis on the policy environment, attention to the involvement of beneficiaries in project implementation, and regard for the political capacity of governments to implement reforms.
- The efforts of nongovernmental groups, including advocacy NGOs, service-delivery organizations, and grassroots organizations representing the poor in developing countries, to bring about changes in Bank policies and programs.
- The preferences of member countries of the Bank that have pursued new agendas either because of their own interests or because of pressure brought to bear by their citizens.
- The goals of World Bank leaders who bring to the institution their own ideas about its appropriate role.
- The priorities of staff members who are committed to certain approaches and practice them in their work.

The first two of these ingredients – shifts in the international context and development ideology – have facilitated institutional change by stimulating new thinking on the part of the Bank and others. The other four ingredients are the actors that have served as agents of change, alone or in concert. These factors have combined in a variety of ways, as suggested by the four simplified models that follow.

The top-down model

Top-down strategies are pursued largely within the institution and depend on the commitment and organizational prowess of individual leaders. This model of change is simpler than the others in that it does not involve a high degree of interaction between internal and external actors. While the tacit agreement of member countries with leadership goals is helpful, their active support is not needed.

When McNamara introduced a poverty focus into the World Bank's work in the 1970s, there was little pressure for him to do so either from within or outside the Bank. The poverty agenda clashed with the Bank's organizational culture and there was resistance to its incorporation. These barriers were overcome by a growth strategy whereby McNamara added new departments and new staff, and rapidly increased the pace of lending. McNamara was able to incorporate the poverty agenda into Bank activities by stressing its importance at a time when the Bank was expanding, by committing significant institutional resources to it, and by creating incentives for Bank staff to increase lending volume in these new areas of activity.

Leaders before and after McNamara have not had the luxury of pursuing their priorities within a similar growth environment. James Wolfensohn's campaign to reshape the Bank's culture is a case in point. Wolfensohn has articulated a challenging agenda for change: to make the Bank more results-oriented and responsive to its clients. He is the first Bank president to announce a shift in the Bank's culture as one of his chief priorities; however, he cannot pursue this goal by rapidly hiring new staff and diluting the Bank's existing culture. Instead, he faces the much more difficult task of reshaping the institution at a time when its lending flows, budget, and staff size are in decline. As a result, Wolfensohn has worked to reorient existing institutional resources by using his bully pulpit as president to stress the importance of cultural change, altering incentives for staff, and opening the Bank to outside influences through exchange programs and other mechanisms. He has also stressed partnership with other organizations, both as a matter of principle and as a pragmatic means of conserving Bank resources and limiting its scope. To achieve results, Wolfensohn has had to enlist the support of mid-level management and lower-level staff and work to build consensus. For this reason, consultative mechanisms, focus groups, and feedback have formed an important part of the process. But while the process of change under way at the Bank appears less autocratic and more consensual than in McNamara's day, there is no doubt that it is still change imposed from above.

Dissatisfaction with the Bank's performance by many of its members and others in the development community lends a certain urgency to Wolfensohn's change agenda. The president has said, for example, that the strategy of moving from an approval culture to a results culture is something the Bank needs to do institutionally in order to survive.[11] It is not yet clear whether this new agenda will be successful. Top-down efforts to reorient the Bank appear to be easiest in a growth environment, but with strong leadership and high stakes they may be successful even at a time of consolidation.

The bottom-up model

On several occasions, new agendas have emerged not from the Bank's leaders but from mid-level staff working in its operational areas. This has been the case for a variety of social issues that gained prominence in the 1990s, including participation, the role of women in development, and the implementation of Bank policies on resettlement and the rights of indigenous people. In all these cases, the on-the-ground experience of individual staff members contributed to a recognition of the importance of these issues to the success of their work. These staff members forged networks among themselves and created alliances with outside groups that supported the same agendas.

The case study of participation included here, as well as recent studies of resettlement policy (Cernea 1995, Fox 1998), gender (Murphy 1995), and sociological issues more generally (Kardam 1993), suggests the importance of interaction between internal advocates and external supporters. Advocates of participation, who practiced it in their own work, joined forces with interested member countries to develop an institutional forum for discussion of participation. The Bank's resettlement and indigenous people policies, crafted by in-house sociologists and anthropologists in the early 1980s, went largely unimplemented until internal advocates and external supporters put greater pressure on the Bank for compliance. Jonathan Fox (1998) finds that, in the case of resettlement, the existence of strong external support changed the incentive structure within the Bank, giving internal advocates greater leverage over the rest of the Bank's apparatus. Nüket Kardam (1990, 1991) shows how internal policy advocates worked to put women in development issues on the Bank's agenda, while Josette Murphy (1995) identifies a series of United Nations conferences in the 1970s and 1980s and attention to women in development at bilateral agencies as having a major effect on the early emergence of gender issues at the Bank.

In all these cases, the creation of alliances between internal advocates and external supporters brought new agendas to the attention of senior management and facilitated their incorporation within the Bank. External support and the formation of alliances appears to have been essential to the success of these bottom-up efforts. In addition, the ability to cast new issues in such a way that they fit with the Bank's institutional norms made these changes more palatable to the organization as a whole.

The outside-in model

Some important new agendas were first formulated by actors outside the Bank. Like the bottom-up model outlined above, change introduced from the outside relies heavily on the interaction of internal and external factors. The goal of incorporating environmental considerations into Bank lending was raised initially by representatives of Northern NGOs, who brought pressure on the Bank in a variety of ways: through grassroots campaigns, by enlisting the support of influential member countries, and by forming alliances with internal supporters. The private sector development agenda originated with the Bank's largest member country, the United States, which used direct financial leverage to force a Bank response.

While these agendas were pushed from outside the organization, they were facilitated by changes in the international context and by the existence of supporters within the Bank. The United States made far greater gains in its pursuit of a private sector development agenda once the Bank had become convinced that it was behind the curve relative to its member countries and the actions of other lending institutions. Similarly, proponents of strong environmental policies were able to team up with individuals inside the

Bank who were concerned about the environmental consequences of Bank lending. In both the private sector development and environment cases, change might have occurred eventually in the absence of external pressure, but it would have taken longer and the resulting policies would not have been as forceful.

Outside-in strategies, of course, do not always succeed. The case of human rights suggests that NGO advocacy alone is not sufficient to bring a new agenda to the attention of the Bank, even within a facilitating international context. The absence of member country allies or strong internal supporters for a human rights agenda at the Bank has meant that it has made little progress, even at a time when human rights concerns are becoming integrated into the aid programs of other agencies.

The inside-out model

A final model reverses the outside-in approach outlined above. In the cases of adjustment lending and governance the impetus for the new agenda originated within the Bank largely as a result of its own institutional learning.

The Bank came up with the idea of policy-based adjustment lending in the late 1970s out of dissatisfaction with the performance of its loans. Several years later, in the context of the debt crisis, the United States seized on the adjustment lending program as a way of channeling new capital to debtor countries while tying these financial flows to neoliberal policy reform. The congruence between the Bank's own institutional needs (to play a central role in addressing the debt crisis) and US priorities (for preservation of the stability of the international financial system) led to a rapid expansion in the levels of adjustment lending and the deep incorporation of these activities across the Bank.

The governance agenda, too, resulted from growing frustration with the results of Bank lending. In this case, the impetus for change that arose internally was facilitated by important shifts in the international environment, such as the spread of democracy and the activities of other lenders. The Bank's governance agenda was also furthered by greater openness from borrower countries who were increasingly willing to accept the Bank's attention to institutional and political issues.

The models presented above suggest strategies for Bank leaders, member countries, and NGOs that seek changes in the Bank's mission or activities. Three broad lessons emerge:

- *The importance of alliances.* Change has occurred most readily when several different actors have shared the same goal. When NGOs or member countries pushed a new agenda from the outside, it helped greatly to find internal supporters who could at the same time pursue it from within. Conversely, when internal advocates introduced new agendas, they were most effective when they could enlist the support of external actors. The formation of alliances appears to be critical to the success of efforts to introduce new agendas at the Bank.

- *Congruence with broader trends.* Changes in the international environment or shifts in development ideology acted as important contextual factors in fostering institutional evolution. The Bank has shown that it is more likely to move when other development institutions are going in the same direction or when there is a sense internally that the Bank is out of step with changes in the international environment. While those seeking to bring about change at the Bank cannot manufacture developments at the international level, they can choose their battles, focusing on those goals that are congruent with international trends and for which broad public and governmental support exists.
- *Fit with organizational culture.* New agendas appear to be incorporated most deeply when they fit with – or can be made to fit with – the Bank's organizational culture. Adjustment lending, private sector development, and environmental concerns have been incorporated at the Bank in large part because they have been approached technically and without violating the Bank's apolitical norm. The poverty agenda posed a challenge to the Bank's technical orientation and the norms of its professionals and thus required the allocation of significant institutional resources to make it a priority across the Bank. Participation challenges the Bank's expert culture, but its supporters have framed the issue in narrow terms and tied it to the achievement of the broader goal of enhancing the effectiveness of Bank programs. Governance comes close to violating the apolitical provisions of the Bank's charter and is difficult to cast in narrow terms; its limited integration into Bank activities is related to these factors. In seeking institutional change, advocates will be most successful if their goals can be presented as providing an answer to institutional needs and fitting comfortably with the Bank's technical and apolitical identity.

The prospects for organizational transformation

Writing about the organizational impediments to the emergence of a strong population program at the Bank in the 1960s, Crane and Finkle concluded that:

> Bank officials have been slow to recognize the extent to which its organizational commitments represent obstacles to the Bank's development goals, particularly in the social sectors; they have been even more reluctant to try to alter these commitments in order to improve the Bank's performance . . . In effect, they continue to fit the task to the organization rather than the organization to the task.
>
> (Crane and Finkle 1981: 518)

This characterization holds true for the agendas discussed in this study. While the Bank has taken on new tasks, its fundamental organizational culture has not changed. The technical and apolitical norms that govern the Bank's approach to development and permeate the values and beliefs of its staff have remained in place even as the scope of Bank activities has widened. The coming decade, however, is likely to bring increased pressure on the Bank for change that does challenge central elements of its organizational culture. Two examples come to mind.

The first is President Wolfensohn's effort to change how the Bank operates. The main goals of this agenda are to deemphasize the volume of lending and stress the results of Bank programs; to become less inward-looking and more responsive to Bank clients; to work more closely in partnership with other organizations; and to inject an element of competition into the Bank's entrenched, bureaucratic internal workings.[12] Wolfensohn's agenda is driven mainly by growing questions about the Bank's effectiveness, declining support from the United States (which has led other member countries to consider whether alternative institutions, such as the EBRD, might more effectively serve their goals), and reduced opportunities for lending as global capital flows rise. Bank management recognizes that the institution simply must become more results-oriented if it is to retain the support of its members. Wolfensohn's approach goes beyond organizational restructuring (although there is plenty of that under way) to include strategies such as opening the Bank to outside influences and altering the incentive structure for staff. It is not clear yet whether these strategies will succeed in reorienting the Bank's internal culture, but they suggest that the president understands the difficulty of reshaping an institution that is characterized by such a strong and well-entrenched organizational culture.

The second example of a new agenda that challenges the Bank's identity is the growing number of calls for it to recognize the centrality of social issues in its work. Over the years, the number of social, as opposed to economic, issues on the Bank's agenda has proliferated. The range of social concerns addressed by the Bank includes poverty reduction, gender, indigenous people, resettlement, participation, and governance.[13] In the past, these issues have usually been treated as "add-ons" to Bank projects that are concerned chiefly with economic impact and financial rate of return. (One NGO advocate calls this the "Christmas tree model," where Bank loans are given "an ornamental poverty component, a gender bauble, and a participation star on top.")[14] In an effort to combat this fragmentation and overcome the lack of connection between social issues and the Bank's core mission of poverty reduction and sustainable development, advocates within and outside the Bank have attempted to raise the profile of social issues. One outcome of their efforts was the establishment of an internal Social Development Task Group, which issued its report late in 1996.

The modest measures called for in the report of the task group disappointed many involved in the effort.[15] The true incorporation of a social development agenda would require a shift in the nature of Bank hiring, training, and socialization so that its technical norms give way to more encompassing notions of development. The current social development efforts under way at the Bank fall short of this transformation, but future initiatives are to be expected. Many of the ingredients mentioned above are in place. The broader development community has recognized the centrality of social issues to sustainable development. The Bank's own experience – particularly the failure of many of its projects to ameliorate social conditions and the negative social consequences of some of its loans – suggests the importance of considering social issues more closely in its work. And both internal and external advocates are involved in seeking the implementation of a stronger social development agenda at the Bank. Yet the changes they seek challenge one of the key tenets of the Bank's organizational culture: its technical orientation.

Will the World Bank be able to reorient its existing identity to accommodate a set of concerns that the Bank itself deems central to the success of its mission? Or will the technical norms that have characterized the Bank since it was founded remain in place, even if they are no longer necessary to (and, in fact, may hinder) the Bank's accomplishment of its goals? The persistence of the Bank's institutional identity through the 1990s, at a time when the conditions that gave rise to it had long since disappeared, suggests that this identity, if not immutable, is at least extremely robust. Bank staff and managers have made great efforts to adapt their work to the needs of a changing world, but throughout they have been guided by values acquired by the Bank more than fifty years ago. As the Bank faces the challenge of development in the twenty-first century, it must also confront the challenge of organizational transformation. The world is moving faster than the Bank. The new agendas introduced in the 1990s represent the organization's best efforts to respond to the momentous changes under way. The Bank's impact has been limited, however, by its institutional identity and organizational culture. Unless members, staff, and management can agree that it is time to move beyond the technical and apolitical norms that have characterized the World Bank since birth, it will find it difficult to keep pace. Consigned to the role of chasing a changing world, the World Bank will become increasingly less relevant and the opportunity for exercising far-sighted and energetic leadership in the field of development will have been lost.

Notes

1 Introduction

1 The World Bank consists of the International Bank for Reconstruction and Development (IBRD), which makes loans at market rates to developing member countries, and the International Development Association (IDA), which provides loans on concessional terms to the poorest of these countries. The two World Bank affiliates responsible for interacting directly with the private sector are the International Finance Corporation (IFC) and the Multilateral Investment Guarantee Agency (MIGA). Together, the World Bank, the IFC, and the MIGA are known as the World Bank Group.

2 In the course of this study, I carried out more than sixty interviews with current or former World Bank staff members, US government officials, representatives of NGOs, and other observers of the Bank. Interviews were conducted between June 1995 and January 1997, with follow-up phone conversations and correspondence through July 1998. The departmental affiliations of those who contributed comments for attribution were current at the time of the interview and, unless noted otherwise, refer to the World Bank.

3 This is a conclusion supported by personal experience. In the mid-1980s, I was responsible for analyzing the investment quality of World Bank bonds for Salomon Brothers. Although I had a high degree of access because of my employer's role as one of the Bank's chief underwriters, information was parceled out "as needed," interviews were hard to come by, and any criticism – even of the most muted kind – was met by anger and paranoia. The climate for research has changed markedly; most staff members now meet outside attention to their work with less resistance and occasionally with enthusiasm (although this spirit of cooperation does not extend across the institution).

4 Two recent works offer a broader view. Catherine Caufield's *Masters of Illusion* (1996) provides a critical, well-documented history of the World Bank. *The World Bank: Its first half century* (1997), edited by Devesh Kapur, John P. Lewis, and Richard Webb, provides a comprehensive thematic history of the Bank, as Edward Mason and Robert Asher did in their 1973 study of the Bank's first twenty-five years.

5 Exceptions are Paul Nelson's insightful analysis of the World Bank–NGO relationship (1995), and Jonathan Fox and L. David Brown's edited volume on the World Bank and grassroots movements (1998).

2 Understanding the World Bank: a theoretical overview

1 The custom of appointing an American to the presidency, in place since the World Bank's earliest days, was based less on the position of the United States as the Bank's largest shareholder than on the importance of securing access for the Bank to US capital markets (Kraske 1996: 5).

2 The "50 Years is Enough" campaign coordinated the efforts of more than three hundred environmental, poverty, and development NGOs to bring public attention to what they considered the negative consequences of World Bank and IMF lending. The campaign reached its high point in 1994, the fiftieth anniversary of these institutions' establishment. Its steering committee included representatives of the Development Gap, the Environmental Defense Fund, Friends of the Earth, US Global Exchange, International Rivers Network, Oxfam America, Center for Democratic Education, and Greenpeace USA. For a statement of its platform, see the International Rivers Network's *BankCheck Quarterly*, No. 8, June 1994.

3 Between 1961 and 1964, the Bank added thirty-four new members, amounting to a 50 per cent increase in its membership (Mason and Asher 1973: 799, Table B-2). Bank membership expanded by 20 per cent between 1990 and 1996, after growing by only 12 per cent during the entire previous decade (*Annual Reports* 1980–96). Most newcomers in this period were from the former Soviet bloc.

4 The World Bank and IMF were both established in 1944 at the Bretton Woods conference. The regional development banks for Latin America (established in 1959), Africa (1963), Asia (1966), and Europe (1990), resemble the World Bank in that they have members from within and outside the region they serve. The regional "club" institutions, like the European Investment Bank (1958), are made up of only regional members.

5 The term "stakeholder" is used frequently by the Bank, which defines the stakeholders in its projects as "those affected by the outcome, negatively or positively, or those who can affect the outcome of a proposed intervention." This definition encompasses the borrowing country itself; the people, communities, or organizations expected to benefit from Bank projects or programs; other groups that may be indirectly or adversely affected by Bank policies or investments, such as the poor and landless, women and children, indigenous people, and minority groups; and others with a vested interest in development, including donors, NGOs, religious and community organizations, local authorities, and private sector firms. See "Social Assessment," Environment Department Dissemination Note No. 36, The World Bank, September 1995.

6 Pivotal work along these lines includes Meyer and Rowan (1977), Zucker (1977), and DiMaggio and Powell (1983). For a discussion of the differences between the new and old sociological institution, see introduction to Powell and DiMaggio (1991: 11–15).

7 David Baldwin (1965) identifies three respects in which the World Bank is political: staff unavoidably take political considerations into account in its lending, despite the formal ban on doing so; Bank activities have political effects in that they alter the distribution of influence within and among international actors; and the Bank acts politically when it attempts to get governments in borrower countries to do things they would not do otherwise. Lars Schoultz (1982), analyzing the change in US behavior toward the multilateral development banks in the 1970s, argues that the World Bank's "separation of

economics and politics was never achieved or even approximated," but that the "fiction of separation was possible" because the United States expressed its political preferences silently and effectively. In light of declining US power within the Bank and increased activism in Congress on issues like human rights, that fiction broke down altogether (Schoultz 1982: 539). More recently, Bartram Brown (1992) has shown how the United States uses its voting power in the World Bank to serve political purposes determined unilaterally by Congress.

8 In this respect the World Bank's staff resembles that of the United Nations and its affiliate institutions. There is an important distinction, however, between the World Bank and IMF on the one hand and the United Nations on the other. In recruiting its staff, the Bank and Fund are not limited by geographical quotas, as are the UN agencies. The language governing recruitment at both the Bank and the Fund calls for giving "due regard to the importance of recruiting personnel on as wide a geographical basis as possible," but "subject to the paramount importance of securing the highest standards of efficiency and of technical competence." (Mason and Asher 1973: 31)

9 Credit ratings are awarded by independent agencies, the two most important of which are Moody's Investors Service and Standard & Poor's. These ratings are used by underwriters and investors as indicators of the credit safety of a given bond issuer.

10 Even with these provisions to ensure the repayment of World Bank loans, a portion of its lending portfolio is in non-accrual status, that is, not being serviced in a timely fashion. At the end of fiscal 1997, loans to six countries, amounting to 2.2 per cent of the IBRD's portfolio, were in non-accrual status (*Annual Report* 1997: 135). The Bank has an obvious interest in minimizing its late payments problems in the eyes of member countries and bondholders. In part because of this, it has never declared a borrowing country in default even when loans have remained in non-accrual for many years.

11 There was concern among investors when IDA was established that it would weaken the Bank's credit standing because it lent at lower-than-market rates for projects that were not commercially viable. In response, the Bank agreed to keep IDA and IBRD accounts separate. (The separation is something of a fiction, since both lending programs are run by the same institution.) The IBRD is allowed to make transfers to IDA only out of its net income for the current year. (See Mason and Asher 1973: 121.)

12 Author's interview with representative of the Young Professionals program, June 1996.

13 Author's interview with member of the Private Sector Development division, June 1996.

14 World Bank, "Employment Information" bulletin, March 1995

15 Author's interview with Eveline Herfkens, Executive Director from the Netherlands, October 24, 1995.

16 For more on the role of social scientists at the Bank, see Michael Cernea (1996) and (1993). For the impact on the Bank's resettlement policies in particular, see Fox (1998).

17 The task group is discussed in more detail in Chapter 6. Its draft report, "Social Development and Results on the Ground" (October 15, 1996), called for, among other things, "stepped up efforts to recruit and retain high-caliber social specialists" (p. 26).

18 Details drawn from transcripts of meetings of President Wolfensohn with senior managers, December 1995 through September 1996.

3 Approaching business: the private sector development agenda

1 See, for example, Bandow and Vásquez, eds (1994) and Paul Craig Roberts, "Development Banks: An idea whose time has gone," *Business Week*, July 11, 1994. For earlier assessments of the Bank by conservative critics see, for example, Phaup (1984) and Representative Jerry Lewis, "The Trouble with the World Bank," *Wall Street Journal*, September 18, 1981, p. 30.

2 This was the premise of the "50 Years is Enough" coalition formed during the fiftieth anniversary celebration of the Bretton Woods institutions in 1994.

3 A sovereign guarantee was not considered sufficient to secure the trust of investors. Many other precautions were built into the IBRD's charter, such as limiting Bank support only to the foreign exchange portion of specific projects. Ultimately, it was the capital backing of the institution by its wealthy members, the United States in particular, that gave investors confidence in the Bank.

4 For details on early Bank lending to national development banks and finance companies, see Mason and Asher (1973: 359–65).

5 The most comprehensive study of the World Bank's policy-based adjustment lending is found in Mosley et al. (1991).

6 Article 11, Section 3 of the EBRD's Agreement stipulates that not more than 40 per cent of its total committed loans, guarantees, and equity investments shall be allocated to the state sector (Shihata 1995: 46).

7 For details on the private sector-related activities of the regional development banks, see Sherk (1994) and Haralz (1992).

8 See Ibrahim Shihata (1995: 45, n. 44); and Inter-American Development Bank, *Annual Report* 1994: 34. Non-guaranteed lending was called for initially by a high-level group appointed to examine the IDB's relationship to the private sector. Although this group suggested a limit of 5-10 per cent of total annual lending, the Bank settled on a 5 per cent ceiling to ensure that its top credit rating was preserved. The non-guaranteed financing facility is available only for large infrastructure and public utility projects providing services generally performed by the public sector. IDB participation may not exceed 25 per cent of each project's total costs, or $75 million, whichever is less. For details, see Tussie (1995: 143).

9 For details, see Stallings (1992).

10 Author's interview with E. Patrick Coady, former US Executive Director, May 14, 1996.

11 Author's interview with Ernie Stern, former Executive Vice President, May 17, 1996.

12 Author's interview with Eveline Herfkens, October 24, 1995.

13 Author's interview with E. Patrick Coady, May 14, 1996.

14 Examples in this section are drawn from the World Bank's *Annual Reports*, 1995–97.

15 For details on the Bank's guarantee program, see "Mainstreaming of Guarantees as an Operational Tool of the World Bank," R94–145, July 14, 1995, discussed by the World Bank board on September 8, 1994; *Annual Report 1995*: 30–1; George Graham, "World Bank Backing for Investors," *Financial Times*, September 13, 1994; Andrew Taylor, "Why World Bank is Shifting Policy," *Financial Times*, October 6, 1994; and Shihata 1995: 758–9.

16 Andrew H. W. Stone, "Private Sector Assessments: Best practice and pitfalls," Private Sector Development Note No. 1, undated brochure; author's interview with Andrew Stone, June 10, 1996.
17 Author's interview with Andrew Stone, PSD, June 10, 1996; Wolfensohn (1996).
18 See Mosley *et al.* (1991: Chapter 3) on the informal bargaining entailed in the negotiation of an adjustment loan.
19 Electronic mail correspondence from Amanda Blakeley, Office of the Vice President, Finance and Private Sector Development, July 10, 1998.
20 Author's interview with Alexander Shakow, Development Committee of the World Bank, May 14, 1996.
21 For a review, see Kapur *et al.* (1997: Chapter 10).
22 The categories reported by the Bank in its "Trends in IBRD and IDA Lending" table havee changed over time. For 1988–93, Figure 3.1 includes loans to development finance companies, the energy sector, industry, and telecommunications. For 1994–7, it includes loans to the energy sector, finance, industry, mining, and telecommunication.
23 Example provided by IFC staff member in interview with the author, January 1997.
24 Figures in this section for the World Bank and the IFC come from the agencies' annual reports.
25 Figures in this paragraph come from the World Bank *Annual Report* 1996: 11; IFC *Annual Report* 1997: 1; and Richard W. Stevenson, "The Chief Banker for the Nations at the Bottom of the Heap," *New York Times*, September 14, 1997.
26 For details, see "IFC Announces Initiative to Reach New Markets: Effort Aimed at Boosting Private Sector in Challenging Economics," IFC Press Release No. 97/27, October 1, 1996; and IFC *Annual Report* 1997: 11. Also, author's interview with Mark Constantine, Corporate Relations Unit, IFC, October 7, 1996.
27 See Paul Lewis, "A New World Bank: consultant to Third World investor," *New York Times*, April 27, 1994.

4 Approaching civil society: the participation agenda

1 On the need for the Bank to modify its project cycle along these lines, see Picciotto and Weaving (1994) and Picciotto (1995).
2 NGOs are defined by the Bank as "non-profit groups whose primary stated goals are to organize in order to use their cooperative influence to better public welfare, health, the environment and/or other social or cultural objectives," including organizations that act at the local, national, or international level (Shihata 1995: 237, n. 2). There are many different types of development NGOs, ranging from large international organizations like CARE or OXFAM to small grassroots organizations of farmers or women entrepreneurs. For typologies of NGOs, see Nelson (1995) and Malena (1995).
3 Information about Bank projects in this section comes from Caufield (1996) and Rich (1994). For a detailed analysis of the evolution of the environmental agenda at the World Bank, see Wade (1997).
4 Author's interviews with David Grey, Africa Region, January 10, 1997; Ngozi Okonjo-Iweala, Institutional Change and Strategy Department, January 10, 1997; and Larry Salmen, Environment Department, January 14, 1997. On rural development, see Cernea (1991); the first edition of this volume was published

in 1985 and is one of the Bank's earliest efforts to encourage development practitioners to think about the needs of project beneficiaries.

5 Author's interview with Charlotte Jones-Carroll, Africa Region, January 10, 1997.

6 Quoted in Bread for the World Institute, *News and Notices for World Bank Watchers No. 19*, December 1997, p. 20.

7 For an analysis of how the 1993–4 resettlement review came about and its impact, see Fox (1998).

8 On these transnational networks, see Nelson (1996) and Fox and Brown, eds (1998). On issue networks more generally, see Keck and Sikkink (1998).

9 For an introduction to this literature, see Paul (1991) and Clark (1994).

10 Author's interview with Josette Murphy, Operations Evaluation Department, January 14, 1997.

11 For background on the learning group, see Bhatnagar and Williams, eds (1992), which contains the papers prepared for the group's 1992 workshop; the report of the group (World Bank 1994c); and Rietbergen-McCracken, ed. (1996), which summarizes some of the studies prepared over the course of the learning group.

12 For an early NGO assessment of the Bank's new disclosure policy, see Chamberlain and Hall (1995).

13 For details, see *The Inspection Panel: Operating Procedures, The World Bank*, August 1994; *The Inspection Panel: Report, August 1, 1994 to July 31, 1996*, The World Bank, July 31, 1996; and Shihata, "The Resolution Establishing the World Bank Inspection Panel: its drafting history and interpretation," in Shihata (1995). For an update on the activities of the Inspection Panel, see its Web site: <http://www.worldbank.org/html/ins-panel/

14 On the Inspection Panel's treatment of the Arun case, see "World Bank Cancels Arun III: alternatives to be considered," *BankCheck Quarterly*, no. 12, September 1995.

15 The Bank's Operations Evaluation Department (OED) has begun a project designed to evaluate participation in Bank operations, scheduled to be completed in 1999. While it is part of the Bank, OED is overseen by a director general who reports directly to the Bank's executive directors; the group is thus able to fulfill an independent evaluation function. The Bank–NGO Committee has also undertaken its own evaluation of the subject.

16 Data in this section come from the Bank's annual progress reports on cooperation between the World Bank and NGOs, 1990–97, available from the NGO Unit of the Social Development Department.

17 Bread for the World Institute, *News and Notices for World Bank Watchers No. 19*, December 1997.

18 Author's interview with former NGO staff member, June 10, 1996.

19 Author's interview with former core group member of Learning Group on Participatory Development, January 1997.

20 Quoted in Robert Chote, "World Bank management criticised," *Financial Times*, November 1, 1996.

21 The Bank's return to an anti-poverty mission was signaled by the 1990 *World Development Report*, which had poverty as its sole focus. Fighting poverty became official policy when Operational Directive 4.15 was promulgated in December 1991. It reads: "Sustainable poverty reduction is the Bank's overarching objective." (Kapur *et al.* 1997: 51)

22 Author's interview with John Clark, NGO/Participation Unit, January 13, 1997.

23 James D. Wolfensohn, "The World Bank and the Evolving Challenges of

Development," speech given at an Overseas Development Council Congressional Staff Forum, Washington, DC, May 16, 1997.

24 Author's interview with Frances Seymour, World Wildlife Fund, January 8, 1997.

25 Author's interview with Michael Cernea, World Bank sociology adviser (retired), January 19, 1997.

5 Approaching politics: the governance agenda

1 While the communist countries of the Eastern bloc, with the exception of Yugoslavia, were not members of the World Bank and received no loans from it, the Bank did lend to developing countries allied with the Soviet Union and to non-aligned countries with socialist regimes. Since 1990, all the former members of the Eastern bloc as well as the countries that emerged from the break-up of the Soviet Union have joined the Bank.

2 Raymond Bonner, "The Worldly Business of Bribes: Quiet battle is joined," *New York Times*, July 8, 1996. See also "Who will listen to Mr. Clean?" *Economist*, August 2, 1997.

3 Letter from Ibrahim Shihata, General Counsel, to the author, June 4, 1998.

4 For details, see Graham Hutchings, "China Worried at Economic Cost of Crushing Dissent," *Daily Telegraph*, June 20, 1989.

5 Quoted in John M. Goshko, "U.S. Censures Nigeria's Execution of Nine Activists," *Washington Post*, November 11, 1995.

6 For broad treatments of the connection between economic and political reform, see Haggard and Kaufman (1992) and Nelson *et al.* (1994). On the need for institutional reform to consolidate and deepen economic reforms, see Moisés Naim, "Latin America: The Second Stage of Reform," *Journal of Democracy*, Special Issue on Economic Reform and Democracy, October 1994. Naim is a former executive director of the World Bank from Venezuela who later served as an adviser to President Wolfensohn.

7 The Bank, in its 1991 *World Development Report*, had concluded that the evidence is mixed about whether authoritarian governments are better than democracies at overseeing economic reform. See also Jose María Maravall, "The Myth of the Authoritarian Advantage," in *Journal of Democracy*, Special Issue on Economic Reform and Democracy, October 1994; and Marc Lindenberg and Shantayanan Devarajan, "Prescribing Strong Economic Medicine: Revisiting the myth about structural adjustment, democracy, and economic performance in developing countries," *Comparative Politics*, January 1993.

8 See, for example, Hunter (1996) and Lawyers Committee for Human Rights (1995).

9 Bank officials draw the distinction between economic/social human rights, which the Bank promotes by furthering development, and political/civil human rights, which it maintains are off limits due to its charter. Human rights advocates contend that these rights are inseparable and that the Bank's distinction is a false one. On the rationale behind the Bank's unwillingness to take political/civil human rights into account in its lending, see speeches by the Bank's general counsel, Ibrahim F. I. Shihata, on "Human Rights, Development, and International Financial Institutions" and "The World Bank and Human Rights," reprinted in Shihata (1995). For critical views of the Bank's stance, see Lawyers Committee for Human Rights (1995) and Sullivan (1995).

10 The new team was headed by Pierre Landell-Mills, who was the primary author

of the revised report. The high quality of the writing in the revised version added to the impact of its findings.

11 See Lancaster (1993) and Kapur *et al.* (1997: 761), as well as Michael Holman and Michela Wrong, "Donors Run Rule over Kenyan Aid," *Financial Times*, July 24, 1995.

12 See "Issues of 'Governance' in Borrowing Members – The extent of their relevance under the Bank's Articles of Agreement," Legal Memorandum of the General Counsel, December 21, 1990 (Sec.M91-131, February 5, 1991). A slightly modified version was published as "The World Bank and 'governance' issues in its borrowing members," Chapter 2 in Shihata (1991).

13 See "Partnership for Capacity Building in Africa: Strategy and program of action," draft report, 1996.

14 Author's interview with Carol Lancaster, Institute for International Economics, June 10, 1996.

15 An overview of legal reform activities and issues, along with a list of Bank projects involving legal technical assistance components, can be found in "The World Bank and Legal Technical Assistance: Initial Lessons," Policy Research Working Paper 1414, Legal Department, January 1995.

16 Extensive details of a showcase legal reform project in Russia, to which the Bank has agreed to commit $58 million, are provided in "Technical Annex to the Memorandum of the President, Russian Federation, Legal Reform Project," Report No. T-6883-RU, Europe and Central Asia Region, May 21, 1996.

17 Letter from Michael Stevens, principal public sector management specialist, to the author, March 20, 1998.

18 Letter from Salvatore Schiavo-Campo to the author, April 24, 1998. Schiavo-Campo is currently Senior Adviser for Public Sector Management and Reform at the Asian Development Bank. While at the World Bank, he was Manager of the Public Sector Group for Europe, former USSR, Middle East and North Africa.

19 See Paul Lewis, "I.M.F. Seeks Argentine Deal Linking Credit to Governing," *New York Times*, July 15, 1997; and "New Yardsticks for Global Banks," *New York Times*, July 28, 1997.

20 Author's interview with Michael Stevens, Operations Policy Department, December 4, 1995; letter to the author, March 20, 1998.

21 Letter from Salvatore Schiavo-Campo, Senior Adviser for Public Sector Management and Reform, Asian Development Bank, to the author, April 24, 1998.

22 This interchange is reported in Chamberlain (1996).

23 Cited in Shihata (1995b: 26, notes 40, 41).

24 See Shihata (1995b); also author's interview with Ibrahim Shihata, December 5, 1995.

25 Author's interview with Carol Lancaster, June 10, 1996.

26 Author's interview with C. Mark Blackden, Africa Region, May 13, 1996.

6 Effecting change: the challenge of organizational transformation

1 Only Article I of the eleven articles in the IBRD's charter is devoted to a discussion of the organization's purpose.

2 For details on the poverty alleviation strategy pursued under McNamara, see Ayres (1983). For a discussion of how the World Bank's attention to poverty changed the broader understanding of development, see Finnemore (1996), Chapter 4.

3 This conclusion is in line with the findings of the most detailed study of

adjustment lending to date (Mosley *et al.* 1991). The authors argue that the emphasis on non-project lending tied to policy change was due to internal pressures, including dissatisfaction with project lending as an instrument for policy reform and McNamara's doubts about the effectiveness of past Bank strategy. For a history of the Bank's move to policy adjustment lending, see Kapur *et al.* (1997), Chapters 9 and 10.

4 Rich (1994) and Caufield (1996) tell the story of NGO advocacy toward the World Bank on the environment. Wade (1997) recounts the institutional history of the Bank's approach to the environment.

5 See Caufield (1996), Chapter 7, for details on this and other ways in which the Bank's lending under McNamara bypassed the very poor.

6 Of course, members of the NGO community and representatives of some member countries argue that economic decisions about how to allocate budgetary resources or the balance between public and private spheres in the economy are inherently political, whatever the Bank claims.

7 See, for example, Steven Greenhouse, "Republicans Plan to Guide Foreign Policy by Purse Strings," *New York Times*, November 13, 1994; and David Rogers, "House Subcommittee Clears Sharp Cuts in Funding for Foreign Development," *Wall Street Journal*, June 9, 1995.

8 See Paul Blustein, "$11 Billion Pledged to World Bank for Poor Nations as U.S. Debates Share," *Washington Post*, March 20, 1996.

9 Private e-mail correspondence from former staff member to author.

10 One argument for the benefits of US participation in the multilateral development banks concerns the money that goes to US corporations as part of procurement by these institutions. The US Congressional Research Service has estimated that through 1995, US firms received a cumulative $20.12 billion in IBRD procurement disbursements, while the amount of US capital paid in to the IBRD was $1.96 billion. The ratios are reversed for IDA, where through 1995 US firms had received $3.81 billion in IDA procurement disbursements, compared to US government contributions of $21.83 billion. (Figures from Sanford 1996: 12–13.) The fact that every dollar contributed by the United States to the World Bank has been matched by money received by US firms for goods and services provided in relation to World Bank loans is a powerful claim to US support.

11 From transcript of President Wolfensohn's meeting with senior managers, January 30, 1996, Washington, DC.

12 Some see this as an effort to reshape the Bank along the lines of a private corporation. There are several problems with this conception, one of the most difficult of which is how to measure performance. Because the Bank's success is determined not by a financial "bottom line" (such as profits or rate of return) but by the more amorphous goal of development impact, it is extremely difficult to assess staff performance. On the president's agenda, see "Mr. Wolfensohn's New Clients," *Economist*, April 20, 1996.

13 Task Group Report, "Social Development and Results on the Ground," October 15, 1996, pp. 5–8. The Bank's list of social issues offered here also includes Country Assistance Strategies, which are supposed to address poverty concerns; social assessments carried out in some countries; social capital; civil society; and Bank involvement in post-conflict resolution. This list includes widely disparate types of activity, reflecting the Bank's tendency to group together every-

thing that falls outside the mainstream of its activity. Whether this contributes to the greater integration or continued marginalization of these concerns is up for question.

14 Frances Seymour of the World Wildlife Fund, in Opening Remarks at ESD Associated Event on Mainstreaming Biodiversity for Rural Well-Being, September 24, 1996, p. 3.

15 The report's most tangible recommendations include a call for the development of a sourcebook on social assessment; the preparation of two or three Country Assistance Strategies in each region that provide a full treatment of social issues; additional training for Bank staff; a new funding mechanism to support pilot social development activities; and the establishment of a multidisciplinary Social Learning Group to follow up on the task group's recommendations. It calls for these initiatives to be undertaken in a "budget-neutral" manner. (World Bank 1996c: iii-iv.) NGO critics believe that these recommendations fall short, citing among other things the absence of targets by which progress will be measured, a lack of attention to incentives for Bank staff and managers, and the unwillingness to spend any net new funds on the task group's program. (Bread for the World Institute, *News & Notices for World Bank Watchers No. 15*, November 1996, pp. 31–2.)

Bibliography

Books, Articles, and Reports

Alexander, Nancy C. 1998. "The World Bank's New Strategic Alliances." Draft paper, Development Bank Watchers' Project. Silver Spring Md.: Bread for the World Institute.

Annis, Sheldon. 1986. "The Shifting Grounds of Poverty Lending at the World Bank." In Feinberg *et al.*, *Between Two Worlds*.

Ascher, William. 1983. "New Development Approaches and the Adaptability of International Agencies: The case of the World Bank," *International Organization* vol. 37 no. 3, Summer.

Ayres, Robert L. 1983. *Banking on the Poor: The World Bank and world poverty*. Cambridge, Mass.: The MIT Press for the Overseas Development Council.

Baldwin, David A. 1965. "The International Bank in Political Perspective," *World Politics* vol. 18 no. 1, October.

—— ed. 1993. *Neorealism and Neoliberalism: The contemporary debate*. New York: Columbia University Press.

Bandow, Doug and Ian Vasquez. 1994. *Perpetuating Poverty: The World Bank, the IMF and the developing world*. Washington DC: Cato Institute.

Berg, Robert J. and David F. Gordon, eds 1989. *Cooperation for International Development: The United States and the Third World in the 1990s*. Boulder: Lynne Rienner.

Blackden, C. Mark. 1996. "Human Rights, Development, and the World Bank: Economics v. politics?" Article prepared for *Trialogue*, April.

Bosshard, Peter, Carlos Heredia, David Hunter, and Frances Seymour. 1996. *Lending Credibility: New mandates and partnerships for the World Bank*. Washington DC: World Wildlife Fund.

Bread for the World Institute. *News and Notices for World Bank Watchers*, Development Bank Watchers' Project, multiple issues. Silver Spring, Md.: Bread for the World Institute.

—— 1996. "Gender Justice and the World Bank," Development Bank Watchers' Project, September. Silver Spring, Md.: Bread for the World Institute.

Broemmelsiek, Michele Foust. 1995. "Encouraging Participatory Development in the World Bank: Confronting the challenge of changing organizational culture." Unpublished research paper.

Brown, Bartram S. 1992. *The United States and the Politicization of the World Bank: Issues of international law and policy*. London: Kegan Paul International.

Cairncross, Alec. 1959. *The International Bank for Reconstruction and Development. Essays in International Finance, no. 33*, Princeton University.

Caufield, Catherine. 1996. *Masters of Illusion: The World Bank and the poverty of nations.* New York: Henry Holt and Company.

Center for Strategic and International Studies (CSIS). 1997. *The United States and the Multilateral Development Banks, Draft Final Report of the CSIS Task Force, March.* Washington DC.: Center for Strategic and International Studies.

Cernea, Michael M., ed. 1991. *Putting People First: Sociological variables in rural development,* 2nd edn. New York: Oxford University Press.

—— 1993. "Sociological Work within a Development Agency: Experiences in the World Bank." Unpublished paper, August.

—— 1995. "Social Integration and Population Displacement." *International Social Science Journal* 145: 1.

Chambers, Robert. 1993. *Challenging the Professions: Frontiers for rural development.* London: Intermediate Technology Publications.

Chamberlain, Christopher and Martha L. Hall. 1995. "The World Bank's Revised Information Disclosure Policy: A report on content and accessibility." Washington DC: Bank Information Center, October 1995.

Charles Stewart Mott Foundation. 1995. "What's Ahead for the World Bank: Interviews on the Bank's role in promoting sustainable development." Flint, Mich.: Charles Stewart Mott Foundation.

Clark, John. 1991. *Democratizing Development*. London: Earthscan Publications Ltd.

Coats, A.W., ed. 1986. *Economists in International Agencies: An exploratory study*. New York: Praeger.

Crane, Barbara B. and Jason L. Finkle. 1981. "Organizational Impediments to Development Assistance: The World Bank's population program," *World Politics* vol. 36 no. 4, July.

Development Committee Task Force on Multilateral Development Banks. 1996. "Serving a Changing World: Report of the Task Force on Multilateral Development Banks," Washington DC: Development Committee Task Force on Multilateral Development Banks, March 15.

DiMaggio, Paul J. and Walter W. Powell. 1983. "The Iron Cage Revisited: Institutional isomorphism and collective rationality in organizational fields," *American Sociological Review* 48, April.

—— 1991. Introduction to Powell and DiMaggio, eds, *The New Institutionalism in Organizational Analysis*.

Escobar, Arturo. 1995. *Encountering Development: The making and unmaking of the Third World.* Princeton: Princeton University Press.

Feinberg, Richard E. 1988. "The Changing Relationship Between the World Bank and the International Monetary Fund," *International Organization* vol. 42 no. 3, Summer.

Feinberg, Richard E. and contributors. 1986. *Between Two Worlds: The World Bank's next decade.* Washington, DC: Overseas Development Council.

Finnemore, Martha. 1996. *National Interests in International Society*. Ithaca: Cornell University Press.

Fox, Jonathan. 1998. "When Does Reform Policy Influence Practice? Lessons from the Bankwide Resettlement Review." In Fox and Brown, eds, *The Struggle for Accountability*.

Fox, Jonathan and L. David Brown, eds 1998. *The Struggle for Accountability: the World Bank, NGOs, and grassroots movements*. Cambridge, Mass.: MIT Press.

Gardner, Richard N. 1956. *Sterling-Dollar Diplomacy*. London: Oxford University Press.

George, Susan and Fabrizio Sabelli. 1994. *Faith and Credit: The World Bank's secular empire*. London: Penguin Books.

Gwin, Catherine. 1994. *U.S. Relations with the World Bank, 1945–92*. Washington DC: The Brookings Institution.

—— 1995. "Conditionality: The finale of foreign aid or the prologue to global governance?" Unpublished manuscript, January.

Haas, Ernst B. 1990. *When Knowledge is Power: Three models of change in international organizations*. Berkeley: University of California Press.

Haggard, Stephan and Robert R. Kaufman, eds 1992. *The Politics of Economic Adjustment*. Princeton: Princeton University Press.

Haralz, Jonas H. 1992. "The Public Sector's Pursuit of Private Sector Development," A study carried out on behalf of the Royal Norwegian Ministry of Foreign Affairs.

—— 1997. "The International Finance Corporation." In Kapur *et al.*, *The World Bank*.

Hunter, David. 1996. "The Role of the World Bank in Strengthening Governance, Civil Society, and Human Rights." In Bosshard *et al.*, *Lending Credibility*.

International Bank for Reconstruction and Development. 1954. *The International Bank for Reconstruction and Development, 1946-1953*. Baltimore: The Johns Hopkins University Press.

International Rivers Network. Bank Check Quarterly. Various issues. Berkeley: International Rivers Network.

Kapur, Devesh, John P. Lewis, and Richard Webb. 1997. *The World Bank: Its first half century*. Washington DC: The Brookings Institution.

Kardam, Nüket. 1990. "The Adaptability of International Development Agencies: The response of the World Bank to women in development." In Kathleen Staudt, ed., *Women, International Development and Politics: The bureaucratic mire*. Philadelphia: Temple University Press.

—— 1991. *Bringing Women In: Women's issues in international development programs*. Boulder: Lynne Rienner.

—— 1993. "Development Approaches and the Role of Policy Advocacy: The case of the World Bank," *World Development* vol. 21 no. 11.

Karns, Margaret P. and Karen A. Mingst, eds. 1990. *The United States and Multilateral Institutions: Patterns of changing instrumentality and influence*. Boston: Unwin Hyman.

Keck, Margaret and Kathryn Sikkink. 1998. *Activists Beyond Borders: Advocacy networks in international politics*. Ithaca: Cornell University Press.

Kenen, Peter B., ed. 1994. *Managing the World Economy: Fifty years after Bretton Woods*. Washington DC: Institute for International Economics.

Keohane, Robert O. 1984. *After Hegemony: Cooperation and discord in the world political economy.* Princeton: Princeton University Press.

—— 1988. "International Institutions: Two Approaches," *International Studies Quarterly* 32, 179–396.

Kindleberger, Charles P. 1952. "Review of the Economy of Turkey"; "The Economic Development of Guatemala"; "Report on Cuba." *Review of Economics and Statistics* 34.

Klitgaard, Robert. 1990. *Tropical Gangsters.* New York: Basic Books.

Korten, David C. 1984. "Strategic Organization for People-Centered Development," *Public Administration Review* vol. 40 no. 5.

Krasner, Stephen D. ed. 1983. *International Regimes.* Ithaca: Cornell University Press.

—— 1985. *Structural Conflict: The Third World against global liberalism.* Berkeley: University of California Press.

Kratochwil, Friedrich and John Gerard Ruggie. 1986. "International organization: A state of the art on the art of the state," *International Organization* vol. 40 no. 4, Autumn.

Lancaster, Carol. 1993. "Governance and Development: The views from Washington," *IDS Bulletin* vol. 24 no. 1, January.

—— 1997. "The World Bank in Africa Since 1980, The Politics of Structural Adjustment Lending." In Kapur *et al.*, *The World Bank.*

Lawyers Committee for Human Rights. 1995. *The World Bank: governance and human rights*, revised and updated, August. New York: Lawyers Committee for Human Rights.

March, James G. and Johan P. Olsen. 1984. "The New Institutionalism: Organizational factors in political life," *American Political Science Review* 78.

—— 1989. *Rediscovering Institutions: The organizational basis of politics.* New York: The Free Press.

March, James G. and Herbert A. Simon. 1958. *Organizations.* New York: John Wiley.

Mason, Edward S. and Robert E. Asher. 1973. *The World Bank Since Bretton Woods.* Washington DC: The Brookings Institution.

Mearsheimer, John J. 1994/5. "The False Promise of International Institutions," *International Security* vol. 19 no. 3, Winter.

Meyer, John W. and Brian Rowan. 1977. "Institutionalized Organizations: Formal structure as myth and ceremony," *American Journal of Sociology* vol. 83 no. 2.

Mistry, Percy S. 1989. "Financing Development in the 1990s." In Berg and Gordon, eds, *Cooperation for International Development.*

Moore, Mick, ed. 1993. "Good Government?" *IDS Bulletin* vol. 24 no. 1, January.

Moore, Mick. 1995. "Promoting Good Government by Supporting Institutional Development" *IDS Bulletin* vol. 26 no. 2, April.

Morris, James. 1963. *The Road to Huddersfield: A journey to five continents.* New York: Pantheon Books.

Morse, Bradford and Thomas Berger. 1992. "Sardar Sarovar: The report of the Independent Review." Ottawa: Resource Futures International.

Mosley, Paul, Jane Harrigan, and John Toye. 1991. *Aid and Power: The World Bank and policy-based lending.* London: Routledge.

Naim, Moisés. 1994. "The World Bank: Its role, governance and organizational culture," In *Bretton Woods: Looking to the Future.* Washington DC, Bretton Woods Commission.

Nelson, Joan M. and contributors. 1994. *Intricate Links: Democratization and market reforms in Latin America and Eastern Europe*. Washington DC: Overseas Development Council.

Nelson, Paul J. 1995. *The World Bank and Non-Governmental Organizations: The limits of apolitical development*. London: Macmillan and New York: St. Martin's.

—— 1996. "Internationalising Economic and Environmental Policy: Transnational NGO networks and the World Bank's expanding influence." *Millennium: Journal of International Studies* vol. 25 no. 3, October.

Ness, Gayl D. and Steven R. Brechin. 1988. "Bridging the Gap: International organizations as organizations," *International Organization* vol. 42 no. 2, Spring.

Organisation for Economic Cooperation and Development (OECD). 1994a. "Participatory Development and Good Governance," Development Co-operation Guidelines Series. Paris: OECD.

—— 1994b. "Support of Private Sector Development," Development Co-operation Guidelines Series. Paris: OECD.

Perrow, Charles. 1970. *Organizational Analysis: A sociological view*. Belmont, Calif.: Brooks/Cole Publishing Company.

—— 1972. *Complex Organizations: A critical essay*. Glenview, Ill.: Scott, Foresman and Company.

Phaup, E. Dwight. 1984. "The World Bank: How it can serve US interests." Washington DC: The Heritage Foundation.

Powell, Walter W. and Paul J. DiMaggio. 1991. *The New Institutionalism in Organizational Analysis*. Chicago: The University of Chicago Press.

Purcell, John F. H. and Michelle B. Miller. 1986. "The World Bank and Private Capital." In Feinberg *et al.*, *Between Two Worlds*.

Rich, Bruce. 1994. *Mortgaging the Earth*. Boston: Beacon Press.

Richardson, Richard E. and Jonas H. Haralz. 1995. *Moving to the Market: The World Bank in transition*, Policy Essay No. 17. Washington DC: Overseas Development Council.

Robinson, Mark, ed. 1995. "Towards Democratic Governance," *IDS Bulletin* vol. 26 no. 2, April.

Ruggie, John Gerard, ed. 1993. *Multilateralism Matters: The theory and praxis of an institutional form*. New York: Columbia University Press.

Ruttan, Vernon W. 1996. *United States Development Assistance Policy: The domestic politics of foreign economic aid*. Baltimore: The Johns Hopkins University Press.

Sanford, Jonathan E. 1982. *U.S. Foreign Policy and Multilateral Development Banks*. Boulder: Westview Press.

—— 1996. "Multilateral Development Banks: Issues for the 104th Congress," CRS Issue Brief, Congressional Research Service, The Library of Congress, Updated May 30.

Schein, Edgar H. 1990. "Organizational Culture," *American Psychologist* vol. 45 no. 2, February.

Schoultz, Lars. 1982. "Politics, Economics and U.S. Participation in Multilateral development Banks," *International Organization* vol. 36 no. 3, Summer.

Scott, W. Richard. 1981. *Organizations: Rational, natural, and open systems*. Englewood Cliffs, N.J.: Prentice-Hall, Inc.

—— 1995. *Institutions and Organizations*. Thousand Oaks: Sage Publications.

Selznick, Philip. 1949. *TVA and the Grass Roots: A study in the sociology of formal organization*. Berkeley and Los Angeles: University of California Press.

—— 1957. *Leadership in Administration: A sociological interpretation*. Evanston: Row, Peterson and Company.

Sherk, Donald R. 1994. "Emerging Markets and the Multilateral Development Banks; Focus Issues: Emerging capital markets," *Columbia Journal of World Business* vol. 29 no. 2, June 22, p. 44 ff.

Shihata, Ibrahim F. I. 1991. *The World Bank in a Changing World: Selected essays*. Dordrecht: Martinus Nijhoff Publishers.

—— 1995a. *The World Bank in a Changing World: Selected essays and lectures, volume II*. Dordrecht: Martinus Nijhoff Publishers.

Simon, Herbert A. 1961. *Administrative Behavior: A study of decision-making processes in administrative organization*. New York: Macmillan.

Stallings, Barbara. 1992. "International Influence on Economic Policy; Debt, stabilization and structural reform." In Haggard and Kaufman, eds, *The Politics of Economic Adjustment*.

Stern, Nicholas with Francisco Ferreira. 1997. "The World Bank as 'Intellectual Actor.'" In Kapur *et al.*, *The World Bank*.

Stevens, Michael and Shiro Gnanaselvam. 1995. "The World Bank and Governance," *IDS Bulletin* vol. 26 no. 2, April.

Stinchcombe, Arthur L. 1965. "Social Structure and Organizations." In James G. March, ed., *Handbook of Organizations*. Chicago: Rand McNally.

—— 1968. *Constructing Social Theories*. Chicago: University of Chicago Press.

Sullivan, David Bryan. 1995. "The World Bank's Governance Efforts and Human Rights." Unpublished paper, May 19.

Tendler, Judith. 1975. *Inside Foreign Aid*. Baltimore: The Johns Hopkins University Press.

Thompson, James D. 1967. *Organizations in Action*. New York: McGraw Hill.

Tussie, Diana. 1995. *The Inter-American Development Bank*, Volume 4 in *The Multilateral Development Banks*. Boulder: Lynne Rienner.

U.S. Department of the Treasury. 1982. *United States Participation in the Multilateral Development Banks in the 1980s.* Washington DC: U.S. Government Printing Office.

van de Laar, Aart J. 1975. "The Young Professionals Programme of the World Bank. An Analysis of an Elite Group," *Development and Change*, vol. 6, no. 3, July.

Wade, Robert. 1996. "Japan, the World Bank, and the Art of Paradigm Maintenance: The East Asian miracle in political perspective," *New Left Review* no. 217, Spring.

—— 1997. "Greening the Bank: The struggle over the environment, 1970-1995." In Kapur *et al.*, *The World Bank*.

Waltz, Kenneth N. 1979. *Theory of International Politics*. Reading, Mass.: Addison-Wesley.

Weber, Steven. 1994. "Origins of the European Bank for Reconstruction and Development," *International Organization* vol. 48 no. 1, Winter.

Williams, David and Tom Young. 1994. "Governance, the World Bank and liberal theory," *Political Studies* vol. 42, March.

Williams, Marc. 1994. *International Economic Organisations and the Third World.* Hemel Hempstead: Harvester Wheatsheaf.

Zucker, Lynne G. 1977. "The Role of Institutionalization in Cultural Persistence," *American Sociological Review* vol. 42 no. 5.

World Bank Publications

Adamolekun, Ladipo and Coralie Bryant. 1994. *Governance Progress Report: The Africa Region experience*, Capacity Building and Implementation Division Study Paper, Africa Technical Department, February.

Agarwala, Ramgopal and Pushpa N. Schwartz. 1994. "Sub-Saharan Africa: A Long-Term Perspective Study," paper prepared for the World Bank Workshop on Participatory Development, May 17-20, 1994.

Beckmann, David. 1991. "Recent Experience and Emerging Trends." In Paul and Israel, eds, *NGOs and the World Bank.*

Bhatnagar, Bhuvan and Aubrey Williams, eds. 1992. *Participatory Development and the World Bank.*

Brautigam, Deborah. 1991. *Governance and Economy: A review*, Policy Research Working Papers, WPS 815, December.

Cernea, Michael M. 1988. "Nongovernmental Organizations and Local Development," World Bank Discussion Paper No. 40.

—— 1996. "Social Organization and Development Anthropology: The 1995 Malinowski Award Lecture," Environmentally Sustainable Development Studies and Monograph Series No. 6.

Clark, John. 1994. "The State, Popular Participation, and the Voluntary Sector." Paper prepared for the World Bank Workshop on Participatory Development, May 17–20, 1994.

de Capitani, Alberto. 1994. "The World Bank and the Right to Development." Presentation before the UN Commission on Human Rights – Working Group on the Right to Development, Geneva, Switzerland, May.

Dia, Mamadou. 1993. *A Governance Approach to Civil Service Reform in Sub-Saharan Africa,* Technical Paper No. 225, Africa Technical Department Series.

—— 1996. *Africa's Management in the 1990s and Beyond: Reconciling indigenous and transplanted institutions.*

Dichter, Thomas. 1992. "Demystifying Popular Participation: Institutional mechanisms for popular participation." In Bhatnagar and Williams, eds, *Participatory Development and the World Bank.*

Frischtak, Leila L. 1994. *Governance Capacity and Economic Reform in Developing Countries,* Technical Paper No. 254.

International Bank for Reconstruction and Development. *Articles of Agreement* (as amended February 16, 1989).

Kraske, Jochen. 1996. *Bankers with a Mission: The presidents of the World Bank, 1946–91.* New York: Oxford University Press for the World Bank.

Landell-Mills, Pierre and Ismail Serageldin. 1992. "Governance and the External

Factor," *Proceedings of the World Bank Annual Conference on Development Economics 1991.*

Madavo, Callisto. 1997. "The Evolving Relationship Between Africa and the World Bank: What we have learned together," James Smoot Coleman Memorial Lecture, Los Angeles, CA, October 8, 1997. <http://www.worldbank.org/html/extdr/offrep/afr/cm100897.htm>.

Malena, Carmen. 1995. *Working with NGOs: A practical guide to operational collaboration between the World Bank and non-governmental organizations.* Operations Policy Department, March.

McNamara, Robert. 1992. "The Post-Cold War World: Implications for military expenditure in the developing countries," *Proceedings of the World Bank Annual Conference on Development Economics 1991.*

Murphy, Josette. 1995. "Gender Issues in World Bank Lending," A World Bank Operations Evaluation Study.

Paul, Samuel. 1987. "Community Participation in Development Projects: The World Bank experience," World Bank Discussion Paper No. 6.

—— 1991a. "Strengthening Public Service Accountability: A conceptual framework," World Bank Discussion Paper No. 136.

—— 1991b. "Nongovernmental Organization and the World Bank: An overview." In Paul and Israel. eds. *Nongovernmental Organizations and the World Bank: Cooperation for development.*

—— 1994. "Does Voice Matter? For public accountability, yes," Policy Research Working Paper 1388. Policy Research Department, December.

Paul, Samuel and Arturo Israel, eds. 1991. *Nongovernmental Organizations and the World Bank: Cooperation for development.*

Picciotto, Robert. 1992. "Participatory Development: Myths and dilemmas," Policy Research Working Papers, July.

—— 1995. "Putting Institutional Economics to Work: From participation to governance," World Bank Discussion Paper No. 304.

Picciotto, Robert and Rachel Weaving. 1994. "A New Project Cycle for the World Bank?" *Finance & Development*, December.

Pinto, Rogerio F. 1994. "Projectizing the Governance Approach to Civil Service Reform: An institutional environment assessment for preparing a sectoral adjustment loan in the Gambia," Discussion Paper No. 252, Africa Technical Department Series.

Rietbergen-McCracken, Jennifer, ed. 1996. "Participation in Practice: the experience of the World Bank and other stakeholders," World Bank Discussion Paper No. 333.

Salmen, Lawrence. 1994. "Listening to the Poor," *Finance & Development*, December.

—— 1995a. "Beneficiary Assessment: An approach described," Environment Department Paper No. 023, July.

—— 1995b. "Participatory Poverty Assessment: Incorporating poor people's perspectives into poverty assessment work," Environment Department Paper No. 024, August.

Salmen, Lawrence and Paige Eaves. 1991. "Interactions Between Nongovernmental

Organizations, Government, and the World Bank: Evidence from Bank projects." In Paul and Israel, eds, *Nongovernmental Organizations and the World Bank.*

Shihata, Ibrahim F. I. 1995b. "Prohibition of Political Activities in the Bank's Work," Legal Opinion by the Senior Vice President and General Counsel, International Bank for Reconstruction and Development, July 12.

Stone, Andrew H. W. (undated). "Private Sector Assessments: best practice and pitfalls." PSD Note no. 1.

Wolfensohn, James D. 1995. "New Directions and New Partnerships," Address to the Board of Governors, Washington DC, October 10.

—— 1996. "People and Development," Address to the Board of Governors, Washington DC, October 1.

World Bank, *Annual Report*, various years.

—— "Cooperation Between The World Bank and NGOs: Progress report," various years, available from NGO Unit, Social Development Department.

—— *World Development Report*, various years.

—— 1981. *Accelerated Development in Sub-Saharan Africa.*

—— 1984. *Towards Sustained Development in Sub-Saharan Africa: A joint program for action.*

—— 1989a. *Developing the Private Sector: A challenge for the World Bank Group.*

—— 1989b. *Sub-Saharan Africa: From crisis to sustainable growth, a long-term perspective study.*

—— 1991. *Developing the Private Sector: The World Bank's experience and approach.*

—— 1992a. *Adjustment Lending and Mobilization of Private and Public Resources for Growth,* Policy and Research Series 22.

—— 1992b. *Effective Implementation: key to development impact*, Report of the Portfolio Management Task Force, September 22.

—— 1992c. *Governance and Development.*

—— 1993. *Portfolio Management: Next steps – a program of actions,* Operations Policy Department, July 22.

—— 1994a. *Adjustment in Africa: Reforms, results, and the road ahead,* A World Bank Policy Research Report. New York: Oxford University Press for the World Bank.

—— 1994b. *Governance: The World Bank's experience.*

—— 1994c. *The World Bank and Participation*, Operations Policy Department, September.

—— 1995a. "Cooperation Between the World Bank and NGOs: FY 1994 Progress Report." Operations Policy Department, February.

—— 1995b. *The Momentum for Change: Lewis T. Preston at the World Bank, 1991-95, Addresses and Statements.*

—— 1995c. *Private Sector Development in Low Income Countries*, Development in Practice Series.

—— 1995d. "The World Bank and Legal Technical Assistance: Initial lessons," Policy Research Working Paper 1414. Legal Department, January.

—— 1996a. "NGOs and the Bank: Incorporating FY95 Progress Report on Cooperation Between the World Bank and NGOs." Poverty and Social Policy Department, June.

—— 1996b. "Participation Sourcebook Launch," mimeographed transcript. February 26.

—— 1996c. "Social Development and Results on the Ground," Report of the Task Group on Social Development, October 15.

—— 1996d. *Working Together: A live sourcebook for the renewal program of the World Bank's Africa region,* July 1.

—— 1996e. *The World Bank Participation Sourcebook*, Environmentally Sustainable Development Department.

—— 1996f. *The World Bank's Partnership with Nongovernmental Organizations,* Participation and NGO Group, Poverty and Social Policy Department, May.

—— 1997a. "Helping Countries Combat Corruption: the role of the World Bank," *Poverty Reduction and Economic Management*, September.

—— 1997b. The Strategic Compact: Renewing the Bank's effectiveness to fight poverty. Planning and Budgeting Department, February 13.

—— 1997c. *World Development Report 1997: The state in a changing world.* New York: Oxford University Press for The World Bank.

World Bank Group. 1994. "Learning from the Past, Embracing the Future." Washington, DC: The World Bank Group.

Index

P^n Agenda

NGO partners may be highly critical

Need for national advocates, networks, sharing experience

Inclusion → responsiveness → success ↑ (cf Others – an end in itself) WB not allowed to be political

NGOs' Comparative advantage p70

Narrow def^n, but still radical potential. Challenge to project cycle (dominant paradigm) + economic + technological change forces.

Poor fit

p71 – list.

Bank rel' to NGOs has to be via govt but practice it of the direct.

* P^n agenda facilitated by:
  NGOs outside the Bk ——— Crit of WB projects → Co-optation
  motivated staff within ——— Shaped arguments + linked with org^n outside
  + programs of a few countries (esp US) [via NGOs + Congress] informal networks / Social analysts
  Also – att^n of Bk leaders
  gradual erosion of dvpt effectiveness of loans – learning curve ↑ – Wapenhans Rept "decline in effectiveness / % of projects with major problems ↑"
  broader changes in LDCs.
  – democracy
  – role of NGOs ↑
  – research results

* Imp. role of a Group in forcing the pace. Strategies up p80

* + Channel of communication